Jews and Christians Together

D1248461

Jews and Christians Together

An Invitation to Mutual Respect

A. Christian van Gorder
Gordon Fuller

FOREWORD BY *Jeff Levin*

CASCADE *Books* · Eugene, Oregon

Cascade Books
An Imprint of Wipf and Stock Publishers
199 W. 8th Ave., Suite 3
Eugene, OR 97401

www.wipfandstock.com

PAPERBACK ISBN: 978-1-5326-9007-5
HARDCOVER ISBN: 978-1-5326-9008-2
EBOOK ISBN: 978-1-5326-9009-9

Cataloguing-in-Publication data:

Names: van Gorder, A. Christian, author. | Fuller, Gordon, author. | Levin, Jeff, foreword.

Title: Jews and Christians together : an invitation to mutual respect / A. Christian van Gorder and Gordon Fuller.

Description: Eugene, OR: Cascade Books, 2020 | Includes bibliographical references.

Identifiers: ISBN 978-1-5326-9007-5 (paperback) | ISBN 978-1-5326-9008-2 (hardcover) | ISBN 978-1-5326-9009-9 (ebook)

Subjects: LCSH: Judaism—Relations—Christianity | Christianity and other religions—Judaism

Classification: BM535 V35 2020 (print) | BM535 (ebook)

Manufactured in the U.S.A.   JULY 24, 2020

You might ask, how I can form a friendship with a Jewish person? It shouldn't be any harder than making friends with a Gentile. Show him by your conversation and actions that you are interested in him as a person. Seek out common interests, such as hobbies, employment, or neighborhood activities as a basis for conversation. Encourage your Jewish friend to talk and you should try to be a good listener. Even if you are only able to do ten percent of the talking it is not how much you say but what you are saying during the allotted time that counts. A good gesture of friendship is to remember to send greeting cards to your Jewish friends at Jewish holiday times like Passover, the Jewish New Year, and Hanukkah. They will greatly appreciate the fact that you respect their religion.

—Moishe and Ceil Rosen, *Share the New Life with a Jew*, 41

Since Messiah has come and offered his culminating sacrifice, there is, as we see it, no temple, no priesthood, no altar, no atonement, no forgiveness, no salvation, and no eternal hope in Judaism as a religion.

—Vernon C. Grounds, "The Problem of Proselytization," in Tanenbaum et al., *Evangelicals and Jews*, pp. 207–8

It (the Holy Spirit) hates them a lot and I do too. / And God hates them and I hate them / and the whole world must hate them / because they do not wish to desist from their errors.

—*The Tale of the Bishop of Toledo*, in Gautier de Coinci, Les Miracles de Notre Dame, II lines 209–12 p.13

If the statistics are right, the Jews constitute but one percent of the human race. It suggests a nebulous dim puff of star-dust lost in the blaze of the Milky Way. Properly the Jew ought hardly to be heard of; but has always been heard of. He is as prominent on the planet as any other people, and his commercial importance is extravagantly out of proportion to the smallness of his bulk. His contributions to the world's list of great names in literature, science, art, music, finance, medicine, and abstruse learning are also altogether out of proportion to the weakness of his numbers. He has made a marvelous fight in the world in all the ages- and has done it with his hands tied behind him. He could be vain of himself and be excused for it. The Egyptian, the Babylonian, and the Persian rose, filled the planet with sound and splendor, then faded to dream-stuff and passed away; the Greek and the Roman followed, and made a vast noise, and they are gone. Other peoples have sprung up and held their torch high for a time, but it burned out, and they sit in twilight now or have vanished. The Jew saw them all, beat them all, and is now what he always was, exhibiting no decadence, no infirmities of age, no weakening of his parts, no slowing of his energies, and no dulling of his alert and aggressive mind. All things are mortal but the Jew all other forces pass, but he remains. What is the secret of his immortality?

—Mark Twain, "Concerning the Jews," in the *Complete Essays of Mark Twain* (Garden City, NJ: Doubleday, 1963), 249

O that man might know; the end of this day's business 'ere it come; But it sufficed that the day will end; and then the end is known.

—Brutus to Cassius in *Julius Caesar,* Act V, Scene I, William Shakespeare

Table of Contents

Acknowledgments

You cannot put "Thank you" in your pocket.
—Yiddish Proverb

I (VAN GORDER) WOULD like to thank Donna Oberstein Allen and Dr. Howard Kenig for their assistance in classes we taught together at Messiah College in Harrisburg, Pennsylvania. Before he passed away, Howard's stoic embrace of life's unfair assaults was a great source of inspiration. This book could not have been possible without Dr. Kenig. In Waco, I have also been grateful for the able assistance of Cantor Monica O'Desky, Rabbi Moti Rotem, and Rabbi Laura Harari from Temple Rodef Shalom.

I (Fuller) would like to thank those teachers who have been committed agents of change in my life and in their communities. Thanks particularly to Congregation Agudath Jacob during my tenure there for the ability to work in the community, and to my teachers, Rabbi Judith Abrams (of blessed memory), Rabbi Yitz Cohen, Danny Siegel, and Rabbi Yosef Leibowitz. I'm also appreciative of my regular colleagues at the monthly multifaith ministers' lunch—Jimmie Johnson, Charlie Packard, Charley Garrison, Rick Koskela, Nathan Stone, and Margo Ford. Rabbi Kerry Olizky of the Jewish Outreach International and Diane Tobin of Bechol Lashon have been crucial in helping me understand "Big Tent Judaism." Special thanks to our mutual friend Dr. Stanley Hersh (of blessed memory) whose wit and wisdom were constant companions to us both.

Special thanks to Heather Carraher, Michael Thomson, and Robin Parry of Wipf and Stock for their tireless support and assistance in this project.

Special thanks to our families especially Vivian Ndudi Ezeife Van Gorder and Sharon Beirne Fuller: We are blessed beyond compare to have known such support. We write in hopes that the Van Gorder children: Patrick, Brendan, Keegan, Michael, Tatijiana, Gretchen, Andrew, Erik, Tristan, Clare, and Grace; and the Fuller children and grandchildren: Evan and Jessica (Maya and Naomi), and Eliana and Gemma (Gabriel and Miriam), will find this book of benefit in their own journeys in interfaith engagements.

Foreword

CHRIS VAN GORDER IS a faculty colleague at Baylor and Gordy Fuller served as my rabbi—and I have heard about their writing project for some time. When I first picked up this book, I expected it to be something of a folksy first-person account of the travails of teaching about Judaism to innocent, young, sheltered Baptists, replete with a litany of semi-foolish quotes that would be lightly cringe-worthy while inducing forgiving chuckles, and that would close with an earnest call for more education, tolerance of diversity, and all manner of positive interfaith goodness. "After all, we all worship the same God, *kumbayah*, etc., good night and drive safely." This is what I was expecting.

What I found when I began reading the manuscript, transfixed almost from the first page, was something entirely different. I am not prone to hyperbole, but here it is: This book is one of the most thought-inducing contemporary works on Jewish-Christian relations that I have read. In places, it is reminiscent of some of the finest works in this genre: Jacob Neusner's *A Rabbi Talks with Jesus*, Elliot Abrams' *Fear of Faith*, Abba Hillel Silver's *Where Judaism Differs*, and Neusner and Andrew Greeley's *A Priest and a Rabbi Read Scripture Together* come to mind. But van Gorder's and Fuller's book is uniquely poignant. It is loaded with first-person accounts of the authors' experiences teaching the impressionable—and somewhat rigid—young minds of undergraduate religion students about a faith tradition beyond their familiar Evangelical orbit. The book also is heavy on the very words of these students as they negotiate, in many instances, their very first exposure not just to Judaism or even to a Jewish person (Fuller) but to *any* religious tradition, belief, or person other than the flavor that they encountered in their home church or community while "growing up."

This book is thus much less a book about abstractions, theologically, culturally, or politically. Rather, it underscores the estrangement of young

Evangelicals from even the most basic information about normative Jewish identity, belief, or practice. By normative I mean the entirety of rabbinic Judaism, almost the entirety of contemporary North American Jewish religious expression, and anything of substantive significance in Judaism's post-Temple era of the past 2,000 years. To most of the students described in this book, the Jewish religion is precisely as described in the literal words of their Bible, no more and no less. For such reasons, then, there is no surprise in reading the jarring words of one student, during a class visit to our synagogue, who asked Rabbi Fuller if he would show them the room where we sacrifice sheep. Remarkably, this book functions as an unexpected Evangelical Christian *apologia* for Judaism. For this, van Gorder is to be praised to the hills (of his native Pittsburgh, at least). It takes considerable courage to stake out the positions that he does, and I suspect that he may receive some pushback from professional colleagues. Likewise, Fuller is to be praised for his sensitive and forgiving, yet quite pointed, reflections on his experiences with college students.

Gordy had a lengthy career in religious education before entering the rabbinate, and he has witnessed the flip side of this issue: the perceptions and misperceptions expressed by young Jews about the Christian-dominant ethos in which they live. My favorite passage in the book is this one; the words are van Gorder's:

> Evangelicals who insist that Jews cannot reach heaven apart from becoming Christians should, at the very least, acknowledge that such a view comes from one specific interpretation of the Christian scriptures. It would be hoped that these same advocates would at least accept that those Christians who disagree with their views—and believe that the Almighty promised an eternal blessing for all Jews that cannot be cancelled—are not, in some way, being traitorous to the historic Christian tradition. As a Christian, I take the Bible seriously and literally when it says—in no uncertain terms—that God has made an everlasting covenant with the Jewish people that cannot be—and will never be—revoked. (170)

The Catholic church has famously acknowledged this same view about the eternal fate of the Jewish people in the Conciliar Document from Vatican II entitled *Nostra Aetete* and subsequently in follow-ups by popes Paul VI (*Guidelines and Suggestions for Implementing the Conciliar Declaration Nostra Aetete*) and John Paul II (*Notes on the Correct Way to Present the Jews and Judaism in Preaching and Catechesis in the Roman*

Catholic Church), as well as in statements by Pope Francis. Mainline Protestant denominations and organizations (e.g., the National Council of Churches) have followed suit, or already had shunned the proselytizing of Jews. Professor van Gorder's statement is the most blunt, straightforward statement of this type that I have read by an American Evangelical leader, theologian, or religious scholar. If indeed Evangelicals too are taking steps in this direction, then I consider this a very hopeful development—very "good news," if you will for the Jewish people.

To be clear, it is not that Jews should really care one way or the other how the theological, soteriological, or eschatological positions staked out by this or that Christian communion sorts them out. We don't have a horse in the race. If some Christians choose to believe X, Y, or Z about Jews or about anything else, then that is between them and God. But, if it means less persecution for us, more informed and respectful coexistence, and even a step toward what would be the best outcome for committed Jews—both Jews and Christians need to work together with shared purpose in the sacred vocation of *tikkun olam* [תקון עולם], i.e., repairing the brokenness of the world—then we are all for it. What more beautiful vision could there be for this world than faithful followers of the Mosaic covenant and of the Abrahamic call to "go forth" walking hand in hand with gentile friends who have accepted Christ's call to take up the cross and likewise "go forth into all the world?" There is a gigantic reclamation project awaiting us, and it requires the labors of committed Jews and Christians working together.

The authors are telling their story through the words of very young, non-cosmopolitan students in an undergraduate class on world religions at a historically Baptist university located in the Bible Belt of Texas. Presumably, undergraduate religion majors taking a graduate-level seminar on the same topic in the divinity schools of, say, Chicago, Princeton, or Harvard would be a bit more exposed to, fluent in, and accommodated to the specifics of faith traditions other than their own. At the same time, I can attest that these young men and women, as narrowly cast as are their past encounters with the fullness of the American religious experience, are for the most part exceedingly polite and good-natured, and are willing to work hard to learn new things, consider new ideas, and better both themselves and the world in which they live. These are all, ideally at least, Jewish religious values of the highest importance.

Say "Baylor" to leaders of North American Judaism and the first thing that comes to mind, besides the medical profession, is liable to be a stereotypical image of an old intolerant, Jew-baiting, Southern Baptist preacher—Bailey Smith, ca. 1980, for example, who once proclaimed that "God did not hear the prayers of the Jews."[1] That was then, this is now. An example of changing times is that fact that Rabbi Gordon Fuller has been so warmly welcomed in our classrooms. The Rabbi is a person who refuses to accept the status-quo. In this book, he speaks with a prophetic voice, in the original meaning of the word prophetic: calling people out of their complacency and transgression, pointing out their mistakes, and encouraging penitence, all in service to an idealized and brighter future. That he does so gently and respectfully is even more impressive.

This book is a wonderful and challenging reading experience—wonderful because the topic is so provocative, the students' remarks are so fascinating, and van Gorder's and Fuller's comments are so unflinchingly honest; challenging for the same reasons: the topic is so provocative, the students' remarks are so fascinating, and van Gorder's and Fuller's comments are so unflinchingly honest. The authors have crafted an accessible piece of work that quickly draws us into the substance and nuances of the serious issues that they raise. It is an unforgettable read and merits a wide audience.

Jeff Levin
University Professor of Epidemiology and Population Health
Director, Program on Religion and Population Health
Institute for Studies of Religion, Baylor University, Waco, Texas

(Endnotes)
1. https://wwwjta.org.baptist-leader-claims-god-does-not-hear-the-prayer-of-a-jew.

Chapter One

Starting Points for Jewish–Christian Dialogue

To every answer you can always find a new question.

—Yiddish Proverb

We need not agree with fundamentalists . . . to accept their prof-
fered friendship on shared worldly concerns. And although we dif-
fer with many of them on particular secular and sectarian issues,
we can no more rationally ascribe deviltry to them than godliness
to ourselves. Given the actuality of their political and social diver-
sity and the pejoration in the stereotype of them as monolithic,
they—and fairness—merit fresh evaluation by Jews even as Jews
have pled for bias-free consideration of their own diversity and
have insisted on the secular merit of their own religiously shaped
values.

—Rabbi Nathan Perlmutter, Anti-Defamation League

"Too bad he is going to hell . . ."

"RABBI FULLER IS SUCH a great and cool guy! His conversational tone
and sense of humor made him the best speaker we had. He didn't leave
us drooling from boredom. Too bad he is going to hell!"[1] So wrote one
college student after hearing Rabbi Fuller speak for the first time.

1

Gordon Fuller is an American-born (Detroit) rabbi who served for eleven years at a Conservative synagogue in Waco and is now in Columbia, Maryland. Chris van Gorder is an American-born (Pittsburgh) professor who is also an ordained American Baptist minister attending an African American church. In 2004, we met to discuss how the rabbi could help teach students about Judaism in van Gorder's World Religion courses at Baylor University, a Baptist institution located in Waco, Texas. The two of us worked on that project for over ten years. Before that, van Gorder taught at Messiah College in Grantham, Pennsylvania. At Messiah, van Gorder taught Jewish-Christian Relations with Dr. Howard Kenig who was from the Community Relations Council of the Harrisburg Jewish Community (part of the Jewish Federation of Greater Harrisburg) along with Rabbi Carl Choper of the Harrisburg Reconstructionist community and Rabbi Chaim Schertz of the Harrisburg Orthodox community. Unless specifically cited, all student responses described in this book spring from our work together in the classroom at Baylor.

We are writing this book to share our experiences and relate how misconceptions by some Christians about Jews and Judaism can be addressed. Each chapter will focus on specific and common "problem areas" in the multivalent interactions between conservative Christians and Jews. Ours is a reflection (not an empirical evaluation) that springs from our experiences with college students at a Christian university. Most Baylor students participate across the wide range of conservative Christianity and this book responds to their frequently expressed statements about Jews and Judaism. We are not social scientists and do not provide a definitive analysis of these students' perspectives. Instead, we will introduce the broad themes that repeatedly occur in our classroom encounters when we discuss Judaism. We make no claim that our students represent the hundreds of millions of Christians around the world, who are as different as can be imagined.[2]

Baylor University, chartered in 1845 while Texas was still an independent nation, boasts of being the world's largest "Baptist and Christian university." Its motto, *Pro Ecclesia, Pro Texana*, emphasizes a distinctly Christian way of engaging the world. For many conservative Christian parents, it is a place where they can send their children without much fear that they will lose their faith due to confrontative ideas, such as those expressed by other faith-traditions. As it relates to other traditions, Baylor's Religion Department, with over twenty full-time faculty members, but only one in World Religious studies, makes few efforts to promote theological reflection about how the Christian faith relates to other faiths. Graduate students in the religion department, for example, are eligible to receive a master's or a doctoral degree without ever once being required to study or read about other faith traditions as part of their final exit examinations.

Specifically, as it relates to Judaism, there are five courses within the undergraduate religion department that frame the pre-rabbinic Jewish Scriptures in course descriptions as the "Old Testament," a term originating in the Christian Orthodox and Catholic traditions. This contested term, according to Walter Harrelson, should be rejected because to do so expresses a "contemporary commitment to avoid pejorative references to the sacred writings of the Jewish people."[3] Harrelson prefers terms such as "Hebrew Bible," a term frequently used by mainstream Protestants and Catholics (even though some of the text is in Aramaic).

Baylor at present (2020) holds a policy of hiring only faculty who are Christians, with the significant exception of Jewish scholars, who can be hired, though not in the Religion Department. In fact, the first non-Baptist Christian professor was in that department just a few years ago. Buddhists, Muslims, Sikhs, Jains, Baha'i, Zoroastrians, Hindus, Unitarians, Taoists, and Rastafarians need not apply. Why is it, then, that Jews are welcome to work at Baylor? Because it has been concluded that Judaism holds—through the shared legacy of the "Old Testament"—a unique connection with Christianity. At the time of this writing, there are six Jewish faculty at Baylor in a wide range of Institutes and various departments.

The first Jewish faculty member to be appointed, Professor Marc Ellis, was also the founder and first director of the Institute of Jewish Studies (now defunct) at Baylor. Dr. Ellis, citing suppression of his academic freedoms, left Baylor in 2012. Although the contentious nature of his time at Baylor would seemingly merit a further explanation about why and how he left the university, this is a labyrinthine topic well beyond the scope of our study. On the positive side, since 1992, at least ten other scholars from Jewish backgrounds have taken teaching positions at Baylor.

Students in REL3345—World Religions come from a broad range of religious perspectives.[4] Because this is a survey of all religious traditions, Judaism is not discussed until near the end of the fifteen-week semester. The broad and generalized survey approach of the course brings with it its own challenges as we try to avoid promoting misconceptions that can easily congeal into a "gumbo" of confused generalities. This kind of broad overview, of course, is exactly how countless collegiates become familiar with the world's religions.

Since this course is not a university-wide requirement, most students graduate and enter their hectic worlds in business, professional, or social services without any introduction to the world's religious traditions. Of course, in some surveys of world history and world cultures, various traditions may be discussed in passing. While two Christian religion courses are required of all undergraduates (Introduction to Christian Scriptures and an Introduction to Christian History), there is no required world religion (or multireligious) component within either of these two required campus wide courses.

Baylor presents itself as a Christian university, yet several students have no religious orientation at all and would describe themselves as agnostics or atheists. There are also Baylor students that we have met who are Wiccan, Muslim, Sikh, Buddhist, Hindu, or even—once in a bright blue moon—Jewish. While the vast majority of the school's undergraduates are from Texas—and often from tiny hamlets where religious difference means being Methodist instead of Baptist—it is also the case that there are students from all over the United States and from across the world. Most students are some variety of Christian. Many follow a deeply cherished version of conservative Christianity that assumes that, based on their understanding of John 14:6 ("I am the Way, the Truth, and the Life. No man comes to the Father except through me."), they themselves hold the only salvific truth about God (see also Acts 4:12).

What is Evangelicalism? The term "evangelical" is a widely contested term that comes from the commonly used Greek term *euangelion*, which means "gospel" or "good news." As a movement, it is both a status-quo majority and a crusade convinced that it is marginalized and persecuted within North American society. Evangelicalism is one of the largest conservative Christian movements within North American Protestantism, spanning a wide range of denominations. As many as fifty million North American Christians call themselves "Evangelicals." It is a largely conservative movement, socially and politically, with roots in the fundamentalist-modernist controversies of the early twentieth century. One often hears about "Evangelicals" in the popular media whenever election pollsters are examining voter backgrounds.

One key idea commonly held is the conviction that the Bible alone presents universal truth. Biblical revelation is central for conservative Christians. Claims about the nature of biblical authority are framed considering divine revelation. Not to accept the authority of the text means that one is rejecting divine truth: there is no middle ground. Conservative Christians' views generally offer little breathing space for a nuanced appreciation of other faiths or the merits of those faiths' scriptures and practices. Paul Holmer joked that North American Evangelicals "look marginal if you are churchly, intolerant if you are ecumenical, and anti-intellectual in their belief that everything is systematic and settled."[5]

For more than a decade, I (Fuller) have met with van Gorder's students to introduce Judaism and to address what I have observed are many students' most commonly held misconceptions. At the start of class, I wrote my contact information on the board and invited students to reach out to me at any time to ask questions. I hoped my accessibility would send the message that I wanted to interact with them on their own terms. Undergrads have told me that I am the first rabbi—or sometimes even the first Jewish person—that they have ever met. This explains why some of their questions seem to be based on stereotypes about Jews and Judaism. A student told me: "No offense, but when I think "Jewish", I think "*Fiddler on the Roof*" and I think that that's what Jews should look like and you don't look like that."[6] Another student explained, "I was taken aback when I met you. I had the foreknowledge that the speaker for our class was from a traditional background and I had a preconceived idea of what he should look like. I imagined you would be a heavy-set long-bearded man in a dark suit with thick, black-rimmed glasses to complete the ensemble."[7]

After I came to a class one student wrote a response to her visit to our synagogue: "It was neat to see that the temple was not a museum and that all the people who went there were normal people. I might have seen any of them around Waco and not even taken a second glance."[8] Waco is a growing community of about 240,000 with a Jewish population of no more than 400 individuals, many of whom do not attend either of the two synagogues (one is Conservative while the other is a Reform congregation) on a regular basis. Central Texas Jews have a long history of dealing with both well-meaning and myopic neighbors who often try to evangelize them into the Christian faith. In response, most at-large public programs co-sponsored by the two congregations tend to focus on education about the Holocaust (*Shoah*).

"The rabbi is basically half a Christian . . ."

What are the various views held by Christians about Judaism? Andrew White thinks that there are three main ways that Christians have approached Judaism: "replacement theology, remnant theology, and recognition theology."[9] The first view, "replacement theology," is widespread among Evangelicals, who often call this view "supersessionism." Christianity has superseded Judaism, a religion that is irrelevant, ineffective, misleading, and, therefore, must be replaced. For some conservative Christians, supersessionism is the logical way to view Judaism. This is a central "elephant in the room" in Jewish and Evangelical interactions.

Jewish-Christian theological dialogue best begins with a few basic questions: What are the goals of our conversations? How should our objectives be articulated? How should discussions about Israel proceed? How do religious and political loyalties affect each other in discussions? What is the relationship between respectful learning and the need to promote mutual respect? How should Jewish presentations of faith proceed in contexts where some Christians openly assume that Judaism is deficient, and that Jews must become Christians in order to please God?

Talking about Judaism is a challenge for some Bible Belt students who have not been raised to equate being Jewish with being an average North American and have no personal frame of reference about Judaism. For some, Jews exist only in the ancient pages of the Bible and they have scant knowledge of rabbinic and modern Judaism. One student wrote, "I knew from my Sunday School that the Jews were the chosen people and that they did not eat hot dogs, but that was about it."[10] "Jew", for this student, was a historical category understood through the filter of their Christian worldview assumptions. Another student perceptively wrote, "I had trouble understanding the rabbi because I feel like I view everything from a Christian perspective."[11] Still another explained that "Rabbi Fuller is basically half-a-Christian because he believes in half of the Bible."[12]

For some conservative Christians, Judaism is reduced to the historically frozen religiosity of the Pharisees who lived during the time of Jesus. One student who visited the synagogue mused, "I felt like I was travelling back in time to the Old Testament. I felt like I got to see my roots. It was so cool."[13] Meeting Jews, in this view, is like meeting ancient religious dinosaurs. When one student visited the synagogue, they realized that "Jews truly value Old Testament culture and practices instead of chasing after modern advances and conveniences."[14] It can be that simple for those who have spent their entire lives hearing about "Jews" in their Sunday school classes. Another student wrote, "I am so accustomed to seeing Christians devoting themselves to worship, prayer, and teaching, and it was surprising to see people from another religion being so devout. This really opened my eyes and spurred my inner questioning about why other people believe as they do."[15] Students are sometimes surprised to discover genuine piety within the synagogue, perhaps based on a superficial reading of the Gospels in which "the Jews" are sometimes presented as a hypocritical foil to the heroic role of Jesus as he confronts formalistic and sanctimonious religiosity.

Christians often learn about the general category of "Judaism" through their church and Sunday school classes, in which biblical-era typecasts have been the unquestioned norm. It has even been assumed that North American Jews still sacrifice animals in their neighborhood temples and dream of one day restoring sacrifices at the temple of Jerusalem so that countless gallons of sheep's blood can soothe the wrath of God. Some repeat the claim of televangelist Pat Robertson that Jews somewhere are secretly breeding red heifers so that they can be sacrificed in Jerusalem's soon-to-be-rebuilt temple. One student wrote, "Judaism was about the same today as it was during the times of the Bible, minus the Temple."[16]

Such a misguided starting point will stubbornly remain if conservative Christian teachers and pastors continue presenting Judaism as an ancient preface to the truths of Christianity. One of the key interpreters of Judaism to conservative Protestant Christians in North American churches is the publisher David C. Cook via a host of Sunday school curricula that they publish which underscore the ancient biblical-era nature of Jews and Judaism. In one example, one lesson taught that "The Jews continued to bring trumped up charges against Jesus." Another widely used Sunday school curriculum publisher, Gospel Light, described Pontius Pilate as a "mere pawn for the Jewish community's animosity toward Jesus."[17] Christians who claim to have no tolerance for anti-Semitic views should recognize that such lessons foster negative views about Jews through caricatures of a people locked forever into a distant past.

Many non-Jews think of Judaism as an exotic religion, remote from their lives. One student, after visiting a Shabbat service, observed, "It was like stepping into a different world. It was a very new and wonderful experience."[18] When people assume everything is different about Judaism it is a challenge to help them gain a more accurate view. Some students have admitted to me that they've yet to meet a real live flesh-and-blood Jew. In some parts of North America, such an experience is almost inconceivable, but it is common in many rural mono-religious towns and villages in central Texas. One student claimed, "In my Erath County hometown our idea of a different religion was the Methodists down the street. There was legitimate panic/controversy when a mosque-lookin' building was constructed near the town that turned out to be the Catholics, though that was really just as bad."[19]

Conservative Christians often assume that all other religions besides their own are false. Israel, as presented in the Bible, is seen as a hard-hearted and stiff-necked tribal people that has already rejected Christ and chosen, instead, a stern, ritualistic legalism. Christians must evangelize Jews because, if Jews do not accept Jesus as their Messiah, they will burn forever in an eternal hellfire for rejecting God's gift of salvation. In many conservative Christian congregations, the idea of interfaith dialogue is of little concern. Students from such churches can live their entire lives without ever hearing a voice from another religious tradition or a citation from the scriptures of another faith. It is far more common for Christians in Central Texas to come from religious backgrounds where the evangelism and conversion of Jews, and not appreciation of them, is the first concern of Jewish-Christian interactions. In fairness, this intent comes from their sincere convictions, learned from an early age, that the religious traditions of others are insufficient, and, because of that, the loving thing is to seek their conversion.

Because of this, simply teaching about Judaism as a broad religious category objectively fails to address harmful preconceptions rooted in understandings of the Bible. Before non-Jews are presented with neutral "facts" about a historically frozen Judaism, one should ask whether they are interested only in such details in order to increase evangelistic effectiveness or whether there is a hope to partner with others in a constructive dialogue rooted in progressive mutual respect.

For many North American Jews, the goals of interfaith dialogue are quite basic: appreciating key similarities and differences. Even such a straightforward objective, however, can go far toward reducing prejudices among those who have never seen interfaith dialogue in their own lives or in the lives of their churches. Conservative Christians who begin with negative preconceptions about the inferiority of the faiths of others can be nudged towards the idea that entering dialogue with those of other faiths serves, at the very least, to deepen their own self-understanding and even lead them into a stronger embrace of their own faith. In an ideal world, the goals expressed by Rosanne Catalano and David Fox Sandmel could become a strong incentive for interreligious engagement: "Jews become stronger Jews and Christians become stronger Christians; through the encounter with the 'other' we come to know ourselves better."[20]

Such a sentiment assumes a greater potential for Jewish-Christian engagement than can be realized in a few hours of one semester during a class for twenty students in Central Texas. How do such ideals relate to those Christians who have never contacted anyone who represents any kind of a lived and actual Jewish perspective? A disquieting sense of smug isolation leads to a sense of religiously relational segregation. History is filled with the rationale for religious ghettos and cultural quarantines that result in the strengthening and elevation of myopic bigotry. The traditional and fear-motivated background of some individuals, convinced that they alone know the truth about God Almighty, makes their desired sense of isolation a sought-for reality to be securely reinforced in order to keep the faith, instead of opening it up to challenge.

Anyone can see, in the most graphic and hellish of all examples, that anti-Semitism in Nazi Germany was directly related to fostering among non-Jews a perception of Jewish otherness and strangeness. While the Jews of Nazi Germany were forbidden to work or to marry non-Jews, there is little need for such restrictions where there are no Jews to be found. Central Texas, for example, is largely a *Juden-Frei* (a Nazi term to mean "free of Jews") zone. While the Nazis of Germany worked hard to create the conditions for the ghettoization of the Jews in order to foster Nazism's brutal power and its passionate nationalism, the modern context of many socially isolated individuals across North America presents no barriers to the creation of a sense of desired exclusion or unchallenged condescension or even revulsion towards "the other." Sadly, false assumptions, rooted in strict exclusivist religious convictions of superiority, are rarely threatened or challenged by the seeking out of direct personal interactions with people of other faiths.

A lack of neighbor-to-neighbor interactions means that Jews are often nothing more than one-dimensional caricatures in the minds of those conservative Christians who are certain that they alone know the truth about God. Because such people may not actually know any flesh-and-blood Jewish people, there is little motivation to empathize with the idea of a Judaism that thrives and gives deep meaning to the lives of its adherents.

At the same time, many already feel that they have learned all that they will ever need to know about Judaism through the clearly delineated explanations of the New Testament bestowed upon them by their trusted religious authorities. The evidence in the Bible is there for all to see. The New Testament shows—without doubt—that Jews are eternally lost, separated from God, and need to accept Jesus as the only possible and long-foretold Jewish Messiah. For some students, four hours in a world-religions survey that introduces them to contemporary Judaism might be all that keeps them from careening into adulthood free from any sense that such a metanarrative might be false. A few remarks from a rabbi are all that they will have to counter the far more pervasive church-based approach to a static and historic Judaism that has rejected Christ, which may be all they hear for the rest of their lives.

Motivations for Writing

A basic question for interfaith discussions is whether Christianity is *inherently* anti-Jewish. Peter A. Pettit claims that a "systematic denigration of Judaism in favor of Christianity became standard in Christian teaching."[21] In fact, the very founding of Christianity, as it gradually emerged from Judaism, was fundamentally a critique of Judaism.

Jon Levenson notes that a neutral observer would assume that Christianity and Judaism share "a basis for good relations," which is rarely actualized because "Christianity, for the most part, has viewed itself as the fulfillment of Judaism, the true and enduring Judaism as it were."[22] While early Christians came to think that Christianity had superseded Judaism, making it of no value, some virulently anti-Semitic Christians later came to see Jews as a community in league with the pernicious deceptions of the devil.

Our hope in writing this book is to encourage learners, students, congregants, teachers, priests, pastors, rabbis, cantors, and people of goodwill to advance mutual respect between Jews and Christians. In many ways, this book can only begin to scratch the surface of achieving such an objective. The ten topics that have been selected are chosen because they might serve as possible starting-points for further discussions between Jews and Christians. The Hebrew word for "friend"—*yedid* (ידיד)—has at the core of its meaning the idea of extending a hand of welcome and embrace to another. How can we reach out across barriers of misunderstanding? Why is this imperative? This book's conclusion explores how discussions between Jews and Christians can overcome what some see as intractable differences along creedal lines by focusing on fostering social justice partnerships. This is a straightforward starting point, even if all other appeals or approaches fail, because both faiths are deeply committed to "mending the world." For both traditions, peace and justice in this world are intimately linked with right worship of a Holy God, and the failure to confront the various evils of a world in rebellion against the Divine is a distorted expression of faith that is unable to bring right reverence and appropriate honor to God.

Jewish-Christian dialogue, of course, has always been in a state of constant flux throughout two millennia. On the positive side, there have been many positive developments over time that have promoted mutual appreciation and genuine respect. A clear example of this includes fresh considerations by both Jews and Christians about the issues surrounding interfaith marriages.[23] Hanspeter Heinz is correct that, within the past forty years, Jewish-Christian relations "have become stable enough" to withstand new "burdens and stumbling blocks."[24] In the last century, the scarring and deep trauma of the Holocaust branded an entire generation. Even the events of history, however, play a fresh role in the ways that adherents of the two faiths relate to each other.

A Multivalent Judaism

It is vital to emphasize to Christians learning about Judaism that there has never been one distinct form of Judaism. Jewish communities are dramatically diverse and have thrived in a wide variety of places as remote as Yunnan, China; Bukhara, Uzbekistan; and in Alexandria, Egypt.[25] There are Black Jews, Yemeni Jews, Asian Jews, and Ashkenazi and Sephardic Jews, to name just a few. Judaism cannot be limited to a narrow frame of reference that includes only the familiar streets and neighborhoods of Israel or North America.

When we teach together, we talk about our own specific starting points to illustrate the inherent diversity that is found within each faith. We also start by stressing at the outset the deep and historic roots that Judaism has within the North American story. There were, for example, strong Jewish communities in the original United States colonies. John Rousmaniere claims that, at the time of the American Revolution, there were about one thousand Jews living throughout the colonies.[26] One of the earliest Jewish communities was founded in Newport, Rhode Island in 1658. By 1763, Newport Jews had built a stunningly attractive synagogue in support of that community. Substantial numbers of Jews, however, did not come to the New World until the end of the nineteenth century when waves of persecution forced the Jews of Eastern Europe and Russia to flee to cities such as New York, Pittsburgh, Chicago, Philadelphia, Galveston, Toronto, and Montreal. Today, more than six million Jews live throughout Canada and the United States. We also introduce students to the terms *Ashkenazim* (Jews originating from Central Europe) and *Sephardim* (Jews originating from the Iberian Peninsula and Mediterranean shores) to help students see how interculturality is another vital point of complexity within the myriad dimensions of the modern Jewish world.

Since the "Survey of the World's Religions" course is tasked with introducing many different faiths, there are only four class sessions allocated in this overview to cover the vast breadth of Judaism. Our first objective is to introduce students to the four major branches of North American Judaism.

We begin our survey with Reconstructionist (now rebranded as Reconstructing) Judaism because of its North American origin. It is also a good starting point because Rabbi Mordecai Kaplan's goal—to help individuals to see Judaism as a "religious civilization and not a religion exclusively"[27]—puts the spotlight on deep-seated issues at the heart of North American Jewish identity. Next, we turn to Reform Judaism, a historical movement that began in Germany (ca. 1810) and instructs modern Jews to accept that the Prophets and their views on social justice are just as important as the divinely inspired Torah. When one student learned that a Reform congregation tends to be more liberal than a conservative one, that student chose to attend the Reform service because "I transposed my experience of liberal verses (sic) conservative churches and assumed that services would be shorter, and people would pay less attention to me at the Reform instead of the Conservative congregation."[28]

Finally, I (Fuller) introduce dimensions of Orthodox and Conservative approaches to Judaism. In our classes, I introduce myself as a representative of Conservative Judaism in relation to my other sympathies towards other forms of North American Judaism. I explain how the Conservative movement began as an attempt to bridge the extremes of a vigorous Reform movement in Europe and North America with the seeming intractability of Orthodoxy. We also introduce Hasidism because many students have heard about this movement through books, movies, and scattered snippets of popular culture. Christians often seem to find the stories of Hasidic teachers who call for an intimate relationship with God in line with their own views on how faith is all about "knowing God," an idea that many assume is absent in other forms of Judaism. We will discuss the ways that we present these various traditions in greater detail in Chapter 7.

In the End is the Beginning

Jacob Neusner noted that the challenge devotional Judaism provides to some Christians is both an inward and an outward dimension: "Christians have typically preferred to dismiss Judaism rather than ask why their own religion has not developed in the same way as others."[29] Even though the road toward respectful Jewish-Christian dialogue seems long, the need to improve such relations is obvious, making the task of removing barriers along the way well worth the effort.

Each reader comes to this book with their own experiences, or lack thereof, in Jewish-Christian interactions. Because the goal of education is always more education, our effort in beneficial Jewish and Christian interactions is an incomplete work in progress. It is hard to disagree with Rabbi Chaim Schertz's (Harrisburg, PA) warning from Jewish tradition that "all beginnings are difficult." Our prayer in this effort is a familiar one: "May the words of our mouth and the meditations of our hearts be pleasing before Thee—the Lord our Rock and our Redeemer."

Chapter Two

Gods of Two Mountaintops

The believer asks no questions while no answer can satisfy the unbeliever.
—Yiddish Proverb

Mountains cannot meet, but men can meet.
—Yiddish Proverb

Mount Sinai and Mount Calvary

FOR CHRISTIANS, DIFFERING THEOLOGICAL assumptions affect how they view the main ideas of modern Judaism. One student commented on a statement I (Fuller) made in class about God's mysterious nature by saying: "He believed God makes mistakes. I found that statement rather off-putting. The two ideas do not fit together."[30] The sum of my one-hour lecture was boiled down into the notion that I saw God rife with flaws, citing the decision to destroy the world during the flood, and later Sodom and Gomorrah. I have no way of knowing how that student came to that conclusion.

For some, Judaism and Christianity are two sides of the same coin. One student wrote: "When I went to the temples of other religions, I felt like I would be sinning if I went there. Here [at the synagogue], it was a bizarre feeling of connection that I cannot describe. Their God was my God, our God."[31] Another student explained: "Even though the temple felt like a library, and the scriptures that they read from is the Old Testament, but still, they see God the same way that we do."[32] This willingness to focus on common ground provides a sturdy starting point for further respectful Jewish-Christian interactions.

The notion that God is something of a schizophrenic combination of Old Testament justice and New Testament grace has been a common refrain that is often heard in contentious Jewish-Christian debates. For two millennia, Jews and Christians have battled over this contested ground while invariably concluding that followers of both faiths worshipped the same God (in contrast to Wotan, Vishnu, and others). Furthermore, no one can deny that Christianity springs from its parent religion, (pre-rabbinic or biblical) Judaism, a fact that implies a clear interrelationship. Theological tensions between these religions have been frequent, but Christians have consistently agreed with Judaism that there is only one God.

In the Academy Award-winning film *Chariots of Fire,* the proctor of an elite English school muses that Jews are different from Christians because they worship a "different god from a different mountaintop." The "God of Mount Sinai" is a vindictive God who hides from individuals while the compassionate "God of Mount Calvary" extends mercy and love. This assumption advances the notion that, even if Christians and Jews worship the same God, the Jewish worship of God is somehow deficient. The God of biblical Judaism, according to this narrative, is a forbidding judge while Jesus is a loving intermediary standing between the wrath of a volatile God and the wretched sinfulness of humanity. Christianity, it is claimed, offers the promise of an intimate relationship with a merciful, loving God while the Jewish path of ritual and formalism offers no such promise. The God of Mount Sinai demands fidelity to the strict law of Moses while the God of Mount Calvary can offer a free pass for eternal forgiveness through Jesus.

This "Two-Mountain Theology" held by some Christians as they define "the Jew" is rooted in negative assumptions about the ultimately spiritual bankruptcy of Judaism. The harsh "Old Testament" ethics of Mount Sinai are caricatured by the stern commands of YHWH and contrasted with the inclusive and embracing love of God in Christ. For some, the demanding God revealed on Mount Sinai is portrayed as a vindictive judge—a celestial terrorist—who calls for individuals to be stoned to death for being gay or for disobeying their parents. One student at Messiah College wrote, "In the past I have advocated for capital punishment and many other Old Testament style beliefs. I now question the legitimacy of this to a New Testament Christian who is taught mercy and commanded to turn the other cheek."[33] This student has driven a wedge between the Old Testament God, who demands harsh justice, and the New Testament Christ, who is forgiving. This view of a volatile and unpredictable God offers one way to explain the relation between the Old and New covenants while also leading conservative Christians to view Judaism as an incomplete, insufficient pathway to eternal life.

Jewish and Atheist?

Students have found it hard to grasp that there are some Jews who deny the existence of God and yet remain as members in good standing within the larger faith tradition. One student pondered "the idea that a Jew could be an atheist and still be Jewish was a little perplexing."[34] For most conservative Christians, such a concept is unfathomable because faith is seen as connected to correct doctrine and a commonly agreed upon litany of theological assertions. At the same time, the fact that an individual can be both Jewish and atheist is an insight that can help some Christians appreciate that being Jewish is very different from their own views when it comes to the need to affirm specific doctrines. (The question of how the "death of God" movement relates to Judaism is beyond the scope of this book. Indeed, this movement, rooted in Christian scholarship, is based on the ideas of the German philosopher Friedrich Nietzsche.)[35]

Students are sometimes confused at the large number of "secular Jews" (*hilonim* [חלונים]) they encounter in our shared North American cultural landscape. "Secular Jews" refers to individuals who identify themselves as Jewish (and are accepted by other Jews) but may never set foot in a synagogue. Some "secular Jews" either openly question God or claim that, after the Holocaust, they are—implicitly or overtly—atheists. These same individuals may also be active in Jewish organizations without being "religious." To further complicate issues for those who are looking for simplistic characterizations, there are some synagogues that describe themselves as "humanistic congregations." They consist of individuals who "strongly identify themselves as Jewish but do not believe in God."[36] They note that none of the Torah's 613 laws prohibits atheism. Nicholas de Lange explains that Jewish atheism has its roots in the *Haskalah* (השכלה), the Hebrew Enlightenment of nineteenth-century Europe, which "shared the antireligious and anticlerical sentiments of the

European Enlightenment in general."[37] This movement was active in advancing the cause of Zionism. One rabbi, Adam Chalom, said that one of the primary goals of this movement, which focuses on cultural identification over theological unity, was to "strengthen the community overall."[38]

God Described

There are countless ways that various Jews or Christians describe their view of God's nature. In fact, the notion of a systematic view of "theology" is far more of a Christian idea than a traditional Jewish one. Leffler and Jones suggest that Christians in conversation with Jews replace the term "theology" with the term "religious ideas" since the two fields of concern, while similar in many ways, are not identical; confusion arises when terms are used interchangeably, allowing for incorrect assumptions.[39] Throughout history, for example, Jewish religious leaders (apart from Maimonides) have rarely systematized their religious assumptions into strict theological categories.

While many assume that both traditions pray to the same God, throughout history there have been thinkers, both Jewish and Christian, who have questioned this underlying premise (for example, the second-century heretical dualist Marcion, who claimed that the Gods of the two testaments were distinct). Moses Maimonides, one of Judaism's most renowned theologians, argued that Christians were not monotheists who worshipped the God that was revealed to Abraham, Isaac, and Jacob. Maimonides believed that Christians were idolaters and that Jews should avoid business dealings with them for this reason. He thought that Jews had much more in common with Muslims than with Christians when it came to describing the unity of God's nature. Maimonides concluded that the Christian doctrines of the Trinity and the incarnation of Christ associate (Hebrew, *shittuf* [שתוף]) another being (Jesus) with God, which meant that Christians were claiming that there was another being who shared in the divine nature.

Variant views about the nature of God among Christians and Jews provide opportunities for energetic discussions of how these differences relate to other shared ideas. David Ellenson states: "Jewish views of God diverge, in several significant ways, from Christian conceptions. Christian worship is not a viable religious choice for Jews. Indeed, there is no reason it should be."[40] For Jews, God is *Ribbono Shel Olam* (של ריבונו

עוֹלָם), the Master of the Universe who is also the essence of all righteousness (Ps 19:2, 8). Samuel Sandmel explains that, in traditional Jewish theology, "God was not a physical being but was intangible and invisible."[41] Both faiths agree that God alone is the sovereign of the universe and has all power. The divine is all-knowing and all-present. God is zealous for justice and calls followers to a life of moral purity. At the same time, the fact that God has all power also means that God is responsible for creating all that is in the world, both good and evil (Isa 45:7).

Jewish and Christian scholars have taught, albeit in different ways, that God is an indivisible unity who is distinct and apart from humanity. At the same time, according to Jacob Neusner, "Judaism locates God's concerns within the realm of human society, and mundane issues such as worship are elevated to questions of divine moment."[42]

Both traditions affirm that God is known by various names, and each of these helps us to know more about the divine nature. The Bible teaches that God is compassionate (Ps 145:8–9) and like a parent to a child-like humanity (Ps 103:13). There is no other God (Isa 45:22) and this God is close to all who call out in prayer (Ps 145:18). God will help us when we are in trouble (Ps 121:1–2) and guide us for eternity (Ps 48:14). These affirmations not only explain something about God but also provide an ethical portrait of how holiness should be expressed within our daily lives of faithful devotion.

Judaism and Christianity teach that God is holy and creates humanity in the divine image so that humanity will strive towards ethical and moral holiness. The divine is met within history; human encounters with God call individuals to a more reverential pathway of worship. The worship of any other "god" will lead to an individual straying from the truth and falling into error. In both traditions, when one speaks of God, they should speak with reverent measure. God's ways are beyond human understanding and categories, such as ideas of gender or other human characteristics. Moses Maimonides, in *The Guide for the Perplexed* (1:59, 88), explained "if I could describe God, God would not be God."[43] Even so, individuals throughout the ages (such as Moses) have asked YHWH (the unpronounceable four-letter Hebrew name of God) to show humanity something of the divine nature (Exod 33:13–20). While humanity will never fully be able to comprehend the mysterious ways of divine providence, believers are called to trust (*emunah* [אמונה]) God and rely upon divine goodness for the various challenges of life.

Every act of revelation is, to quote Elliot Dorff, the "continual entry of God into the experience of each individual's life."[44] Because God loves all within the created order, a divine desire is loose in the world to help creation transcend the temporal with that which is eternal. Judaism does not call followers to escape into fogs of escapist mysticism but to live ethical lives in concrete realities. The best way to understand the nature of God in Jewish thinking, according to the great Hasidic philosopher and writer Martin Buber, is dynamically through relationships with people and in relationship with the world around us. God is not a remote abstraction or a theoretical idea but has a unique personality and is in distinct and direct relationship with all of creation. Because we seek to honor God, we also honor each other with a willingness to live lives that are open, mutual, present, and equitable.

God's Oneness

The declaration of the *Shema Israel* (שמע ישראל) (Hear, O Israel) rings out with the bold assertion that God is One (Deut 6:4). Franz Rosenzweig claims that the revelation of God's oneness is the truth that outlives all who acknowledge it and outlives any name that can be given to God.[45] Jewish monotheism is not a negotiated exercise in mystical obtrusion but a rational conviction that the oneness of God is a foundational truth revealed in scripture. God's oneness means that there is no place for the worship of any other as a complementary or secondary deity (Deut. 4:4, 35–39). This belief is not only to be embraced intellectually but is to be "cleaved" to (Deut 4:4) in the same way that a wife and a husband cleave to each other (Gen 2:24).

Most Jews and Christians readily acknowledge that the concept of God within these two traditions is radically distinct. As mentioned earlier, some Jews throughout history have felt that the Christian doctrine of the triune nature of God (or "Trinity") is idolatrous (*avodah zarah* [עבודה זרה]). Although many Jewish scholars know that Christianity speaks of the Trinity, most also appreciate that the doctrine does not portray three distinct and separate forces with different and conflicting wills. Rather, the Trinity represents three aspects of one God. While Jews are forbidden to hold such a belief, it is not *avodah zara*. The discussion of how idolatry relates to the concept of God is a discussion that few Christians have considered from a Jewish perspective. While teaching at Messiah College in

Grantham, PA (van Gorder, 1997–2003), one of my students wrote that "because polytheists are equal to pagans, I was shocked, personally, to find out that some Jews consider some Christians to be pagans. Obviously, the belief that Christians are cannibals is a misconception, but the way some people talk about Communion it is nonetheless understandable."[46]

Widely held theological assumptions can also influence relational dynamics between Jews and Christians. While many prefer a "live and let live" approach, such a view may be naïve given the negative implications of Christian supersessionist assumptions. It may even be impossible because some conservative Christians may feel that they have no choice but to obey the command of God to evangelize Jews until they accept Jesus as their Savior. One student explained how this mandate frustrated him after the rabbi visited class:

> The Jews do not believe that Jesus Christ is the Son of God sent to the world to save us and that only through him do we receive eternal life and enter into eternity. This, for me, is an incredibly tough thing to understand. Rabbi Fuller seems like an incredibly intelligent and kind man and yet he has a complete lack of acceptance of Christ as Savior. That is just mind-boggling to me. However, although I am a believer, I am also a believer in good people and Rabbi Fuller is obviously a good person.[47]

In this student's worldview, the only consolation that he could find was a bridge of ethical respect while the larger issues of the rabbi's faith forever consigned the rabbi—and all non-Messianic Jews—to an eternal torment because they have failed to accept Jesus Christ as Savior.

Chapter Three

Living in a Broken World

*Rich men are often lean and poor men are often fat. When the
sin was sweet the repentance is not so bitter. Of two evils choose
the lesser, of two women choose the third.*
—Yiddish Proverbs

Inherent Evil or Goodness

MOST CONSERVATIVE CHRISTIANS ASSUME that people are born into sin
with an inherently sinful nature. In contrast, Judaism embraces a positive
view of human nature, rejecting any notion of original sin. While Adam
fails God according to Genesis, his actions do not consign all humanity
to an eternally inherent sinful nature. Each person will be judged on their
own individual merits; the actions of Adam countless years ago have no
bearing on the ontological character of people born into the world today.
These two distinct views about the fundamental nature of humanity may
also have a dramatic effect on how people view their own moral standing
in the world.

Christians and Jews both teach that God created humanity from
dust (Gen 2:7). The very name "Adam" (the word for earth is *Adamah*
[אדמה], for the red clay) reminds humanity of this earthy and mundane
status. One rabbinic commentary notes God did not create *Homo sapiens*
until the sixth day as a lesson of humility because "even the lowly insect
precedes man in the order of creation."[48] At the same time, individuals
are invested with the image of God, and are cherished as God's precious

21

creation. The Divine has placed a divine breath (*neshamah* [נשמה]) within all mortals. God shares with Adam the task of naming the animals as a way of involving the first human in a "shared" process of creation (Gen 2:20).

God also calls humanity to "rule" as stewards over creation (Gen 1:28–29). The Psalmist exalts that God made humanity "a little lower than God [*Elohim*]" (Ps 8:5–6). Although there is some debate among modern Jewish scholars about the question of whether humans have such a thing as a "soul" these questions are relatively recent in origin. For most Jews, each person has a soul that makes them responsible for their own moral actions. The soul distinguishes humanity from other animals, who cannot be said to have a sense of moral responsibility but simply live their lives out of a sense of base instinct. For most Jews, this soul, which is a gift from God, is eternal and will one day return to its creator (Eccl 12:7). Therefore, one should engage in a life of soul-searching (*Heshbon ha-nefesh* [חשבון הנפש]) through devoted prayer and study.

Original Sin

Jewish tradition has taught that, since humanity is created through God's power, it is essentially good in its basic form. Genesis declares that when God created humanity that it was "very good (Gen 1:31)." It is offensive to Jews to suggest that God created humanity to be inherently evil. They see life as a holy gift from God, even if humans continue to sin. Some Christians, but not all, would also find the suggestion that humanity is created inherently evil to be offensive.

Many Jews have often recited a daily morning prayer: "O God, the soul which you have implanted in me today is a pure one—you created it, you molded it, you breathed it into me, and you will someday take it away from me."[49] This positive view of human nature contrasts dramatically with some Christian views that people are basically sinful and born with a corrupted nature in need of salvation from an eternal fire of damnation. One scholar notes that "even during Biblical times there was no Temple sacrifice that addressed original sin nor did any of the prophets refer to it. For Jews, Christianity offers a solution to a Biblical problem that simply does not exist."[50]

A consequence of Jewish ideas about humanity's goodness is the fact that most Jews have avoided anti-materialist views which saw the body as evil, calling for asceticism free from the sin-generating stains of sexuality as described by St. Augustine and others. When Jewish teachers retell the story of Adam and Eve in Eden, the moral is often that those who rebel against God do so at their own peril. Eden was a time of ideal interactions between God and humanity; it is now an aspiration. The "curse" that came to Adam was not leveled against his soul or spirit but against the nature of his toil and its subsequent difficulty.

Many conservative Christians assume that all humanity was affected by Adam's sin in Eden (Gen. 3:17–19) because all future generations were irreparably tainted by this decision of one person. In Judaism, sin is a human action for which every individual is responsible. Sin is not an ontological condition but relates to ethical actions and individual choices. For many conservative Christians, apart from Christ, humanity is incapable of reformation or moral goodness. In contrast, Judaism teaches that every command (*mitzvah* [מצוה]) and the practice of every ritual leads progressively to a more moral life. Even though everyone sins (Eccl. 7:20), humans can also overcome their errors through a life of service and just action.

Considering this emphasis on individual, personal responsibility, it is ironic that one of the major critiques of Judaism extended by some is that Jews are too rooted in a communitarian sensibility when thinking about how an individual relates to God. The Jewish view of sin is rooted in intentional choices that make each of us responsible for our own actions and choices. Because individuals are made in God's image, they brim with the potential for loving acts of kindness (*gemilut chasadim* [גמילות חסדים]). Any moral act imitates God's righteous behavior. Just as God covered Adam and Eve after their sin in the Garden of Eden, so should we graciously clothe those who sin with a heart of acceptance and forgiveness. In contrast, some Christians claim that we can do no acts to please God until our basic sin-nature is transformed by Christ.

The two most familiar Hebrew words used to describe what some conservative Christians call "sin" in the Bible are the terms *chet* (חטא) and *avon* (עון). The first term speaks of a mistake (Exod 34:7); the second term might better be translated as a "transgression." Such actions affect our relationship with God and bring dishonor to the divine name.

Obviously, both faiths recognize that evil exists in our world filled with suffering and woe. A traditional Jewish view that humanity is inherently good, however, provides a safeguard against any claim that God is responsible for human evil. God has given all of us free moral agency and a mission in life to be moral and every moment of life offers one the opportunity to practice *tikkun olam* (תקון עולם)—repairing the world—and to fulfill the mission of being "a kingdom of priests and a holy nation" (*mamlechet kohanim v'goy kadosh* [ממלכת כהנים וגוי קדוש]; Exod 19:6).

Judaism's ritual calendar reinforces the need to repent for past mistakes and strives to be virtuous in words and actions. Whenever a person repents (*teshuvah* [תשובה]), they are seeking, in a life-long process, to enter God's "gates of repentance," which are always open to those who are sincere and open-hearted. Repentance for mistakes and moral sins is at the heart of the commemoration of Yom Kippur, the Day of Atonement. Worshippers ask a God of grace and mercy to forgive them from misdeeds (*avon*), for deliberate acts of rebellion (*pesha* [פשע], literally a "crime"), and for mistakes that may have been inadvertent (*chet* [חטא]).

The experience of forgiveness is also different based on the nature of a specific sin. For those sins that are *bein adam l'makom* (בין אדם למקום)—"between humans and God"—, such as ritual transgressions or omissions, a person prays directly to God. For sins that are *bein adam l'chaveiro* (בין אדם לחברו)—"between fellow humans"—however, (such as gossip, theft, etc.), the tradition is that Jews should directly entreat those they have offended before they can proceed to God in worship.

In Judaism, individual sins are usually framed within a communal context of a shared responsibility. The prophets Amos, Hosea, and Isaiah speak of the rottenness of sin in a communitarian sense (see Hos 5:1; Isa 1:15). God judged the entire people of Israel for individual acts of transgression. Such a view dramatically affects any ideas about the role of the Levitical priesthood and teachings about national atonement through sacrifice. Yet, the Bible does not create an artificial barrier between "sin" and "sinners." Nor is it accurate, as one conservative Christian claimed, that "traditional Judaism has lost" an "essential insight" into the true "sinfulness of sin."[51] The view that sin is both individual and corporate has been consistent throughout Jewish theological interpretation. Professor Jacob Neusner teaches: "Corporate Israel forms a whole that exceeds the sum of its parts. The parts, the individuals, attain individuation only on the terms dictated by the whole, all Israel viewed from God's perspective."[52]

The entire world waits for God's saving work of redemption (Isa 11:6–11; Hab 2:14). This is also a New Testament theme (see Rom 8:18–25; Eph 1:9–11) that is often de-emphasized by those who stress the individual nature of the sinner before God Almighty. The New Testament passages that affirm these ideas borrow heavily from Genesis 3. It is not accurate, however, for Christians to dismiss the communal dimension of Jewish views about sin as a mere "typological understanding."[53]

A Jewish response to those who embrace the concept of original sin as the basis for thinking about interactions between God and humanity is that such a view puts an undue focus on sin instead of ethical and moral obligations to honor God through right living. It must be stressed, however, that those Christians who fixate on sin at the expense of ethical obligation contrast noticeably with other Christians (such as Orthodox and Anabaptist Christians) who note that the Bible says that *death*—and not sin—was the universal result of Adam's action (Rom 5:12). This is not a minor distinction. Indeed, the inevitability of our death, according to Orthodoxy, is the reason why people ultimately fall into sin in the first place. Most Evangelicals would agree with Michael Lotker: "Jesus came to solve a singular problem in a singular way. The problem was original sin."[54] This idea also explains, understandably, why Catholicism puts an emphasis on infant baptism. The Catholic tradition sees baptism as essential to the cleansing of sins before God (Rom 6:3–11), and if all children are born affected by original sin then it needs dealing with through baptism. All camps of Christians agree that after we are forgiven of our sins, a person should continue to seek forgiveness for their mistakes (see Matt 5:23–25; Deut 30:1–3). All forgiveness is ultimately rooted in Christ, who offers forgiveness to anyone, even a tax-collector willing to give everything away (see Luke 19:1–10) or a woman caught amid her sin (John 8:1–11).

I (Fuller) have taught that the Jewish tradition considers all sins to be actions, not simply thoughts or ideas. Of course, people often act on malicious thoughts, but many conservative Christians go one step further and claim that such thoughts confirm that people are evil at the core of their identity. An exploration of these distinctions can generate constructive discussions between Jews and Christians about basic ideas regarding human nature. Some conservative Christians, for example, look to the anguished statement attributed to King David: "In sin did my mother conceive me" (Ps 51:7) to show that the Bible reveals our inherent sin nature. Jewish commentators, in contrast, often reduce this passage to simply being a declaration of frustration on the part of David and not a general statement about the basic condition of human nature.

A Jewish Satan?

Aside from the biblical book of Job, Jewish legends are largely bereft of a "Satan" figure who represents an oppositional power to God. The heavens are not filled with two competing supernatural rivals. Instead of locating evil in a separate satanic being, each person has the capacity within themselves to be either good or evil (see Gen 6:5). A mythological Satan does appear in Jewish legends but he does not have supernatural powers. In the book of Job, "The Satan" (literally, The Adversary) is presented as a being who is a prosecutor and an accuser, whose task was to test those who challenged God. Christian mythology, in contrast, sees a Satan figure in the Garden of Eden story in the form of a conniving serpent who misleads our first ancestors into sin. Jewish renderings of this serpent show a being that has been made by God and sent to Eden to tempt humanity to rebel against the commands of God and not specifically a rebellious fallen angel named Satan.

There is a story in Genesis (6:1–4) in which it states that the "sons of God" had sexual relations with some of the women of the earth. Some rabbis have concluded that this passage refers to "fallen angels" forced to leave the heavenly realms because of carnal instincts. Over time, both Jewish and Christian scholars began to speak more of a Satan who had once been an archangel, but now has the function of tempting people in the world to be disobedient in rebellion to God. Legends in Aggadic writings (and a few times in Halachic writings) spoke of an evil fallen angel who had many underlings, or demons, which did his evil bidding. This creature was said to live in the underworld and cause harm to people who succumbed to various temptations.

This angel of death may well have had more connection with medieval Christian notions of Satan than to historic Jewish teachings. Some scholars have noted that the biblical word *satan* simply means "adversary" (1 Sam 29:4; 2 Sam 19:23) and that it is possible that God has created Satan to test us as an adversary for our souls. The Bible, some note, also speaks of an angel who is sent by God to obstruct the travels of the prophet Balaam (Num 22:32). Later Jewish literature mentioned a ruler of hell, or a "Prince of Gehenna," but these descriptions are probably borrowed from Christian sources. It is likely that such notions parallel dualistic ideas about a force of evil as described by Persian Zoroastrianism which were encountered during the Jewish diaspora in Persia. Early Jewish writers were slow to ascribe power to any other supernatural being beside God Almighty; this may explain why some Jewish theologians through the ages have seen notions of a devil and physical demons as instances of a false, dualistic view of divine power.

Living in a Broken World

John T. Pawlikowski claims that one of the "greatest moral challenges of our time comes in the area of ecology" as we become increasingly aware that "the continued destruction of our biosphere may reach the point where any possibility of healing the world has effectively vanished."[55] The pressing environmental crisis that faces our world in these times is an area where sincere and concerned people of all faiths can unite. Both Jewish and Christian faiths provide adherents with ample moral and theological resources to respond thoughtfully and constructively to our world's increasing environmental challenges. Liturgical traditions that affirm our responsibility to care for the earth, for example, should join with creative expressions of worship and education to underscore God's call for environmental stewardship.

In Judaism, Genesis describes the creation and foundations of the natural world as inherently good. One can see in this affirming claim the heart of Jewish ideas about the promotion of environmental justice. Adam and Eve were called to carefully guard and preserve the Garden of Eden through their work and were not given a license to plunder it carelessly for their own selfish benefit. An individual cannot fulfill God's charge to preserve the earth's resources while at the same time relentlessly disregarding, abusing, exploiting, or destroying those resources. The scriptures, for example, command that farmers should leave their properties fallow every seventh year and that they should not immediately eat the fruit of certain trees but rather wait several years (Exod 23:11). The Bible also contains many verses that speak of protection for animals (e.g., Deut 25:4; 5:14; Exod 20:10).

The lesson of the Tower of Babel is that trouble ensues when humans go beyond their role in the natural order of things. Creative and innovative abilities, gifts of God to humanity, should not become tools for callous exploitation or self-aggrandizement. The most glaring example of this is in Deuteronomy 20:19, where it states that one is not allowed to destroy (lo-tashchit) fruit-bearing trees in order to lay siege against a city. Even in the most life-threatening situations of war, one is forbidden to use trees for weapons or to waste them on the creation of weapons of warfare. If such is the prohibition during a stressful time like war, how much the more so is it forbidden during times of peace? This phrase is the source text for almost all the environmental laws expounded by scholars who study the Talmud.

Humans should derive pleasure from the blessings of the physical world, made for our nurture and enjoyment. Some Jews have even claimed it is a sin when any individual does not fully embrace all the pleasures that the Almighty has provided for all of humanity to enjoy. Food, and all other sensual pleasures, are pathways to worship, not as evils to be avoided, except in unhealthy excess. When a person "blesses" bread and wine at a table (or numerous other encounters in nature), they are simply acknowledging with gratitude to God its inherent characteristics, as opposed to bestowing on it some magical power such as a transfer of goodness. One student said that the idea of *tikkun olam* seemed to counter what she had learned about how humanity was to "take dominion" over the earth (Gen 1:28):

> Because Christians believe the earth is only temporary, their goal on this earth is to get to heaven. That is why in the past, taking care of the environment was not the focus of Christianity. Growing up in a Pentecostal community, I was brought up not to pay too much attention to the world and my own body because the world and my body were only the temporary address for my soul. Now environmentalism is becoming very prevalent in various Christian communities. Even my own views about the environment and my own body have changed.[56]

No Jewish Hair-Shirts

A fundamentally different view about our human nature also leads to two distinct views on asceticism—rarely practiced in the long history of Judaism. Rabbis have long explained that God has given everything within our lives to be celebrated; nothing that God has created for our use is to be understood outside of the active presence of God's love (Ps 16:8) . Humans are commanded to multiply (Gen 1:28), thus making celibacy rarely practiced (except for a time during the Second Temple period) in Jewish history.

When individuals choose to fast, it is better that such efforts result in blessings for others (Isa 58:6–8) and are not done only for personal, spiritual gain. Material self-denial is expressly forbidden on the Sabbath and during times of feasting. The Nazirites, who made a vow (Num 6:1–21) to God not to cut their hair or drink wine, also had to bring a sin offering to the altar for their choice of seeking to know the Divine apart from the standard practices of the larger community. What is their sin? Perhaps it is that they are choosing not to enjoy some of the blessings that the Almighty has put on earth for their benefit.

Christianity has been heavily influenced by Greek and Roman ideas about the inherently inferior nature of the physical world. St. Augustine brought the ideas of a dichotomous and fallen world into the heart of the Catholic tradition with his teachings on the superiority of the spiritual over the physical. It is possible that Christ had some ascetic practices, in keeping with John the Baptist and others who stressed fasting and denial much more than other Jewish teachers of his time. When Jesus, for example, condemns the rich man and claims that a rich man cannot enter heaven easily (Luke 18:25), such words could also have been proclaimed by those Hebrew prophets who condemned those choosing a life of comfort instead of generosity.

Christians should appreciate how differing views of sin and the idea of an inherent sin nature affect varying Jewish and Christian considerations about the nature of the afterlife. A theological focus within Judaism on the inherent goodness of humanity has also played a role in why Jews seem far less concerned with grim and punishing visions of hell than some conservative Christians. These topics, of course, are mentioned, but with far less frequency in synagogues than in churches. Jews are encouraged to use the gift of time on this earth to sanctify *this* life and not to fixate on their eventual, possible status in the world beyond. Every day is a gift given by a God of love and mercy for our nurture and enhancement. One cannot escape living in this life by dreaming about the promise and hope of an ideal, future heaven.

Teaching Circumcision

The ritual of circumcision is a familial reaffirmation of faith before God and the entire Jewish community. God commanded that Father Abraham first administer this rite to himself, and then to his son Isaac on the eighth day after birth (Gen 17:10–12). It is not merely a surgical operation but an act of obedience to a divine command, and some Jews throughout history have chosen to die rather than cease to practice this ritual. Some rabbis have even claimed that the divine command to circumcise male children is more meaningful than any other commandment.

Rashi, an eleventh-century commentator on the Torah and the Talmud, imagined a story illustrating the centrality of circumcision. He wrote that Kind David himself, who was physically fit, had just finished competing in his generation's equivalent of the athletic Olympics. Since that kind of time and effort in athleticism and shaving the body was contrary to Jewish practice, David sitting in the bathhouse relaxing began to feel guilty that he was indiscernible from his non-Jewish competitors. When he looked down and saw his circumcision, he was comforted in remembering that he had not completely abandoned his commitment to his people.

Adherents of both traditions accept that actions in the physical realm, such as circumcision, are related to an unseen spiritual dimension. The Passover meal and the ritual of the Eucharist (for Christians) are also material ceremonies that point to a higher spiritual meaning. All of life is to be united, not divided between that which belongs to God and to the realm of the physical.

Conclusion

Various Jewish rituals are practiced as concrete reminders of how the faithful should perceive the world. At the heart of many rituals is an emphasis on the daily responsibility that individuals have for their own ethical choices. Even emotions must conform to a commitment to relate to other Jews worldwide as they struggle to serve God despite pressing obstacles and difficult circumstances. One of the reasons why Jewish newlyweds smash a glass on their wedding day is to remind themselves— in their greatest joy—that individuals within their cherished community have suffered (and continue to suffer) as they remain faithfully devoted to the faith.

The Jewish mandate for peace—*shalom* (שלום)—is a call for wholeness deeply rooted in this tradition of individual responsibility for moral actions and intentions. The message of *tikkun olam* is a call to bring justice and peace through good deeds into all our relationships in a world filled with evil and injustice. While conservative Christians celebrate the redemptive work of Jesus as Messiah on their behalf, Judaism teaches that individuals cannot stand by with passivity and expect God to forgive their sins through the whims of unmerited, divine actions. Jews, of course, believe that God is merciful and forgiving and has done (and will continue to do) many miracles on their behalf, but there is no understanding that salvation from sin is realized through the shedding of a divine savior's holy blood. Some Christians use the story of Leviticus and the practice of the ancient sacrificial system to confirm their views that God's eternal plan for salvation was to be expressed in a blood sacrifice. In contrast, Jewish teachers have called the community to live as a faithful people before God and to serve others with love and justice as "a kingdom of priests and a holy nation" (Exod 19:6). When Jews live in such a way, they will not live only for their own good but to meet the needs of others. They trust that—as it relates to their eternal destiny—the "God of all the earth will do right" (Gen 18:25).

The central focus of Jewish moral teaching is the command for ethical actions expressed in right relationships with others. Martin Buber explains that God is both the "wholly other" and the "wholly present" who is the "mystery of the obvious that is closer to me than my own I."[57] One knows God through knowing the divine creation, and one shows love to God through loving one's fellow humanity. While all of us aspire to personal spiritual and moral growth, none of us can do this independent of others because we are all interrelated, and all share the mark of our common creation in the image of God Almighty.

In contrast, some conservative Christian pastors preach that—while ethics is important and many even speak of the "fruits" of a genuine believer ("by their fruits ye shall know them" [Matt 7:16])—it is not ethical action that is at the heart of God's eternal plan of salvation. God in Christ is the perfect sacrifice, which erases the blot of all human sinfulness inherent at birth in all sinners, and only the acceptance of a divine blood-sacrifice can appease the demand of a righteous and Holy God for moral purity and perfection.

Chapter Four

Covenant, Atonement, and Sacrifice

Without the shedding of blood there is no remission for sins.
—Hebrews 9:22

The anti-Judaic root of Christianity cannot be torn out until the church's Christology is rid of its negation of the ongoing validity of the Jewish faith.
—Walter Reuther

The Only Path to Salvation

CHRISTIANS SOMETIMES ONLY LEARN about Jews from the pages of the Bible and view Judaism as a historic and ancient form of "Christianity without Christ."[58] They cannot help thinking about Jesus when it comes to learning about Judaism, because Jesus is the primary interpretative lens for their conclusions about any other faith. One way to encourage conservative Christians to consider this preoccupation from a more "Jewish perspective" is to ask how they feel when Muslims ask them to realize how the claims of the Prophet Muhammad relate to Christianity. Just as Muhammad post-dates Christianity, so also the message of Jesus originates from pre-rabbinic Judaism, having no bearing on the tradition of rabbinic Judaism.

For many conservative Christians, the "Old Testament" unambiguously points to the centrality of Christ as the Son of God in both religions. One student explained, "The Bible shows that Jesus brought the new covenant making the old covenant invalid .... Their remission of sins came through animal sacrifices. Yet Christ's sacrifice nullified all that and remission of sins now comes through him and only him. It isn't the politically correct answer, but it is what the Bible teaches."[59] Jews have no other savior and no other hope for eternal salvation beyond accepting Jesus as savior. Being Jewish is being an individual without any secure and confident certainty of eternal salvation. One student explained: "Whenever I hear of the struggles of the Jewish people, I wonder what it would be like to be a Jew. But I am a Christian and one of the best benefits of being a Christian is that I have a savior."[60] Some people simply know that they are right and claim to be certain beyond any shadow of doubt about their eternal destiny. Such a posture is framed as the love of a God-given truth over any form of compromise. One student mused:

> The concept of pluralism doesn't really fit into my worldview. There is a part of me that really wants to be a pluralist. It would make life so much easier. But alas, I believe in absolute truth. If one thing is true, then the opposite thing cannot be true. Therefore, I know that a flower is red even if my friend believes that a flower is blue. I think that my friend is wrong in his belief about the flower. I know we are not supposed to say that people are "wrong" or "right" currently, but I really don't see a way out of it. Now, if I was a pluralist, I would be able to say we are both right. I would not have to conflict with my friend but, when it comes to hell, I would have to watch him suffer his choice for all eternity. There can only be one ultimate and absolute truth.[61]

The logic of the Christian faith for this student, and many others, is a comforting straitjacket that allows for no consideration that there might be any kind of saving truth in any faith other than Christianity. Even if the student is right and that some truth claims entail the denial of incompatible truth claims, we all need a big dose of humility to stop us claiming unchallengeable certainty for claims that are beyond checking and testing, such as belief about the afterlife. And we also need to think very carefully before asserting that a certain truth claim requires the denial of a certain other truth claim. Some assertions appear contradictory at first sight but upon reflection need not be. More than that, we need to be very cautious about claiming that a person's final destiny is fixed by the accuracy of their beliefs. We might consider the possibility that God does not make salvation depend on only correct belief.

For some Christians, there is a major focus on two specific passages in the New Testament, which are appear to teach Christian exclusivism. These two verses—Acts 4:12 and John 14:6—seem to affirm that only Jesus provides eternal salvation from death and hell. In John 14:6, Jesus declares: "I am the Way, the Truth, and the Life, no man comes to the Father except through me." For many, this is the end of the debate; no need for any further discussion. Judaism may be beautiful or filled with sage wisdom, but it offers no salvific truth and cannot lead people into an eternal and intimate relationship with God. The Jewish people have been "John 14-sixed." There is no room to consider any other option beside the resounding certainty and truth of Christianity and the evident falsehoods of all other misguided religions.

Is this what John 14:6 means? Our goal is not to suggest that there is only one way to read certain biblical passages, but one interesting alternative interpretation of John 14:6 is found in the *Jewish Annotated New Testament*. It refers to the term that "Christ-believers" used to call themselves—"the way" (Acts 9:2)—and says that the references to truth and life are meant to emphasize that "knowledge of truth is more like a personal relationship instead of an intellectual experience."[62] Considering this seeming impasse, Franz Rosenzweig suggests that the phrase "no man can come to the Father except through me" could be read as a statement of the need to live the same kind of sacrificial life as Jesus. In other words, walking the way Jesus walked is the only way to come to the Father. Christian theologian Clark Williams claims that both John 14:6 and Acts 4:12 are "theocentric instead of Jesus-centric."[63] Williams argues that both passages affirm that salvation only comes through the "Name" of God, as cited in Acts 4:12, and the "I AM" cited in John 14:6 (which alludes to Exod 3:14–15, *Ehyeh asher ehyeh* [אהיה אשר אהיה]), and notes that the Hebrew name Y'shua (יהושע) means "YHWH Saves." Others have seen these (and other) passages as confirmations of the specific need for *non-Jews* to embrace God through Jesus. Some Christians fail to interpret these passages in the context of their larger themes—such as humility, as advocated in John 14:1–5, and the progressive insights being gained in the life of Peter (e.g. Acts 4:12 understood considering Acts 10:34–35). There are many other passages in John's Gospel that affirm Jesus has come to make, in the words of Exodus 19:6, the Name of God "resound throughout the earth" (see John 5:34; 10:25; 12:13; 17:6).

The theological loyalty to Christian exclusivity convinces individuals that Christians alone have the truth; to think otherwise would be un-Christian. They tend to ignore passages that focus on the fact that God has *already* "reconciled the world to himself" (2 Cor 5:18–19); and claim that verses that show that the entire world will be saved (see John 3:17; 1 Tim 2:4; John 1:29; Rom 5:18; Col 1:19–20) are misinterpreted by liberal, inclusivist universalists. I have yet to hear—in any conservative Christian service that I have attended—a sermon that takes seriously the message of Jesus in John 4:22 that "salvation is from the Jews." How can this clear statement be read to imply that salvation is outside of God's eternal salvation story? Some conclude that salvation "is from the Jews" because Jesus was Jewish. In contrast, the controversial Anabaptist theologian John Howard Yoder notes that John 4:22 should make moot the question of how Christians should bring salvation to the Jews.[64]

What some Christians might call "gray-areas" or points of "nuance" are deep chasms that lead one straight into hell and godless compromise. To ask certain questions is to invite a level of unbelief. Even the very process of exploring an unknown idea needs to be safely framed within the confines of assurances that eventually everything will become reconciled to the larger scope of their secure presuppositions about the true nature of the world. As the Danish philosopher Søren Kierkegaard claims, for some Christians, a sense of certainty and the claims of faith are synonymous. Absolute truth is "owned" and has already been fully embraced by many conservative Christians. This provides great comfort and a sense of being free from all uncertainties. The knowledge that one has the truth provides a comforting steel-framed shark tank to rest within even as looming monsters of the deep, dark approach and threaten to destroy us. One student explained, "The Jewish people do not have that reassurance of us Christians that once we commit our lives to God and accept the sacrifice of Jesus then we are saved and that no other works are required."[65]

One student reflected: "When people think about Jews, they usually think of individuals that have denounced Jesus Christ."[66] My response (van Gorder) was that most individuals that I knew would not have that as their first conclusion and that this student was probably referring to *Evangelical* responses to Jews. It is hard to imagine how the entire sum of a person's life can be viewed through so constricting a lens, but this is exactly what happens when that is what many conservative Christians see as most central to their own lives. In contrast, some Baylor students hold much more tolerant views. One student wrote: "Being from Kansas City instead of the extreme Bible Belt of Texas I grew up with a lot of Jewish friends."[67] The student contrasted her own first-hand experience with

Jews and those of her classmates from rural towns and villages in Texas, whom she assumed had no such similar experiences.

Sacrificing Animals in Central Texas

Jews have not participated in sacrificial rituals for almost two thousand years. That compelling fact, however, is not always known by some Christians that we have encountered. The emphasis on rituals centered on animal sacrifices relates to how conservative Christians view the role that Jesus plays in providing—as the "Lamb of God"—a conclusive sacrifice to appease the wrath of a holy God. Rituals of killing animals to satiate God are now unnecessary because Jesus is the once-and-for-all Lamb of God who takes away the sins of the world.

Some undergrads that we have met have even assumed that the sacrifice of animals is either continuing or that many Jews would think it would be ideal if these ritual practices were reestablished (a theme emphasized in the *Left Behind* series). One student asked sincerely, "What do Jews do for their sins now that they no longer offer animal sacrifices?"[68] This student's question is genuine because the assumption that has been taught in Sunday school classes is that Jesus completed the codes that required an animal sacrifice and that their absence would pose a central problem to the practice of Judaism. James Yaffe reported that one Sunday school teacher asked a local rabbi if her class could visit a synagogue when animal sacrifices were being carried out.[69]

Many conservative Christians conceive of a Judaism from the first century that looks nothing at all like modern Judaism. This caricature of Judaism is a religion of Sadducees, Zealots, Essenes, and Pharisees. Since they view the early followers of Jesus as Jewish, it is often seen that Christianity has arisen as some sort of reform to a stale religion. In fact, rabbinic Judaism was a reform of biblical Judaism. The rabbis taught that several things now replace sacrifices, including prayer and charity. And while rabbinic Judaism has flourished for two millennia, the relatively recent arrival of movements within Judaism, including Reform, Conservative, Reconstructionist, and others, shows that Judaism continues to evolve in new contexts and in response to new questions.

Concepts of Covenant

Judaism and Christianity are both traditions rooted in a concept of a covenant. Covenants, or contracts, were formal agreements common among individuals in the Middle East. Judaism transformed this idea to include a dynamic relationship between the Almighty and the created order. The first covenant was forged between God and Noah; this agreement was sealed with the sign of a rainbow in the sky, which served as a confirmation that the Divine would never again destroy the earth with a flood (Gen 9:15).

Seven commandments, compiled together in the Talmud, were seen to have been given to Noah with the intention that they should be followed by all humanity; a covenant universal in scope. The covenant between Abraham is then made as an everlasting promise to his descendants (Gen 17:7) and a covenant for the entire people of Israel (Deut 30:15–16). Although the story of the binding of Isaac by Abraham (Gen 22) is not initially an anti-human sacrifice text, it does lead the reader towards that stark and chilling conclusion. In the biblical account, Abraham sacrifices a ram in Isaac's stead, which was perhaps the beginning of animal sacrifice for the Jews, and which continues throughout the rest of the Torah in intricate detail.

Indeed, God authored many differing covenants with Israel; each of them is a call to reciprocate, with thanks and offerings, a commitment of fidelity to these covenants. Modern Christians need to recapture an appreciation that God has established multiple covenants—a doctrine long-affirmed by early church fathers, St. Irenaeus, and others. Each covenant has lost nothing of its original integrity, and it should not be assumed that each is a theological stepping-stone to the establishment or authority of the next covenant.

God makes covenants with the Jewish nation, first and foremost, and not with self-concerned individuals within that nation.[70] Judaism does not promote an individualized ethic, but *the entire community* is called to reveal the nature of God through their moral and ethical actions. As the nation fulfills these moral laws, they will become known by God (Exod 19:6-7) and will be a light to all other nations (Isa 42:6). There is no room for arrogant boasting, as God's blessings of mercy and grace are never given to encourage Jews to think that they are superior to other nations, because God is the Lord of the entire universe (see Isa 2:1–5). At the same time, every covenant God makes with humanity is a reassertion that human beings are invested with a fundamental worth and value.

Some conservative Christians believe that their Jewish neighbors can only merit God's acceptance if they convert to Christianity. They come into our classes stating the conclusion that Judaism came to an effective end with the rejection of Jesus, their only hope for salvation. They became "cut off" from the "tree of the covenant" while non-Jewish gentiles "became grafted in" as their replacements (Rom 11:17–24). On this phrase the *Jewish Annotated New Testament* counters supersessionist claims: "The tree is not described as Israel and Paul does not draw the inference that non-Israelites become members of Israel. The tree appears to represent all who are in the family of God, Israelite branches as well as ones from other nations."[71]

Bringing Down a Curse?

A casual observer, outside of our own context of engagement, may be forgiven for assuming that the issue of "who killed Jesus?" was a remote memory from the horrors of Europe's medieval past, dating from long before the coming of the Enlightenment. Certainly, most Christian communities of faith, one of the last being the Roman Catholic Church, have recognized the inherently anti-Semitic quality of repeating such assertions encouraging their congregations to step back from the issue of culpability for the death of Jesus. Most Protestant traditions have done the same.

Because those who supported the crucifixion of Jesus were Jewish, some Christians have claimed that this brought down a curse on all Jews. This view—common in historic Christian teachings—is rarely, if ever, heard among modern Catholics, Orthodox, or mainstream Protestants. Proponents claim support from the Gospel of Matthew (Matt 21:39, 43; 27:25), although many biblical scholars would contest this interpretation of the passages in question. John's Gospel shows the Roman Governor Pontius Pilate repeatedly declaring the innocence of Jesus while the Jews refuse to call for Christ's release (John 18:38; 19:4, 6). North American Evangelist Howard Taylor explains, "Israel's sin is the refusal to accept God's even deeper election in Jesus."[72] Christians are now the "true Jews" and descendants of Abraham (Rom 9:6–9). These same biblical literalists forget that the New Testament, indeed the very biblical passage just appealed to (Rom 9–11), says that the "gifts and callings of God" to the Jewish people are *eternal and irrevocable* (Rom 11:29; Lev 26:44).

The idea that, collectively, Jews "killed Christ" and thus have faced the wrath of God is an arcane slander that has survived into the present among a tiny minority of conservative Christians. What is the reason for this? In churches across North America every Easter Sunday, passages are repeatedly read that indict the Jews for killing Jesus. Some Christians study their Bibles and note that the Jewish leaders played a central role in the gruesome death of Jesus and conclude that such deceptive behavior set the stage for a hardening of their individual and corporate hearts to the truth about Jesus. In these renderings, the powers of evil risk becoming personified by deceptive and scheming Jewish leaders who condemn Jesus to death while the role of the Roman soldiers is downplayed as if the unwilling Romans were helpless under the sway of demanding Jewish leaders.

Although it is an anti-Semitic claim that the Jews killed Jesus, one can find traces of this view among a handful of conservative Christians. One student thought about the role that the Jews played in the death of Jesus: "Jesus could not have been resurrected, overcame death, and paid the penalty for our sins if he had not first been killed by the Jews."[73] At the other side of the spectrum, another student wrote, "I would never think of accusing a modern Jew for killing Jesus and using that as a reason to hate them, nor have I ever heard anyone speak like this. I often think that it was my own sinfulness, and not that of the Jews, that nailed Jesus to the Cross."[74]

Confronting Supersessionism

A familiar perception that some Christians bring to their views about Judaism is the idea that it is a faith of antiquated values. It is sometimes seen as a religion entombed within a distant history, no longer relevant to the modern world. Judaism has logically been replaced by Christianity. One student wrote, "I have always been taught that much of the laws of the Christian Old Testament were relevant practices at the time but have since been outdated and are no longer necessary. Though these religious laws are no longer practiced they are still part of a Christian's heritage. I admire the Jews for keeping such accurate record of their ancient laws and religious beliefs."[75]

This kind of inverted compliment is reflective of an aggressive theological assertion about Judaism often described as "supersessionism." Anything of merit that was once inside Judaism has safely transitioned into Christianity, leaving only a decaying shell of formalistic rituals without any capacity to touch God's heart or provide eternal security with God.

Supersessionism is accepted by some Christians as an obvious truth. Jesus completed the covenant of Judaism and made it forever irrelevant with a new covenant based on grace. The death of Jesus, the Jewish Messiah, encourages some Christians to view Judaism as an ancient relic of the past and something of a fossilized version of what was once a dynamic, but now bankrupt, faith. The devout Christian is a warrior for the truth and a prizefighter living in a hostile world under the dominion of Satan. Jews and others are facing an eternal hell filled with endless torments and punishments. Rabbi Michael Cook writes that "early Christianity's need to justify its separateness from Judaism required of it expressions of negativity towards its parent."[76]

Conservative Christians sometimes downplay the Jewishness of Jesus even though it is not difficult to see how the teachings of Jesus are quite "Jewish" in their presentation and content. Amy-Jill Levine explains, "Historically, Jesus should be seen as continuous with the line of Jewish teachers and prophets for he shares with them a particular view of the world and a particular manner of expressing that view."[77] In another book, Levine writes, "Jesus of Nazareth dressed like a Jew, prayed like a Jew, instructed other Jews on how best to live according to the commandments given by God to Moses, taught like a Jew, argued like a Jew with other Jews and then died with thousands of other Jews on a Roman cross."[78] In response, the supersessionist view that Christianity replaces Judaism sees in the promotion of such Jewish Jesus ideas an inherent challenge to their own assertions that Jesus has "completed" Judaism. Jesus was a revolutionary against the entrenchment of established Jewish power-structures instead of a supportive insider and a willing participant within a calcified tradition he boldly confronted with prophetic authority. Jesus gives an efficacious new covenant which makes the old pathways to faith in God irrelevant. Jesus taught a dynamic faith while the Judaism of that time was mired in cold, legalism.

Some Christians point to the destruction of the temple in 70 CE as being foretold by Jesus as the final proof that Christianity had superseded Judaism. While the destruction of the temple was obviously a traumatic event for early Judaism, Judaism was not as dependent on the temple as some have assumed. The Jewish community through the ages (and before this tragedy) had already focused on core ethical values instead of rituals and ceremonies. The centrality that conservative Christians give to the import of sacrifice also explains why many develop misunderstandings about Judaism, including the idea that all modern Jews are still looking for a messiah. Indeed, it is helpful to show non-Jews that the *Amidah* itself expresses such a messianic hope. For many, however, the notion today is that what is hoped for is a messianic age.

Legalistic Bondage

Christianity, for some, is contrasted in bold relief with blind adherence to the formalistic rituals of Judaism. Trying to fulfill the elaborate and extensive proscribed laws and practices of Judaism would, it is assumed, be a demanding task. One student lamented: "I have always wondered why Jews have so many rules. It seems so exhausting to keep up with all of them."[79]

Some Christians assume that modern Judaism teaches that these rules are to be obeyed even when they are no longer relevant to daily life. The idea, for example, that the adherence to the Sabbath in Judaism is a gift, not an onerous religious burden, sometimes comes as a surprise to our students. For many of them, a legalist is an individual who focuses on outward form, not underlying meaning. Such views rule out any possibility that the Judaism of Jesus' day was a religious tradition that allowed certain legal codes to be broken if a higher need arose. Such a view also overlooks the many times in Matthew's Gospel where Jesus calls for the observance of all the commandments (see Matt 5:19; 7:21; 25:31; 28:19–20). These views limit the appreciation that students might have that Jesus, himself, as a Jew, was far more conversant with the supposed legalism of the Pharisees than the more philosophical ideas of the Sadducees.

How do these views affect the way that some Christians understand Jewish views of salvation? They are often taught that the pathway of Jesus is opposite from those who try to please God through works of righteousness, to "build a ladder" to God through good deeds. One student wrote: "Personally, I don't believe that by abiding by the Law we can ever completely mend human brokenness. A divine act of God is necessary."[80]

This student seems to think that Judaism is, ultimately, a futile attempt to attain salvation through what she calls a "series of dos and don'ts." While such students see Christianity as a religion of redemptive grace, Judaism is viewed as a religion that relies upon demanding laws. Religious rules, such as dietary regulations, are spiritual boa-constrictors that choke out any possibility for genuine personal worship of God. Some Christians focus on the obligatory nature of Jewish law to such a degree that they forget that there is any element of healing grace, forgiveness, and mercy within Judaism. Even the idea of an act of ethical kindness, a *mitzvah*, becomes (in this rendering) the attempts of lost souls to please a distant God they do not know, but fear.

The heart of this miscalculation springs from the singular interpretation that the apostle Paul gives to the covenant that God made with Abraham. Paul wrote that passages such as Genesis 15:6 assert that Abraham was accepted by God as being righteous purely on the fact that he had faith and not that he was obedient to the other conditions God gave him in the Mosaic law. In Romans 4:1–25, for example, Paul claims that Father Abraham was not justified through the law but through faith. The specific context for this argument is Paul's desire to allow gentiles to enter the church without needing to be circumcised. This historical context is often lost, however, for those who assume that the authority of the new covenant has replaced the old. What these Christians need to appreciate is that such a view argues, in effect, that Christians—and not Jews—truly understand the Jewish heritage.

Explaining Judaism to Jews

Jews have always believed that it is the covenant that God made with Moses, and not with Abraham, which is of the greatest importance to their faith. Further, even the Abrahamic covenant is not seen as a covenant that disregards moral obedience to divine commands. At the very least, the Abrahamic covenant is based upon the expectation that the faithful will follow the same seven commands God gave to Noah and the entire world. From a Jewish perspective, some New Testament texts conflate the Abrahamic and Mosaic covenants into one "old" covenant (see Heb 8:6, 13 as examples of this conflation). For Paul, Abraham's faith is the same kind of faith that Christians should now show towards Jesus. Paul uses the story of Abraham as a backdrop to prove his conviction that faith, and not ethnicity, is central. Amy-Jill Levine argues that Paul's reading of the story of Abraham effectively "disenfranchises the Jewish people and replaces them with Jesus-believers, both Jewish and Gentile; belief comes to replace ethnicity in determining the heirs of Abraham."[81] Clearly, Paul (and the author of Hebrews) have distinct definitions of such words as "grace," "covenant," and even "Israel" (more about that later) that are unique to their own intended audiences.

The supersessionist idea asserts that the "old testament" is a covenant that has been replaced by Christ and nullified by God. Some Christians have dismissed the idea that the first covenant has any value any longer and emphatically state that "a two-covenant theology is unacceptable."[82] The question of "old" and "new" covenants goes to the question of whether Judaism has "failed" in some intrinsic way. This becomes a foundational issue whenever Jews and Christians discuss how one best relates to God. Anti-Semites throughout history have relied on the irrelevance of a discarded covenant to disprove the efficacy of Judaism while Jews have used this language to show how many Christians negatively view their faith. For many Jews and Christians hoping to foster respect and mutual understanding, issues of the clarity in language are front and center. For example, as mentioned earlier, some Christians have repudiated the use of the term "Old Testament" for the first part of their Bibles out of concern that this term reinforces the idea that the new covenant has fully replaced the efficacy of the "old" covenant.

Students sometimes claim to understand Judaism better than Jews and hope to explain to them how Jesus is their true Jewish Messiah. The logic is unilateral: if Jesus is the Jewish Messiah then Jesus is also the Messiah for all peoples. The logic of their exclusivist worldviews often creates fundamentally anti-Jewish sentiments where Christians express frustration that Jews do not see the obvious truth about their own faith. What also galls some conservative Christians is that most Jews that they meet find the question of the status of Jesus completely irrelevant to their lives. One student explained:

> I have been taught that Christianity is special above all other religions. God is the One True God and Jesus is the only way to get to heaven. I have found these statements consistent with, even essential to what I have found in the Bible. This view, that Christianity is set above all other religions is not consistent with the rabbi's statement and the broader observation that religions are essentially created to provide meaning in life. The problem I face

is that, unlike most statements on religion, this generalization is very objective rather than subjective and can be empirically proven. At the same time, I cannot accept the idea that there may not be a true God that sent his Son to die for our sins. My faith relies on the fact that Jesus is the one true way to eternal salvation. I have no problem putting my faith in something I cannot see and cannot fully understand or comprehend, but I cannot put my faith in a figment of someone's imagination.[83]

The ways Jews and Christians talk about the "covenant" are distinct and there is no simple parallel between the two views. Discussing the divergence over this contested term will help Christians avoid unnecessary misunderstandings originating from supersessionist views. Christians should be warned that such explorations of this theme in the long history of Jewish-Christian relations will lead straight to confronting problems that relate to historic anti-Semitism. On the other side of the coin, Christians can be reassured that Jews are not asking that they delete all references to covenant in their hymns, liturgy, and preaching. To the contrary, the centrality of this theme within Christianity can help underscore the differences between Christian and Jewish views.

St. Paul and Jewish-Christian Interactions

Is it possible that Paul "diverted" from the "ideology of Jesus" which also "represented a departure from Judaism and marks the beginning of a theological structure that could not possibly be acceptable to Jews"?[84] Amy-Jill Levine observes: "Although Paul . . . is sometimes charged with transforming the message of the Kingdom of God that Jesus proclaimed into a proclamation of Jesus himself, the charge is an overstatement."[85] For Levine, the claims of Pauline Christianity provides an intriguing starting point for Jewish-Christian discussions about the nature of salvation. For example, Paul writes that faith, and not works of righteousness, is what justifies a person. For Paul, righteousness by works is not even humanly possible given the way human beings express sinful behaviors. Further, it can be argued that Paul does not have a firmly stated doctrine of original sin. Such a concept will emerge much later in Christian theological history, drawing inferences from the assertions of Paul's writings. The writings of St. Paul (and the book of Hebrews) in the New Testament are oft-cited sources for the extrapolation of Christian theological ideas about God's covenants. While these passages have provided the groundwork for many supersessionist ideas, one should not automatically assume that the original authors framed their views with that intention. Paul, in fact, began his life as a devout Pharisee; he boasted of his strong Jewish credentials and his deep training within the Jewish theological tradition (Gal 1:14; Phil 3:4–6).

Of course, Paul is not a "Christian" and never uses the term to describe himself because there were no set Christian-versus-Jewish categories at that time (see Acts 11:26). On the other hand, Paul was completely Jewish and understood non-Jews through the frame of his Jewish identity. Amy-Jill Levine explains, "Paul, good Jew that he was, knew about righteous Gentiles. He also knew that the God of Israel was also the God of the Gentiles. . . . For Paul, the Gentiles would come into the messianic realm as Gentiles. They did not have to be Jews in order to be in right relationship with God."[86] Paul believed that he was preaching the message, revealed in Jesus, that was first preached by Abraham and those Jews who were the "first to receive" the truth before it was given to the rest of the world (Rom 1:16).

In the New Testament book of Hebrews, the language of "new covenant" (Heb 8:8–12) is quite like the writings of the Hebrew prophets such as Jeremiah (31:31–34) and these passages are quoted at length. These scriptures warn against individuals forsaking the original covenants and call adherents to "receive what was promised" (Heb 10:35–36). In none of these references are followers of the first covenant described as distinct from those who were now following Jesus. The same focus on the forgiveness of sins is maintained: Jesus brings a "better covenant" directly tied to Jesus serving as a more effective high priest on the model that God has already established (Heb 8:6–8).

While it is probable St. Paul was not the author of the book of Hebrews, this book offers a clear perspective on Judaism that is a distinct departure from previous New Testament books. It uses emphatic language to argue that, after Jesus, Judaism is now obsolete. Ideas about the "obsolete" (see Heb 10:9; 8:13) nature of the first covenant probably refers to the fact that the destruction of the temple ended sacrifices and not as a blanket statement against all Judaism. There is no inherent denigration of the "old" by the coming of the "new." Indeed, one cannot fully appreciate the work of Jesus independent from what God has already done through the Jewish community from which Jesus came. Even so-called "replacement theologies," which assert that the way of Jesus has replaced previously cherished Jewish understandings of right relationship with

God, cannot proceed without referencing existing Jewish normative explanations.

Instead of "using" Paul's writings to promote the idea of Christian superiority over Judaism, these same texts can become resources to stress the interconnectedness of the two traditions. Paul joins Ezekiel in calling us to return with freshness to God's singular intention throughout time (Ezek 16:60; 34:25; 37:26). Paul forever places the language of the "new" covenant in reference to the Lord's Supper (1 Cor 11:25–26). The "new-ness" of this covenant is not contrasted with some perceived deficiency in the "old." Paul's focus was usually on gentiles who were never Jewish. Even though he had this focus, in every instance Paul asserted that those who are chosen can aspire to the blessings of Israel (Rom 9:3; 11:26–27). To suggest that such an idea was not conversant with Judaism, however, would be to suggest that Judaism is inherently xenophobic, which is inaccurate.

We should not bring our own assumptions about modern Jewish-Christian interactions to the letters of Paul, written two millennia ago. In these letters, Paul described himself as a "minister of a new covenant" (2 Cor 3:6) in response to those who challenged his apostolic authority. He wrote that the "old" covenant was veiled (2 Cor 3:14), but not abrogated, by those who rejected it. Paul draws a compelling comparison between Hagar and Sarah (Gal 4:24–33; 5:1) both of whom are "Old" Testament figures, to make a point about following God with one's whole heart instead of a blind slavishness to the "letter of the law." Whatever else Paul is asserting by elevating the status of Sarah over Hagar (or Abraham over Moses; see Gal 3:15–18), these passages do not suggest that Paul rejected the legitimacy of a dynamic spirituality that pleases God through Judaism. The *Jewish Annotated New Testament* explains, "Paul posits a mutually exclusive relationship between the covenant, the promise, and the inheritance on one side and the law on the other."[87]

Only in hindsight can one read into the text any sense of rivalry between what God has done through the divine covenant with Abraham and Moses and what God is doing in the world through Jesus. Paul, and the author of Hebrews, uses the assumed legitimacy of the first covenants to affirm the work of Jesus and does not negatively contrast the work of Christ as being independent from the promises God gave at Mount Sinai (see Heb 9:18–20). Of course, Paul also appreciates that the Passover story is a specific event in time and place that describes the specific experiences of the Jewish people and, as such, is not technically relevant for all peoples. Paul's letters to non-Jews seems to strive to find a way that their practices can remain congruent in some form with his own self-proclaimed Judaism. One vital fact is that all of Paul's writings (and the Book of Hebrews) came at a time when the authority of the Jewish tradition was unquestioned and its legitimacy before God was assumed. It was also a time when these first Christians were trying to codify their own beliefs while thinking that, all along, they themselves remained securely within the Jewish tradition.

St. Paul's writings are filled with labyrinthine challenges that defy simple conclusions such as emphatic claims that he was anti-Semitic (or that he was not). In discussing Paul's writings there are several ways to proceed. A few passages to keep in mind are those verses where Paul teaches that God has never rejected, and will never reject, the Jewish people (Rom 11:1–2) and the assurance that "all Israel will be saved" because the eternal "gifts and callings of God are irrevocable" (Rom 11:26, 28–29).

Perhaps the clearest note in all of Paul's writings on these issues is Romans 11:33 where he exults, "O the depth of the riches and wisdom and knowledge of God. How unsearchable are his judgments and how inscrutable are his ways!" Whatever else that can be said about Paul's views of the people of Israel, this note of humility and trust in God's redeeming goodness offers a key step in countering supersessionist, triumphalist perspectives and a step closer to affirming that God's mercy extends to everyone, both Jews and Christians.

Election: Jewish and Christian

According to the Anglican Bishop Kenneth Cragg, in the Jewish doctrine of election there is "a sense of exceptionality built into its very essence."[88] Is this election unique to Jews or Christians, or does a degree of election extend to every group of people around the world? Some Christians struggle with the idea that God can have more than one "chosen people." There must be only one group, by definition, who are the chosen "elect." At one time, the Jewish people held this divine mandate but failure to faithfully carry out their mission to live and preach the way of God led to the intervention of Jesus in the world. What was once a divine mandate and mission is now an outdated and formalized religious Judaism.

Most Protestants have little interest in what is written in Vatican II and is being preached by contemporary Catholicism. In contrast to many Protestants, however, the Catholic tradition has no problem in accepting the "chosenness" of the Jewish people alongside the uniqueness of Christianity. Vatican II affirms that "the Jews are to be presented as the people of God of the Old Testament which has never been revoked by God and as the chosen people."[89] This clear assertion by the modern Catholic church provides a constructive starting-point for Jewish-Protestant discussions when exploring such issues. Differing Christian and Jewish ideas about "election" are also explored, as we have argued, in the writings of the transitional Jewish-Christian theologian, St. Paul. Those who have thought themselves among the "elect," such as the Pharisees or St. Paul, have sought to distinguish themselves from others in certain ways. Circumcision was one of the first rituals designed to highlight the difference between the elect and those outside of God's grace (Exod 24:3-8). For some Jews, observance of the Sabbath holds a similar function in the modern age, as does the observance of dietary laws.

For some, because Christians are now God's elect, an individual Jew either needs to accept Christianity and reject Judaism or choose to remain bound by the heavy chains of legalistic Judaism. Another path might be that all are elected as they embrace God's eternal covenants and that the elect people of God exists to "be a blessing to all nations" (Gen 12:3; 17:1-22) instead of using their sense of election to raise their own sense of self-worth. Still another way to think about the language of "election" in both Judaism and Christianity is to talk about those who strive for holiness (see Neh 10:29-30). This underscores that one who has been elected is not necessarily spiritually above others.

Redemption is at the heart of God's election, as is establishment of covenant in both the Jewish and Christian traditions. This common ground should be emphasized whenever some Christians assert Judaism does not teach a message of grace. God blessed Israel "to be a treasured possession" (Exod 19:5-6) by delivering the chosen people from disaster. The miracle of Passover is for all God's people and for all time (Exod 13:10). For early Christians like St. Paul, the message of grace had been extended to gentiles—"those who were far off" but now could be "brought near" (Eph 2:13) because of Christ's new covenant. Paul, along with other early Christians, was reframing the Jewish faith considering his understanding that Jesus was God's Son. Beker explains: "The early Christians accomplished a highly sophisticated transition from the old faith to the new. While they differed with their Jewish forbearers on the fundamental nature of God's presence in the world, they agreed on practically everything else."[90]

Jews cannot accept the idea, which traditionally St. Paul has been thought to teach (though some now argue that he did not), that Christians have been grafted into Israel (see Rom 3:28; 8:14–19, 9–11; Gal 3:10 ff.). This does not mean that the Jewish tradition believes that non-Jews will not enter the gates of Paradise. *All* who are righteous, Jew *and non-Jew*, will have a reward in the "world to come," and this is not contingent on virtuous individuals converting to Judaism. It does mean that "Israel" is composed only of Jews and that non-Jews do not become Jews simply by sharing points of agreement. When the Bible speaks of "Israel," it refers exactly to the historic people of Israel; there is no hint that such language is in any way metaphoric or general. Implicit in the Pauline (also in Islam—Qur'an 2:83–87; 2:122–123; 4:46; 5:20–21) assertion that gentiles have been "grafted into Israel" is that Christians have now "inherited this designation from God after the failure of the Jews to satisfy His demands."[91] The promise that God will send a "new covenant" to replace the "old" (Jer 31:31) does not mean that the initial election of the Jewish people is compromised.

Just as the historic Jewish people needed to be saved from Egypt, every person needs to be cleansed of enslaving sins because these sins affect one's right relationship with God. Just as the Egyptian slave masters stood between Jewish freedom and bondage, so the chains of sin hold individuals from the freeing gift of salvation. Even though sin separates God from the "elect," that divide can be bridged by God's mercy. For Christians that is done through the redemptive death of Jesus. For Jews, God restores humanity through the revelation of the Torah and the life-giving law. God redeems the people of Israel at the edge of the Red Sea with a miracle of grace, and God redeems the gentiles with a miracle of saving grace at the cross of Christ. Adherents of Judaism, Christianity, and Islam are all called to be witnesses of the transforming grace they have received from God.[92] A life of faithfulness to God's path, as revealed in the scriptures, brings with it its own sense of assurance of salvation because a God of grace and mercy never will ignore or forsake those who genuinely and sincerely seek salvation.

Conclusion

In Judaism, salvation and redemption (*ge'ulah*) are, first and foremost, acts of national liberation (as in the case of deliverance from Egypt) for all Israel. God saves the entire nation (see Exod 6:6; Jer 32:36–37). For Jews, salvation "takes place publicly on the stage of history and within the community."[93] Any idea of individual salvation is understood within the larger context of national salvation and is linked into the larger community of a shared heritage.

In contrast, many modern Protestants (unlike some Orthodox and Catholic Christians), tend to view salvation as primarily a private experience of an individual soul in personally accepting the atoning gift of Christ's sacrifice. Everyone joins the corporate body of Christ, the church, in a personal way (1 Cor 12:27) and each person has a direct and personal, private encounter with God that leads to eternal salvation. Further, this path of salvation, is only available through one's personal and sincere acceptance of the saving power of Jesus, the promised Messiah. Because of this view, Judaism is ultimately seen as a religion unable to save a person from sin and bring them into right relationship with God. Judaism is seen as a "dead" religion in the historical sense that Jews have emphatically rejected Jesus as their Messiah and personal savior.

Part of the reason for this difference about seeing salvation as personal or corporate relates to divergent theological assumptions. Christians and Jews have often focused on differences and some have stressed the merits of one faith over another. Jews, unlike conservative Christians, have no concept of original sin and the need to be saved from that sin by a pure and holy human sacrifice. In this chapter, we have modeled how these two themes of atonement and covenant, which are central to both traditions, can provide a constructive resource to see a shared sense of identity instead of seeing these themes becoming roadblocks to mutual appreciation. While common themes of covenant and atonement are stressed in distinct ways, perhaps this is because the same source is being revealed to different people at different times. While Jews celebrate the miracle of deliverance taking place in the Passover and at Mount Sinai, and Christians celebrate deliverance at Mount Calvary, both faiths witness to the same message of divine grace and forgiveness.

Most centrally, we serve the same God of love and share a common history in faith. It is easy to create a sense of oppositional confrontation between adherents of our two faiths. Those who find a fundamental contradiction between Jewish and Christian views of the atonement, for example, do so out of an interpretative set of assumptions that emphasize our differences in stark contrast instead of celebrating our much more expansive common ground about the nature of God as loving. The intent of this chapter has not been to create something uniquely un-Christian or un-Jewish but to encourage creative and relational ways to talk about such themes with respect and reflection while also guarding the cherished legacies of both great traditions.

There are obvious differences between how many Christians and Jews think about salvation and such differences should not be ignored and need not be reconciled. At the same time, both religions reveal a personal and loving God who seeks healing relationship with creation. The shed blood of the covenant—be it in the lives of generations of faithful martyrs or in the life of Jesus—becomes a confirming seal of redemption that calls both Jews and Christians to respond with lives of communitarian commitment and personal, moral holiness.

Shared stories of loyalty to our respective communities—as well as efforts to reach across communitarian boundaries—offers hope for an increasingly fractured and divided world. Covenant is at the heart of both traditions and just as covenant is a ground for encounter with God, it can also serve as a shared ground for respectful interactions. In this encounter, historic lessons of paternal dismissiveness or supersessionist boasting should be thoroughly confronted. Christian and Jew can bear witness to the same story of deliverance and the same shared promises of election and covenant that bridge the gap between our sinfulness and God's mercy.

Chapter Five

Prophecies about the Messiah

"Understanding" Judaism

CHRISTIAN CLERGY OFTEN PREACH that Jesus fulfilled (or will fulfill) every prophecy in the Bible about the coming Messiah. Because of this, Jews and Christians have developed an entirely distinct understanding of the nature of a messiah as well as of the nature of salvation. Christians ask, *"who* is the Messiah?" while Jews ask the question: *"what* is the Messiah?" Gershom Scholem explains that "a totally different concept of redemption determines the attitude to messianism within the two faiths. What appears to the one as an indication of its understanding and a positive achievement of its message is unequivocally belittled and disputed by the other."[94]

Student class responses have illustrated this fundamental tension of divergent views about the Messiah. One student wrote that they were "shocked to hear that the Jews may not be looking for a world leader who will be the coming Messiah."[95] The idea that Jews are waiting for a messiah is so deeply ingrained in presuppositions about Jesus that it is inconceivable that this is not the case. Another student explained, "My experience with Jewish people has been limited to what the Bible says about ancient Hebrew people. I had always expected Jews to be hoping for a messiah. Basically, I expected Judaism to be a Jesus-less Christianity. For me, Christianity was nothing more than Judaism that has found its Messiah in Jesus."[96] Another mentioned a particular passage to underline that Jews were misreading their own Bible: "While different instances of God appearing as human beings are plentiful, it is difficult to see some passages as anything but an instance of the triune representation of God."[97]

There is a long history within the Christian tradition for this argument. Whenever the first Christians—who had previously been identified as Jewish—read the Hebrew Bible, they discovered repeated passages that they claimed foretold the coming of Jesus. This also led them to conclude that any Jew who rejected Jesus was also failing to properly understand prophecies that foretold a messiah. Some students are shocked to hear that most Jews only believe that Jesus was a great man, a rabbi, or perhaps even something of a prophet for the times. These same students sometimes also conclude that Jews are being defiant in rejecting Jesus and are overlooking compelling proofs that Jesus was the prophesied Messiah.

Such assumptions create thought-provoking dynamics when the rabbi meets such students. Conversations can become quite spirited and, in the process, some students have written that they became uncomfortable whenever classmates defied the rabbi in ways they viewed as disrespectful. One student, responding to a visit from Rabbi Chaim Schertz of the Kesher Israel Congregation (Harrisburg, PA) wrote, "I was embarrassed when some in the class challenged the rabbi. It appears they were trying to disprove him. They pretended like they had more knowledge than the rabbi. When you discuss issues with people of higher knowledge you need to be humble and realize you do not know everything."[98]

Christians claim a unique understanding of the term "Messiah." Some Jews find these views confusing and question whether Jesus even actually claimed to be the Messiah. These questions arise from passages—like those in Mark's Gospel—portraying Jesus as appearing to be reticent to accept this title. For Jews, the term simply meant "anointed one." Nonetheless, as exile followed exile, many Jews began to hope for a larger-than-life "messianic" figure who would lead them into a time free from oppressive war and injustice as foretold by the prophets. Roman soldiers at the crucifixion used the political term "King of the Jews" for Jesus; placing this title on the cross as a mark of contempt. Christians have come to see this statement as a truth deeply resonant with prophetic meaning.

Concepts of a Messiah

Jewish views of a messiah contrast Christian conceptions of how Jesus fulfills biblical prophecies. In the first place, the term *Messiah* (*mashiach* [משיח]) simply means an "anointed one" and is used in reference to the priests (*ha-kohen ha-mashiach* [הכהן המשיח]) who were anointed for their administrative and liturgical duties (Lev 4:3–5). The hoped-for Messiah was either a strong political or a military leader but clearly only a human being. Each king was also a "Messiah" as their coronation featured a ceremony of anointing (for example, 1 Kgs 1:39; 1 Sam 10:6; 1 Sam 16:11–13; 1 Kgs 1:38–39). A prophet (Isa 61:1) and even a non-Jewish king—such as Cyrus the Great of Persia—could be described as a messiah (Isa 45:1). Reform and Reconstructionist Jews, for the most part, are not looking for an individual Messiah but speak rather of a "messianic *age*" of world peace.

The prevailing Jewish conception of a messiah focuses on redressing the grim problems of this world, not the soteriological issues of a distant, unseen world to come. Further, it is not a central concept of Judaism—much to the chagrin of those Christians who wish that it was. Robert Schoen explains: "Jewish people believe that when the Messiah comes there will be an end to world suffering (Isa 2:4). Jews do not believe the Messiah has come and they do not recognize Jesus as their savior."[99] The Messiah, a descendant of King David, will bring universal peace and restore Israel to its ancestral homeland. It was only over time that a concept of a messiah as an anointed one morphed into the view held by some at the time of Jesus. Others thought that the nation of Israel itself would be a "Messiah" for the nations of the world.

The destruction of the temple in 70 C.E. was a low-point in history that gave further credence to the idea God would send a messiah to deliver Israel from its shame. One passage in the Midrash Aggadah states: "on the day that the Temple was destroyed the Messiah was born."[100] A sense of hope helped individuals sustain their hearts in confusing and uncertain times of trouble. Under the brutal Roman occupation, this hopefulness reached its zenith with the Bar Kochba Rebellion of 135 C.E., when many Jews hoped that Bar Kochba was the "Messiah" who would deliver them from political domination and oppression. This same type of political hope for a messiah led to the rise of many false claimants, such as Shabbetai Zevi in the Ottoman Empire (1626–76), who, when offered the choice of conversion or death, renounced Judaism and embraced Islam.

Jewish Problems with Jesus as Messiah

Some Christians fail to recognize how their Jewish neighbors find it easy to dismiss Jesus from their consideration as a messiah. Did Jesus break the law of Moses? The New Testament claims that Jesus interpreted and extended, rather than abrogated, the teachings of Moses in several ways, such as Christ's choice to provide healing to a person in need on the Sabbath or the choice to pluck grains of wheat on the Sabbath in order to avoid personal harm.

In a series of "but I say unto you" statements, Jesus is presented as the primary authority in interpreting ancient Jewish laws. Such a posture was, by traditional Jewish standards, proof that such a speaker was a false prophet (Deut 12:2–6). Rabbis have taught the Messiah will come as a humble sage who will not make arrogant, boastful claims about divine authority. The idea that Jesus claimed to be the divine incarnation of God is also without precedent in any Jewish traditional expectations of a promised Messiah.

The early Christians seized on the idea of Jesus as the Messiah and developed the concept into something beyond the Jewish understanding of the term. Problems arise from the distinct ways that rabbinic Judaism and Christianity tend to view the nature of prophecy. Biblical prophecy in the Jewish tradition is primarily a moral response to social injustice where God sends prophets to confront a host of social evils and who call the faithful to righteousness. In contrast, many Christians see prophecy as that which primarily foretells the coming of Christ as well as Christ's second coming in the end times. Because Christians and Jews often begin with distinct assumptions about the nature of prophecy, it is necessary to clarify these differences.

Was Jesus rejected as Messiah by the Jewish people of the first century time because he was not a political Messiah as many Christians assert? Not all Jews at the time of Jesus were looking for a political deliverer from God. The assumption that this is the case helps some Christians rationalize their concerns about why it is that Jews do not consider Jesus to be a viable candidate for Messiah. Further, there was no tradition—contrary to Christian claims about Isaiah 53—that the Messiah of Israel would be crucified and raised from death. Amy-Jill Levine explains: "No Jewish source, outside those associated with the followers of Jesus, show any expectation that the Messiah would be killed and after three days rise. The closest possible reference is Hos 6:1–2 . . . [where] the reference is not to a single individual but to the people of Israel."[101]

The fact Jesus dies is further proof to Jews that this candidate is not the Messiah because the nation continues to suffer, and this suffering worsens after Christ's brief life on the earth. While the Hebrew Bible focused on many leaders who were anointed, the Christian tradition focused all those ideas into one divine personage. Therefore, Jesus is linked by Christians to a wide range of different Jewish "Messiahs" such as Moses, Joshua, David, Solomon, and others. Further, none of these "Messiahs" possessed a divine nature while that belief became central for Christians. Such divergent views explain the need some Christians feel to explain to Jews that they do not understand the true meaning of their own scriptures.

One of the most compelling themes in biblical prophecies emphasized by some Christians relate to unusual statements that the Messiah will be born of a virgin. Jesus was conceived of the Holy Spirit (see Luke 1:35; Matt 1:20) and was born in Bethlehem, the city of David. He was born the "Savior" of the world but also as the "King of the Jews." Therefore, King Herod responds to the birth of Jesus with fearful dread and bloody aggression. Matthew reports Jesus was born of a virgin (1:18–25) and the same fact is retold in Luke's Gospel (1:26–38). According to Matthew, this miracle is seen as the fulfillment of Isaiah 7:14, Micah 5:2, Hosea 11:1, and Jeremiah 31:15. Amy-Jill Levine acknowledges that one of the possible translations of the term used is "virgin" and that it is understandable, that some early Christian translators used that rendering. For Levine, however, the larger issue is how such a view fits into historic Jewish understandings of the biblical concept of the Messiah. She writes: "Historically speaking, the idea that Isaiah, sometime at the end of the eighth century B.C.E., predicted a virgin birth to occur seven hundred years later strains credulity."[102]

Some Christians are surprised that the Hebrew term 'almah (עלמה), translated into Greek (and later English) as "virgin" only meant "young maiden" in common parlance. Another phrase, b'tulah (בתולה), is also translated as "virgin" on some occasions, but is more accurately translated as "unmarried woman". A clear example is found in Genesis when Abraham sends his servant, Eliezer, to find a wife for Isaac. Rebekah, the young maiden who meets all the criteria, is described as both a "b'tulah", and as a woman as one whom "no man had known" (Hebrew: ish lo yidaah [איש לא ידעה] (Gen 24:16). The use of both phrases here would be unnecessary if *b'tulah* truly meant a physical virgin. The dramatically distinct ways that Jews and Christians interpret this highly metaphoric and symbolic language of the prophet Isaiah explain these differing conclusions. It also raises the more fundamental question of how such a view relates to issues of how human sexuality might be sinful and how such views have led, directly or indirectly, to centuries of oppressing women.

In reference to the death of Jesus, Christians in the past have pointed to passages in Isaiah (especially chapter 53) that speak of suffering while others find in the imagery of Psalm 22 a parallel to the events surrounding the crucifixion of Jesus and even a promise in this passage that Jesus would die and rise from the dead. Jews may look with befuddlement at such renderings because a logical assumption could be posited that, if Jesus truly were the Messiah, as Christians claim, then God would have spared this messenger from death and suffering in the first place.

The "Suffering Servant" passage of Isaiah 53 has been cited by Christians to reveal how the sufferings of Jesus are a redemptive gift from God (see Acts 8:32–33). This seems to imply that God is responsible for commissioning, and demanding, a human sacrifice. The key verse is Isaiah 53:5 which announces: "He was wounded for our transgressions, crushed because of our iniquities." Jesus as "Lamb of God" is innocent of all sins and yet "bears the sins of the world (John 1:29)." Jesus seems to point to this passage when stating that "the Son of Man will have to suffer"(Mark 8:31). At the Last Supper, Jesus told followers the wine of communion was his own blood "poured out for many for the forgiveness of sins" (Matt 26:28). Those who follow Jesus should expect to give their lives in death and suffering (Mark 8:34–35) as they take up their own crosses in life. Paul warned Christians that God had given them the gift of suffering (Phil 1:29) and they should expect trials (1 Cor 10:13). These verses explain what the German theologian Dietrich Bonhoeffer meant when he warned, "when God calls a man, he bids him come and die."[103]

Some Christians return to one explanation for the seemingly inconceivable Jewish rejection of Jesus as the Messiah: Jews are hard-hearted. It is the fundamental hard-heartedness of Jews who do not follow Jesus that makes the birth of Christianity a necessity in the first place, so that all the peoples of the world can now come to know the truth about God. As one student explained, "Frankly, it makes more sense to say that Christians exist to spread the scriptures all over the earth than it does to say that Jews exist to retain them."[104] Jews, it is assumed by some Christians, do not understand their own scriptures. Therefore, it is a loving act to explain to them the meaning of the Bible with the story of the Ethiopian Eunuch as prototype in Acts 8:26–40. Many Christians seem to choose, instead of confronting the implications of such views, to refrain from mentioning these challenges at the heart of Jewish-Christian relations.

When some Christians think of Christ's second coming, they predict that Jews will convert *en masse* to Christianity as foretold in the New Testament. One noted series of best-selling novels by Tim LaHaye and Jerry Jenkins, the *Left Behind* series, talk about how Jews will become Christians at the end of the world. Reading these books, Daniel Kadosh wrote,

> Jewish characters in *Left Behind* are given three choices: join the antichrist and go to hell; resist the antichrist and go to a concentration camp (and eventually to hell); or become a Messianic Jew who believes in Jesus. And although it's a relief that the Jews are not actually cast as villains—though there is some cryptic talk of conspiratorial gatherings early on—there is a definite sense that they lack any real worth.[105]

Kadosh then cites a response to this series by the Anti-Defamation League who said that "Jews are not hated in the *Left Behind* books. They are merely different: not-quite-human pawns in God's plan, cosmic curiosities."[106]

Ultimately, the most obvious reason that Jesus was rejected as the Jewish Messiah was simple: the prophecies attributed to a messianic figure were not fulfilled by Jesus. Before and after Jesus lived, wars have continued, and the lion has yet to lie down with the lamb. When the Messiah comes the nations will beat their weapons into plows and farming tools. Those messianic prophecies found in the book of Isaiah foretold an era of world peace and political harmony. The opposite, in fact, occurred during (and shortly after) the life of Jesus; Jews lost control of Israel and the temple was destroyed by Roman invaders. The Prince of Peace will bring peace, and that hoped-for peace has yet to arrive.

Some Christians claim that the messianic age has already begun and that the kingdom of God is present through the agency of the Holy Spirit and in the church. For Jews, the messianic age (or the Messiah) has yet to come, and humanity must continue to work toward God's rule on earth by following the *mitzvot* (commands) and doing *tikkun olam*—"repairing of the world." When enough individuals work for social justice, there may well be an era of world peace. Until that time, Jews remain determined to live ethical lives in preparation for such an ideal era. When we compare today's world with the harmony of a messianic age, it is easy to see that we are far from those pristine hopes. Although many preachers, including Jesus, claimed they were the Messiah, the world is still filled with rampant war and entrenched injustice. Perhaps most essentially, Marc Saperstein observes, "For Jews, the idea of vicarious atonement—that the Messiah takes upon himself the suffering that would otherwise come as punishment—seems totally alien," because individuals are directly accountable themselves for their sins before Almighty God.[107]

Conclusion

Revelation, Jewish and Christian, is the "breaking of the infinite into the finite to reveal to the finite the infinite life."[108] Jesus for Christians is the ultimate revelation of the nature and purpose of God Almighty. This explains why Christian students, responding to Rabbi Fuller, often ask how Jews view the teachings of Jesus. One student wrote, "Jesus said a lot of things that sounded radical to pious Jews like the Pharisees. His audience was often astonished. Is he viewed as a respectable Jewish teacher or a madman?"[109] While the Jewishness of Jesus is a frequent starting point for Jews and Christians in conversation, it brings with it clear challenges. When one reads, for example, the "Lord's Prayer" in Luke 11 (or Matt 6), it becomes apparent that its content is entirely consistent with the Jewish heritage of Jesus. Cardinal Carlo Martini asserts, "Without a sincere feeling for the Jewish world, and a direct experience of it, one cannot fully understand Christianity. Jesus is fully Jewish, and the apostles are Jewish."[110]

While Christianity is rooted in Judaism—and there was a time, in the first century, where the two faiths were close—that era has long since passed. A constant focus on that period sends the wrong message about what Jews and Christians really share today, which is a mutual ethical and moral frame of reference. While both Christians and Jews believe in the oneness of God, the *imago dei* of humanity, and the vital centrality of the Sabbath, even these ideas, or the notion of a revealed and shared authoritative scripture, are fraught with complexity.

Michael Kogan summarizes this issue: "When my students ask me if Jesus is the Messiah I usually reply, yes and no, depending on how you define the term *Messiah*."[111] Over time, Christians became more certain

Jesus was the Messiah and Jews became more certain that Jesus was not the Messiah. The issue of the messiahship is bound to how Jews and Christians read the Bible. For Christians, their faith stands or falls on the uniqueness of Jesus, God incarnate. From a Jewish perspective, such theological ideas are both "implausible" and "incomprehensible."[112]

Chapter Six

The World to Come

*While Israel's sons, by scorpion curses driven / Outcastes of earth
and reprobates of heaven / Through the wide-world in friendless
exile stray / Remorse and shame sole comrades of their way, /
With dumb despair their country's wrongs behold / And dead to
glory burn for gold.*
—Reginald Heber, *Palestine, 1803*

*One cannot imagine the sorrows of another. One is certain only
of death. After death one becomes important. Heaven and hell
can both be had in this world.*
—Yiddish Proverbs

A Question

A STUDENT'S PAPER GLOWED about the visiting rabbi from the local synagogue only to conclude, "I know that Christianity is the true religion and
that unless one accepts Jesus as Lord in their heart they will be damned,
but I have a hard time believing that the people chosen by God will not be
in Heaven when I get there. Maybe God will work out something special
for them after they die."[113]

How best to respond? First, it is helpful to note that, in the Torah,
there is no mention of a heaven or a hell and the phrase used to explain
what happens after we die is that we are "gathered to our ancestors." The
Bible reveals an insurmountable gap between this world and the next.

Therefore, the rebellious King Saul is chastised for trying to communicate with the dead via a necromancer (1 Sam 28:7).

There are only a few passages in the Hebrew Bible that speak of the world to come (*olam haba*); even these can be interpreted to explain our search for hope amid daily trials. Ezekiel 37:12 tells of a "valley of dry bones" in a vision of the prophet where God prophesies "I will open your graves and bring you out of your graves." In addition to discussions about the after-life, the other verse that might possibly speak of either a spiritual or an actual resurrection is Isaiah 26:19 which states, "Your dead shall live. Their corpses shall rise; awake and sing, you who lie in the dust." Daniel foretold a time when "many who sleep in the dust of the earth shall awake, some to everlasting life and some to shame and everlasting contempt" (Dan 12:1–2).

Rabbis throughout the ages have offered various statements about what will happen after death. Some "focused on the immortality of the soul" while others posited a form of reincarnation.[114] There are, however, no detailed statements from the Hebrew Bible about the nature of the afterlife. Most Jews believe in the eternal nature of the soul, which will one day be reunited with God, without feeling a need to explain how the world to come will be populated or what its characteristics will include. Only God knows "who is in and who is out" of such an abode of bliss. The people of Israel will be saved (Isa 60:21), but so will many righteous gentiles (Isa 26:2). God can choose, as was the case with the people of Nineveh (Jonah), to save pagans, or he can choose to save those within his covenant. We are called to be humble and trust God's goodness. Such weighty decisions are left to God's holy nature. All that is certain is "the judge of all the earth will do right" (Gen 18) towards all on earth's final day.

There are clear differences between Jewish views of the afterlife and Christian teachings. Many Jews do not hold any clear notion of a heaven or hell after death. What this underscores is that the theme of an afterlife is not a central teaching of the tradition. One student after hearing the rabbi explain this responded, "Since the Jews believe they are saved by merit rather than faith—and that must be from the amount of tradition in their religion—it was surprising to hear that the afterlife is not a big issue."[115] The fact that such an idea, so central to conservative Christians, is barely discernible within Judaism should help Christians appreciate a basic difference between the two religions.

According to one widely asserted scholarly perspective, it is not until the exiles returned from the captivity in Persia, and from living amongst Zoroastrians who believed in a heaven and a hell, that such ideas were first found within Judaism. Even when the question of origin is debated the Zoroastrian and Jewish views do mirror each other. At the same time, most Jews do not accept that physical death is the last act in the drama of the human experience. Many hope for a return to Eden and the avoidance of *Gehinnom,* the idea of a hellish place of punishment named after the Valley of Hinnom (near Jerusalem) where children were sacrificed to the Canaanite god Molech (also *Mikom*). Many have conjectured that Gehenna was a place of punishment or a purgatory. This particular location was chosen to metaphorically represent such a place of gruesome judgment because of two passages in Jeremiah: "And they have built the high places of Tophet, which is in the Valley of the Son of Hinnom, to burn their sons and their daughters in the fire; which I commanded not, neither came it to my mind" (Jer 7:31, see also Jer 2:23; 32:35; 2 Kgs 16:1–17; 23:10). The concept of hell is one with widely varying opinions in Jewish tradition. The logical belief behind the doctrine is that, because God is just, there should be some place where punishment is meted out for wickedness just as there should be a place of reward for the righteous. There is no specific dogma asserted by any Jewish tradition about this doctrine. Even those who have taken the greatest delight in describing the agonies of hell within the tradition have admitted such views are drawn from their imaginations.

Jewish theological traditions also have little to say in the way of specific details about a heavenly place of eternal reward for the righteous. Beliefs about a heaven after death mirror conceptions about the original Eden (Gen 2–3), a realm of pure innocence and delight. One Talmudic passage (*Berakhot* 17a) claims heaven will be filled with comfort and material ease: "In the world to come there is no eating, drinking, begetting of children, commerce, envy, hatred, or competition. There is only this—where the righteous sit with crowns on their heads and take delight of God's splendor."[116] While most Jews do not presume to know what happens after this life, such teachings reveal an assumption there will be some form of life after death. There is also a generally accepted belief that there will be a day of judgment, but there are no details about such events. Rabbi Simon Greenberg explains: "Jewish literature furnishes a wealth of widely varying interpretations on the nature of life and death.

But one thing on which rabbinic literature is unanimous and unequivocal is that the grave is not the end."[117]

The Rabbi Asks a Question

After years of visiting the class, I (Fuller) felt emboldened one day to ask the students directly, "Am I going to hell?" Perhaps this was the outgrowth of a question I had asked a class of students two years earlier during a similar encounter: "What kind of God do you believe in that would condemn good people to an eternal hell of flames just because they did not accept Jesus?"[118]

When I asked the students if they thought I was going to hell, a vigorous conversation ensued. One student responded, "I have been told for so many years growing up in my church that Jews and others would go to hell no matter how nice they were."[119] Another rationalized: "When I heard his question my first thought was that of shock but my second was I *have* to say something before the other overtly conservative Christians in this class open their mouths! It seems that an overwhelming number of Christians go around telling people of other religions that they are going to hell. Unfortunately, my classmates got to him before I did."[120] One student declared: "I must respect everyone who answered honestly. Despite all of the various views there is no need for hatred, even if we think someone is going to hell."[121] This is a stimulating framing of this question because it showed that, while students may (or may not) think I am on the way to the fire, they are also concerned no one becomes offended by such views. This reflects the challenges faced by conservative Christians in an increasingly globalized and pluralistic context.

On the issue of my going to hell another student articulated, "I was stunned and had no answer for him. Now that I have had more time to think about it I can give a biblical answer but it was a great experience because I will have to answer such questions when I am a pastor someday."[122] The student tactfully did not tip their hand as to what was the biblical answer they had found to this provocative question, but it is not too hard to imagine what conclusion was reached given such categorical statements as John 14:6 and Acts 4:12. Another student pronounced: "Since God gave Jesus to the Jews they have to accept him. The Jews even had the first chance at Jesus. I did not make the rules."[123] The conclusion articulated is that, sad to say, I would indeed go to hell because I had fallen outside of the "rules" laid out in the New Testament. One student mused, "I found it funny how my classmates responded since the Jews probably do not have the same concept of hell as Christians. Even if Rabbi Fuller does believe in a hell, I am not sure he is overly frightened by the thought of being condemned there by a roomful of undergraduate students."[124]

Hellfire Pedagogy

One written response, however, raised a series of interesting pedagogical questions. Allow me to cite this response in its entirety:

> I found Rabbi Fuller's question, "Am I going to Hell?" which he directed toward the class, interesting on several different levels. First, the question was interesting in that he, obviously a Jew, asked this question to a group of predominantly Christian students within a Baptist university. This question's context alone provokes my interest. The question was so directed, so unadulterated by polite sensibilities that I will never forget it. I do not mean to say that the question was rude or should not have been asked, but I felt as though Rabbi Fuller had forced the discussion from a mere intellectual context regarding the tenets of Judaism into an actual Jewish-Christian dialogue in which Christians brought the real conclusions of their faith to bear. We cannot leave religion, what we hold to be most vital to our existences, out of a discussion and call such a discussion meaningful. He was even met with a definitive, memorable, though not commendable, "Yes, you are going to Hell." This response only forced me to struggle more resolutely with an issue that had already been on my mind.[125]

The implications of such an "atomic bomb" of a question are multifaceted. Some students felt comfortable telling me that I was going to spend eternity in hell, while others assured me that God would certainly accept my soul, as a good rabbi, into an eternal reward. I am relieved! Of course, not all Baylor undergraduates are from a Christian background and one student responded, "I am a Hindu so of course I do not believe the rabbi is going to hell. All he might face is reincarnation multiple times, but it is already decided anyway."[126] Most students had no answer or concluded wisely that it was up to God to make such weighty determinations.

The wide divergence of answers reflects both the trials and opportunities that arise when such a query is framed with straightforwardness to an audience of (mostly) conservative Christians. On the positive side of the ledger, the question concretizes amorphous sensibilities and reveals differing views among students. It can also be argued such a loaded question is unfair in that it presupposes students are inherently judgmental. One student wrote that it was the "most thought-provoking and controversial questions I have heard in a long time."[127] Another reflected on the larger dynamics at the heart of Jewish-Christian interactions: "Our relations between each other can be rocky because of how Christians behave in accord with this question. Pushing your religion on people usually just pushes people away."[128] One student wrote, "I am not a Christian, but I think many Christian students are uncomfortable with the implications of their own beliefs about hell. If hell is a real place as they believe, I am glad people find the idea disconcerting."[129] Another student reflected, "At first, I thought he would be going to hell. Since then my position has changed completely. The question made me see the arrogance of my preceding understanding and that I might be condemning others that God might not condemn."[130] While insight, and not simply stimulating conversation, is the goal of any interfaith discussion, there is a benefit for such confrontative questions if framed in a larger context where people feel they are not being judged.

Chapter Seven

Revelation and the Bible

Judaism is just about as far removed from the Hebrew Bible as Christianity is. Yet despite this obvious fact it is not uncommon to find that Christians studying the Old Testament think that they are studying Judaism. Just as the history of Christian doctrine is hardly the same thing as a history of biblical interpretation, so the study of Jewish thought is completely different from the study of the Hebrew Bible. This is mainly because the written Torah cannot be read apart from the Oral Torah as recorded in Talmud and Midrash.
—John A. Sawyer

The Bible—Jewish and Christian

BECAUSE THE BIBLE PLAYS such a central role in the way many Christians frame their faith, it is instructive to think about how revelation and the role of the scriptures are viewed within each tradition. The Bible both separates and unites Christians and Jews. One student explained, "Since Judaism has the same scripture as the Old Testament for Christianity I felt that I would not learn much."[131] After I (Fuller) came to class another student responded by saying, "He is a very nice man but I find it almost funny how differently he sees the Old Testament in the Jewish Bible compared to how I see the Old Testament in the Jewish Bible. He claims that it talks nothing about a savior. When I read the Old Testament, I can see it pointing directly to Christ."[132]

Some Christians find it surprising that the two faiths view the Bible through such different lenses. Of course, Christians realize that their Bible is composed of two testaments, the first of which is the foundational scripture of another of the world's religions; an arrangement unique amongst religious traditions. The challenge this offers interfaith dialogue is the question of how to read the scriptures free from presuppositions. One student expressed frustrations after the rabbi shared his views of the Bible, "Their Bible has way too many components to it and it all just seems so confusing to me. I am so glad ours is so much simpler."[133] Daniel Radosh explains:

> The problem is Christians and Jews have very different ideas about what the contributions of the Old Testament are. For starters, Christians—or at least the ones that build theme parks based on it—tend to see the Old Testament as an elaborate game of connect the dots. Do it right and it spells out J-E-S-U-S. Jews like to think that it stands well on its own which is why we call it not the Old Testament but the Bible.[134]

Also, the order of the books of the Hebrew and the Christian Bibles are slightly different, but shared readings should bring Jews and Christians to a common ground about characters such as Adam, Abraham and Sarah, Moses, Kings David and Solomon, and the prophets. The Torah (תורה)—the five books of Moses—is sometimes described as the soul of historic Judaism. This is not to suggest that the Jewish community does not also cherish the historical narratives, the Prophets (*Nevi'im* [נביאים]), as well as the eleven books of sacred writings (*Ketuvim* [כתובים]).

While many Christians, interacting with Jews, focus on Isaiah and the Psalms, such a privileging among Jews is reserved for the Torah. In fact, Jewish scholars have posited all other books of the Bible are, in some degree, commentaries on the ethical teachings of the Torah (Pentateuch). The Torah deals with a vast ocean of both practical and theoretical issues, and learned Jews are called to spend a lifetime studying its many currents and concerns. Besides the Torah, all other writings are generally seen to be of a "lower order of revelation."[135] Even the order of the books of the Bible in the two traditions are telling—the Jewish canon often ends (there are other, variant endings) with the decree of Cyrus in the Chronicles about the return to Israel, while the Christian version ends with Malachi promising the return of Elijah before the Day of the Lord.

Orthodox Jews see the Torah not only as a completed revelation from God, but also as an ongoing process that continues to exist between God and humanity. The Torah contains the literal words of God. Jacob Neusner explains this means that Orthodox Jews believe they can "enter into the intellect of God. We know not only the Word, but the words, the wording, the grammar of thought and the cognition that the Creator of the world has found self-evidently reasonable."[136] For more progressive theological perspectives, the Torah is not only an authoritative revelation about the history of early Israel but is also a living commentary that explains how those first Jews understood God's covenantal relationship with humanity. The Torah is also the place where individuals come to understand their own spirituality. Rabbi Louis Finkelstein taught "When I pray, I speak to God; when I study Torah, God speaks to me."

The Hebrew Bible stands as an eternal reminder to Jews that God requires a life of holiness. The revelation reveals a God who thunders in the fires and in the winds of Mount Sinai. Only the high priest could enter the holy of holies once a year and offer sacrifices. Even Moses could not talk with YHWH "face to face" (Exod 33:11) and was only allowed to see God's "hindmost parts" (Exod 24; 33:20–23). Devoted scribes (*sofrim*) recorded God's words and these have been preserved through the generations as a source of hope. The Torah has always brought solace and strength, it is a guidebook and a mirror. Some Jewish scholars have described the Torah as humanity's primary source for knowing God's will.

According to most Jews, was the Bible dictated by God to humanity or was it simply written under divine inspiration? Indeed, is there any divine role or is the Bible seen to be a purely human contrivance forged out of ritual necessity? These questions (and others) are compelling for those Christians who place such a centrality on the Bible that they get to the heart of the larger question of whether the Jewish tradition can lay claim to the divine influence of the earlier biblical community. Was Judaism revealed by divine influence or simply manufactured by earlier Jewish writers? There are a host of scriptures in the Bible that rumble with unmistakable authority. For example, in Exodus 20:2, God declares "I AM the Lord your God."

For most conservative Christians, the problem of scriptural inerrancy is often the linchpin that informs every other dimension of faith. One student responded to my (Fuller) comments that some Jews do not feel every verse in the Bible is divine by saying,

> I do not understand this. Over the centuries the Jews have been perpetually persecuted and left homeless with only a few brief reprieves and yet they still have faith in a scripture that may not be divine? To me that is astonishing because, for better or worse, I cling to the idea that the Bible is the only tangibly inerrant object on the entire earth. Admittedly, I know that my faith is greatly nourished by that comforting notion.[137]

Such views makes it difficult to grasp a more nuanced appreciation of how scriptures relate to the authority of divine inspiration.

Orthodox traditions teach that the Torah, both written (Pentateuch) and oral (Talmud), is the inerrant word of God and cannot be changed. What remains is for Orthodox rabbis to respond to a host of specific questions of jurisprudence, which cannot be easily answered from the original text. This view most closely approximates the ways many Christians view the entire Bible. For many recent Jewish religious movements, there is a willingness to consider—and even encourage—biblical critical theories that root the text in the historical, literary, political, and cultural contexts of their time. For many Conservative, Reconstructionist, or Reform Jews, the Torah is holy but not penned by direct transmission from God to individuals without any human error or human element.

When students visited Congregation Agudath Jacob while I was there serving as the rabbi, I (Fuller) took them to the front of the synagogue and opened the Torah scrolls to help them see what these scrolls looked like and how they are reverently handled by our community. I explained the role of skillful scribes in the completion of the intensely laborious and expensive task of copying out each Torah by hand and discussed how these scribes are not only trained in Hebrew calligraphy but also in a host of specific laws pertaining to how holy documents should be written and handled. I related how Torah scrolls must be inscribed onto parchments that originally came from kosher animals and the pens used must also originate from the quills of birds that are kosher. The process of writing an entire scroll will take the scribe at least one year to complete, which helps explain why these scrolls are revered as the most holy articles within any Jewish community. Even after the scrolls are completed, from time to time scribes must check them to make sure they are still functional, and if not, they must be repaired or buried in graves. I explained, if a Torah scroll falls to the ground, any adult witnessing it is supposed to fast for forty days (daylight only). I clarified that when a Torah scroll is taken out of the Holy Ark to be used in a service, it is customary that everyone in the congregation stand in its presence, and many even kiss the scrolls when they are paraded around the sanctuary. Only once the scrolls have been set in a resting position may the congregants take their seats.

Christians are familiar with the Ten Commandments and often ask if these commandments are central in Jewish practice. This question provides an opportunity to help Christians appreciate the ways certain passages become more relied upon than others, and how this is also a characteristic of how many Christians look at the Bible. I expand on this theme by explaining how, in *Mishnah Peah*, there is a section of scriptures detailing several commandments that are the "favorites" of the authors, because believing in them leads to deeds of tremendous loving-kindness. The conclusion of the section reads, "But the study of Torah is equal to them [the other commandments] all." Studying the Torah leads readers into all other elements of divine revelation. For most communities, the Torah provides access to the wisdom and moral guidance of past generations. Another passage puns, "if one has no flour, (i.e. physical sustenance), one cannot access the Torah, (i.e. spiritual sustenance), and if one cannot access the Torah, one has no flour."

For many Jews, learning Torah—its practice in daily behavior—and the ascension of spiritual growth are interconnected. What happens when a worshipper immerses themselves in Torah? The scriptures are not only read as a religious duty but as a source for intellectual and spiritual inspiration. The study of Torah can inform a way that a person prays. Appreciating the centrality of the Torah among most Jews helps bridge the gap between perceptions about Jewish forms and ideas that no longer exist (or are practiced) and the dynamic experience of modern Judaism. The Torah provides today's Jews with a vital link back to the experiences of previous generations. It has been passed down with care by rabbis who for generations have felt it is almost impossible to approach the Bible—as many Christians do—without any working knowledge of the Hebrew language. Any translation is a commentary, and idioms and other parts of language further complexify any attempt of a reader to comprehend biblical teachings apart from serious language studies.

The Hermeneutical Tradition

Judaism and Christianity have developed in the last two millennia along distinct lines when it comes to the ways the scriptures are interpreted.

Jewish scholars of the Hebrew Bible note that the text is sometimes literal and sometimes allegorical but always authoritative. It is a place where God meets humanity in a way free of miracles and visions: "Did anyone ever hear the voice of God from within the midst of the fire as you have heard and still live?" (Deut 4:32–33). The Torah is God's gift to the people of Israel so that they can become "a wise and understanding people" (Deut 4:6). Revelation speaks both of a revealer and the ones to whom revelation "comes." There is a partnership at the heart of divine revelation. This raises the intriguing question of who is to initiate such interactions and on what terms? These are the questions discussed when rabbis and scholars explore questions of covenant.

Sadly, the Bible has become something of a platform for a "family feud" between Jews and Christians. In history, there were frequent expressions of rancor between the first Jesus-followers and the wider Jewish communities of their day. Some of these tensions are reflected in New Testament renderings of the Hebrew Bible. Stories such as the battle between Cain and Abel (Gen 4:1–16) become, according to later New Testament commentators, a story of the tensions that exist between Judaism and Christianity. St. Augustine, for example, equated Abel with Christ and identifies Cain with the Jews, "Cain is banished from the land and doomed to wander . . . and a corresponding punishment should determine the destiny of the Jews."[138] Of course, as Paula Fredricksen has written in her article "Augustine and the Jews," Augustine is a complicated saint of the church and his views on Judaism defy simple summation.

As Christian history advanced through the early centuries, there was an increasing number of instances where the Bible was given a typological interpretation. These typologies emerged independent of Jewish ways of reading these texts as historical narratives. At the same time, some Christians resort to typologies when reading the Hebrew Bible, while also claiming to be biblical literalists fighting determined battles over minor details to affirm their fidelity to divine truth. Christ is foretold in prophecy and events of history, such as the story of Jonah, foretell Christ's work while these same narratives are also historical beyond any doubt. While biblical literalism seems at odds with a reliance on allegories and typologies, there is no such contestation among some Christians who seem to know when one should be allegorical (e.g., the typologies that refer to Christ) and when one should be literal. Such selectivity remains an unexplored conundrum for obvious reasons of logic.

One of the problems with biblical literalism, according to Michael Kogan, is that "it distracts the reader from the main point of the story at hand" and Kogan cites the preoccupation with the issue of Jonah's "big fish"/whale as an example of this problem.[139] While the real message of Jonah is to "love your enemies," (even the hated Assyrians), the focus for many readers turns to the issue of a great fish with a seeming appetite for prophets. Such literalist views are selective and are often recalibrated in a few specific instances. Speaking of those who view the creation of the world as occurring within six literal days, Kogan writes,

> They insist on the six-day creation of the world—six 24-hour days. Why: Because the Bible says "day." But a biography of our first president might also include the sentence "in Washington's day, men wore powdered wigs." Would any intelligent reader conclude from this that Washington lived for only one day?[140]

Jewish Traditions

For many conservative Christians, understanding the oral tradition is frustrating because their faith has nothing similar. One student felt particularly frustrated and obviously confused with this issue, "I wonder why it is that Christians have removed the Talmud from their Bible and why it has become the primary Jewish text."[141] Even though it is a holy document, the Torah is not a complete document.

One example from the Decalogue, which appears in both Exodus 20:8–11 and Deuteronomy 5:12–15, has to do with the commandment about the Sabbath. In one place it reads, "Remember the Sabbath and keep it holy." In another it reads, "Observe and keep it holy." Regardless of this minor linguistic discrepancy, neither place tells *how* observant Jews are supposed to fulfill this commandment. According to some, the sages who wrote the Talmud are the ones who filled such gaps with the oral law. The process of arriving at such rabbinic decisions followed carefully agreed upon exegetical rules: precedent held significant weight and decisions were always quoted in the name of the principal rabbi (or rabbis) who derived them. It is believed that this oral tradition began sometime in the first or second century B.C.E. and continued through the entire second century C.E.

Misconceptions about the oral law are not new: Rabbi Joseph Soloveitchik lamented, "Christians have never tried to penetrate the soul of the Jews. They have read the Bible but neglected the Oral Tradition by which we interpret it. This makes a different Bible altogether."[142] Soloveitchik's frustration underscores another theme Christians should understand about the interpretive function of the Midrash. The Midrash is a collection of moral teachings used to illuminate the messages of the Torah. For three centuries, new generations of rabbis studied, discussed, and applied them.

Their discussions are called *Gemara* (גמרא) from the Aramaic word for learning. The Mishnah and Gemara together comprise the Talmud. Amazingly, they were both taught and learned in an oral fashion until being written down at the end of the fifth century C.E. Until that era, they were handed down from rabbis to students who eventually related them to scribes. The Midrash came in two styles: *Midrash Aggadah* (מדרש אגדה) was homiletic material, whereas *Midrash Halacha* (מדרש הלכה) was legal in nature. Both legal documents—the Torah and the Talmud— are believed to be the word of God and, therefore, immutable according to Orthodox Judaism. That is why the Orthodox movement has made fewer changes than any of the other movements. Their only recourse for any significant change is what is referred to as "Responsa Literature." These are rabbinic responses made by Orthodox authorities to questions raised by local rabbis unable to answer problems posed to them by their communities.

As mentioned in the introduction of this book, a major focus in teaching Judaism to college students is helping them appreciate the different movements within the tradition. We explain that these movements are a relatively recent, European and North American phenomenon. Throughout Jewish history there has been a plurality of thought: the Hellenists and the Hasmoneans; the Sadducees and the Pharisees; the mysterious Kabbalists of the sixteenth century; and the Hasidim and the Mitnagdim, to name only a few.

We explain that Judaism's Reform Movement began in Germany in the early nineteenth century and grew in strength in the United States and Canada with the migration of German Jews a few years later. This post-emancipation movement had as its major goal not only to modernize the religion, but to make it more of "just a religion". German Jewish immigrants wanted badly to be accepted by their North American counterparts, so they built temples modeled after churches and created rabbinic roles modeled after pastors and priests. An introduction to Reform Judaism stresses the emphasis on the freedom of the individual to choose her or his observance rather than to feel bound by command as well as the focus on the social justice teachings of the Prophets rather than more legal documents. It is also noted that Reform Jews built the first seminaries for the training of modern rabbis.

In response to this movement, Conservative Judaism was born at the end of the nineteenth century by traditionalists who felt that the Hebrew Union College was going too far in their reforms. We usually tell the story of the "last-straw" that came at a graduation banquet where shrimp (a forbidden food according to Jewish law) was served as *hors d'oeuvres.* The traditionalists stormed out and formed the Conservative movement based on their philosophy of "tradition and change." They reverted to the "Halachic process"—the same exegetic rules decided upon by their rabbinic ancestors—but decided that just as rabbis in the past had the power to make rulings of law, so should their rabbis be empowered; leading to the birth of the Jewish Theological Seminary.

When introducing the Reconstructionist Movement, we outline that Rabbi Mordecai Kaplan, who taught at the Jewish Theological Seminary, was interested in the studies of philosophy and theology and began to develop a set of ideas that increasingly distinguished him from his colleagues. Rabbi Kaplan was too traditional for the Reform movement but too innovative for the Conservative movement. This led Kaplan to found the Reconstructionist movement in the middle of the twentieth century and to launch the Reconstructionist Rabbinical College in Philadelphia in the 1960s. Rabbi Kaplan's most radical ideas were that God was not a "being" but rather a force for good in the universe, a trans-natural godliness that he termed "predicate theology." This view of God made Rabbi Kaplan see the authority in Judaism resting in the community rather than in a divine being. One of his most-quoted sayings was, "history has a vote but not a veto" when discussing the relationship between the historic traditions and modern reason. Rabbi Kaplan was a strident advocate for individuals to approach faith with a sense of creative engagement.

In North American Jewry, individuals relate to—or affiliate with— congregations for a whole host of reasons that may have nothing at all to do with the theologies that we have been introducing in this section. One can find a wide spectrum of observance and belief within each of these movements; none of them are monolithic. *All* these traditions, however, refer to the Torah as the most sacred document of faith and the most cherished possession of the Jewish people. It is the various ways that these different traditions read these texts, relate to their message, interpret their meanings, and apply their teachings to their daily lives where they differ.

In the next section of our lectures, we introduce several ways that some Christians in history have used the Torah to attack Judaism. What is vital to note is how rarely Christians reference the Midrash and the Talmud in their discussions with Jews. This is telling given their central role in the development of Judaism. Further, some Christians are surprised to learn that it is probable (although impossible to confirm) that at least portions of the Midrash would have been familiar to Jesus. Many of these were not written down but handed down from rabbis to their students and to scribes. Early rabbinic decisions became known as the Mishnah ("repetition" or "second telling," also translated as "teachings") and the Mishnah was one form of commentary on the Torah. It was written down in Judea but became accepted by the Jewish scholars of Babylon. One of the leaders of this community was Rabbi Hillel, who moved from Babylon to Israel (around 30 B.C.E.) and lived there shortly before the time of Jesus. This historical fact might shed light on why many of the teachings of Rabbi Hillel seem to be directly rephrased in the teachings of Jesus.

After the scriptures are explained, it is helpful to stress the need for students to appreciate the role of the Talmud in Jewish intellectual and cultural life. Perhaps the most central question is how do the ways that modern Jewish communities relate to their scriptures parallel or contrast with various Christian views about the Bible?

Arguments about the Bible

Christians have sometimes read St. Paul's comments in 2 Corinthians 3:12–16 as an assertion that the eyes of Jews are "blinded" by a "veil," which keeps them from clearly seeing Jesus in every page of the Bible. Such a negative assessment of the capacity of the Jews to understand their own scriptures goes to the heart of many of the tensions between the two religious camps. We should not avoid the fact that many of the ways that Jews and Christians understand the Bible are not only divergent but also mutually exclusive. Christians who interact with Jews confront another fundamental problem when they fail to appreciate the role that the Mishnah, Talmud, and other interpretative and historic tools from the rabbinic tradition play in how Jews read the Bible. Of the challenges of interfaith hermeneutics, Jon Levenson warns, "commonalities and differences are not simply opposites and their relationship is far more complex than that dichotomy suggests."[143]

While there are clear distinctions in the way that Jews and Christians appreciate the nature of divine revelation, it is also the case that these differences can be overemphasized. For both traditions, the Bible is the bedrock of faith. For both religions, adherents are called to a life of faithful study of God's word. The Bible teaches Jews and Christians how to follow God and live within community. It is a sourcebook for understanding our individual and corporate lives in relation to God. The Bible is a book to be studied but also a place for devotion to the God of its revelations. Jews and Christians are called to live out the message of the Bible in their daily lives.

At the same time, it is misleading to say that Judaism and Christianity share the same Bible. Such an overstatement has encouraged conservative Christians to sometimes feel comfortable in reading the New Testament as a commentary on the "Old Testament." This problem is visible in the ways some Christians try to explain to Jews, using Christian presuppositions, how Judaism understands grace. Some Christians have tried to advance the idea that the God of Judaism calls for the observance of law and deemphasizes the blessings of abundant grace. While there are differences about the content of God's revelation, both Jews and Christians agree that God loves all of humanity and seeks our good with nature's many blessings.

Conclusion

Many Christians read the "Old Testament" from the vantage point of the New Testament. There are many ways that some Christians use the Bible to promote and denigrate interactions with their Jewish neighbors. The way someone interprets the Bible is an indication not only of their theological point of orientation, but also of their ethical and relational values. It is hoped that, over time, all Christians can ask the question posed to them by Amy Pessah: "Can Christians live out the depth and beauty of their Bible without simultaneously denigrating their Jewish neighbors?" and the related question: "Can Christians make room for other understandings of the Bible and continue to affirm its authority as divinely given."[144] The answer to this second question will encourage Christians to shift toward non-supersessionist views of the Bible. Everyone should approach the Bible with humility and with the appropriate recognition that all of us are "looking through a glass darkly" (1 Cor 13:12).

Christians should remember that the acceptance or rejection of the validity of certain texts as authoritative is much more an expression of a communitarian mindset than it is an individual choice. While Christians accept the New Testament, others, such as the Mormons, add the *Book of Mormon, The Doctrines and Covenants,* and *The Pearl of Great Price.* Muslims, of course, accept the New Testament in theory while denying its present form and challenge others to accept the authority of the Holy Qur'an. We dismiss without challenge what our communities have not recognized. Logic or careful investigation has nothing to do with such decisions.

The truth claims of the various religions about the veracity of their texts are beyond demonstration and are accepted (or rejected) by faith. As Kierkegaard stated, "those realities that seem to be the most objectively uncertain are believed in with the most intense subjective certainty."[145] Christians dedicated to working for better interactions with their Jewish neighbors should be encouraged to embrace both an internal and a more objective (and external) view toward the role that scriptures play in the development of their respective communities of faith.

It is hoped that, while Jews and Christians see the Bible in different ways, they will be able to mutually appreciate the various angles each faith provides on these texts. As Jews and Christians both allow God to speak to them through the Bible, perhaps we can respond not only to the text but also to the energy found in the powerful ethical and spiritual messages of the Bible. It is constructive for Jews and Christians to appreciate that the same text means very different things and has a distinct focus within each community. When Episcopal priest and scholar Bruce Chilton explained to Jacob Neusner that the New Testament revealed an ultimate victory over sin and death, Neusner replied, "God has taught us more, about more things, than even an empty tomb conveys. Victory over death is one thing, but not the main thing. For this world the Torah bears a far broader range of messages."[146]

While the Bible has been a thorny battleground for varying interpretations, it can become a welcoming meeting ground that engages all to be humble before God. As Abraham Joshua Heschel noted,

> If God is alive then the Bible is His voice. No other work is
> a manifestation of His will. There is no other mirror in the
> world where His will and spiritual guidance is as unmistakably

reflected. If the belief in the immanence of God in nature is plausible, then the belief in the immanence of God in the Bible is compelling.[147]

Chapter Eight

The Sharing of Rituals

Every story has something in it that is concealed. What is concealed is the hidden light. The Book of Genesis says that God created light on the first day and the sun on the fourth day. What light existed before the sun? The tradition says this was spiritual light and that God hid it for future use. Where was it hidden? In the stories of the Torah.
—Rabbi Nachman of Bratislava

"HEBREW SOUNDS SO COOL!" wrote one student, "Do the people know what they are saying? I got lost in the prayer book a few times. First the pages were numbered backwards and then songs would cross pages without warning."[148] Every year students attend services at local synagogues and write about their impressions of these visits. Sometimes, they describe these visits as being stressful. One student commiserated, "When I went, I felt very uncomfortable. Before entering the room, they handed me a book which I assumed was the Old Testament. However, it was a book full of prayers and songs that we read and sung throughout the service. I clung to the book like a life-preserver."[149]

Most undergraduates, however, have positive views about their initial encounters. Some note the similarities between their own rituals. One example is the reverence shown for Torah scrolls. The pageantry surrounding the arrival of the scrolls is appreciated by those who hold the Bible in high regard. One student also wrote with fascination about *yarmulkes*: "Matt found a white yarmulke, but all the rest of the ones left were pink and purple. I wasn't sure if it was okay to wear a pink one thinking that they might be a girl yarmulke or something."[150] Another student was intrigued when first experiencing the rituals surrounding the *Kaddish*, explaining, "At first I thought it was kind of morbid, but then you have to get over necrophobia and realize how awesome it is that people cherish the memory of those who have died."[151] One element frequently mentioned is the serving of wine (or other alcoholic beverages) during *onegs* after the services, which challenges presuppositions about the relation between alcohol and spirituality. After reading in their textbooks about Purim, one student wrote that they were disappointed because of heightened expectations after attending a local Purim celebration: "I expected to find people hissing, blowing noisemakers, wearing three-cornered hats, and getting extremely drunk as I had pictured in my mind."[152]

In several discussions, I (Fuller) have talked about Christians who have converted to Judaism, including the experience of my wife. Sometimes students have had casual discussions at the synagogues with individuals that they had met who had once been Christian before converting to Judaism. These encounters can be disconcerting to some because it challenges assumptions about Christianity's obvious and inherent superiority over Judaism. One student wrote, "Maybe it is just somewhere that I thought it was not an option to reject Christianity for any other religion. But I now see that for some there are other options."[153] Another student was mystified when meeting a former Christian who had converted to Judaism: "It was problematic for me that she had rejected Jesus since she had grown up in a Christian home. How exactly do you forget to give Jesus credit for what he has done for you when you have grown up praising him?"[154] One student summarized feelings about meeting former Christians who are now Jews by stating, "As a Christian, I do not like hearing stories of people leaving my faith. So, listening to her story was very disturbing to me. I am not really sure what to think about it."[155]

After attending a Shabbat service, a student wrote they sensed "a sense of family and community in Jewish life" lacking in the experience of their own church.[156] Another student wrote about how their visit to the synagogue made them feel uncomfortable: "I felt weird sitting there while thinking about the Jesus that I worship; knowing that the people who surrounded me did not believe all the things that I believed about him."[157] Such views help clarify the assumption raised a few years ago by the President of the Southern Baptist Convention, Reverend Bailey

Smith (mentioned in the foreword), who explained that "God Almighty does not hear the prayers of the Jews."[158] Some students have commented that watching Jews pray reminded them of their own spiritual longings and the sincerity—as opposed to the ritual formalism—of Jewish prayer touched their hearts. As Christians and Jews join in prayer, they better appreciate what Martin Buber described prayer as "pregnant expression" of the "speech of man to God" asking for a "manifestation of the divine presence."[159]

Shabbat and the Role of Rituals

Jewish rituals for differing times and seasons of the year have played a key role in the preservation of Jewish communities through the ages. Traditions have been a force for education as well as for personal moral sustenance. They have been a source for hope in many situations where people did not know where to turn or how to protect their children from the Christian majority. In these ways, Judaism (as is true for other religions) offers adherents an array of symbols that shape a person's worldview while also evoking feelings of reverence.

Students often state that the rabbi's focus on the centrality of the Shabbat in Jewish life has been very instructive. One student mused, "The observance of Shabbat is very appealing to me. I'd love to have time to devote a day of my life every week for family and the study of God's Word. This is one thing I think that many Christians don't take seriously enough."[160]

The twenty-five hours of every Shabbat beginning at sundown on Friday are an expression of the sanctification of all time. It is not a restricted time but a dedicated time to focus on that which truly matters in life. Even though Shabbat comes once a week, it is considered the most vital of all sacred days (along with the Day of Atonement). In the Bible, God commands the people of Israel: "Remember the Sabbath day to keep it holy" (Exod 20:8). Jews who obey this command are promised great blessings. Even leaders of early Christianity, such as the apostle Paul, were said to attend services at the synagogue every Sabbath (Acts 18:4). Rabbi Philip Lazowski explains, "throughout the ages, the Sabbath has been the great solidifying force that has welded the Jewish people together and united them in their belief that they are destined to exist to the end of generations."[161] It is not simply one day among others but also a vessel within time to bring holiness into everyday life. In his book, *The Sabbath: It's Meaning for Modern Man,* Rabbi Abraham Joshua Heschel exalted that the Sabbath was a "palace in time" where people came together—not only for the warmth of family and delicious food—but also to reflect on God's goodness. It is a day to be set aside for prayer, meditation, and to get away from what Rabbi Kerry Olitzky describes as the modern, "incessant call of commercialism."[162] Israeli writer Ahad Ha'am (nee Asher Ginsberg) quipped, "More than the Jews have kept the Sabbath, the Sabbath has kept the Jews".

When economic, political, or social circumstances were difficult during dark periods of Jewish history, it was the Sabbath that brought a little security, a measure of peace, rest, and perspective for embattled communities surrounded by hostile majorities. The Sabbath is a refreshing delight to the soul and a precious gift from God. It is a renewing foretaste of the harmonious world to come. Martin Buber exults, "the Sabbath is a day of stability, of untroubled serenity and peace between Heaven and Earth . . . . This achievement of peace in the creation" is part of a God-ordained "rhythm that runs uniformly through the whole year and through all the years of time."[163]

Discussions about the Sabbath are only one context for engagement. In Jewish-Christian discussions, however, it is vital not to lose the "forest for the trees." Whenever one is explaining the cherished rituals of another tradition, it is helpful to keep in mind how the other person processes what they are hearing based on the preconceptions and their own experiences. There is often a vast difference between the role and reason for ritual within each distinct tradition.

Jewish Holidays

Jewish holidays offer ideal teaching tools to help non-Jews learn more about what values are central within Judaism. The logic of each ritual or ceremony (and its location within the liturgical calendar) can help Christians appreciate the empowering structures of the faith and the way that Judaism is lived in daily life. For example, the ritual year begins with the celebration of Rosh Hashanah. This holiday is a call for spiritual renewal and moral contemplation. It is a humbling time of awe and a reminder of our own mortality. One Yiddish proverb states that individuals should pray, not because prayer makes sense, but because life makes no sense unless we pray.[164]

Ten days of contemplation and repentance are followed by the holiest day of the Jewish year: Yom Kippur. It is during these ten days, according to tradition, that the books of life and death are opened in the heavenly realms, and God chooses who will live for another year. The term *Yom Kippur* means "Day of Atonement" and the focus of this day is on the centrality of moral reflection and repentance (*teshuvah*). It is a holiday mentioned four times in the Bible (Lev 16:29; 23:27; 25:9; Num 29:7) and, in each instance, the focus centers on self-denial and fasting. While there is no holiday that directly coincides with Yom Kippur within the Christian liturgical calendar, Ash Wednesday is similar in that it is a time for personal confession and focused self-examination.

Judaism has three pilgrimage festivals rooted within its long history. The first pilgrimage festival, during the spring planting season, is Pesach (or Passover); the second is the festival of the first harvest, called Shavuot; and the third is the pilgrimage at the end of summer (and the final harvest) called Sukkot. When students read about these traditions, they sometimes assume that these festivals exist in the modern era in the same way that they did during ancient Bible times. One student, a theology major, sincerely questioned, "How can any typical Jewish family in America go about and get anything done at all in their lives if they have to go and travel to Jerusalem for all of these festivals?"[165]

Although Shavuot (or "Weeks") is tied to the agricultural cycle of the ancient world (Exod 23:16), this second of the pilgrimage festivals is primarily a two-day celebration that the early rabbi's designated to commemorate the giving of the Torah at Mount Sinai (Deut 16:9–10; Exod 34:22). Shavuot reminds the people of Israel of their eternal redemption as well as their temporal blessings. Of note to Christians is that, according to the book of Acts, it was during their celebration of Shavuot that the first Christians experienced the supernatural, heaven-sent powers of Pentecost (Acts 2:1–4). Some have described this holiday, seven weeks after Passover, as the conclusion of the Passover celebration. It is a time of hope and a call to see God's role at the heart of daily society. At the start of Shavuot, the Ten Commandments (or "Decalogue") are read to remind believers of the moral compass that God has given for their daily lives. Another passage recited during Shavuot is Ps 118, which encourages individuals to worship God with their actions as well as their observance of rituals and financial offerings. This holiday is linked to the

Passover celebration of freedom by showing that the blessings of freedom are maintained through living out the divine teaching. It is a holiday filled with bright flowers and opportunities to thank God for the abundance of all that sustains us in life.

Sukkot, the third nature festival (Lev 23:33–36), is a seven-day (or eight in the diaspora) nature festival held five days after the end of Yom Kippur. It is a holiday to take time to stop and thank God for life's many blessings. The calendar turns over around these three cyclical times of remembrance. Jews are called to rejoice (Deut 16:14–15) with a spirit of gratitude for their deliverance from Egypt. It is this emphasis that leads some to equate Sukkot with the North American Thanksgiving celebration. The most well-known part of this holiday is the requirement to build a temporary structure, a *sukkah*, of more than two walls and at least big enough to take meals inside (Lev 23:42–43).

To honor the revelation of the first five books of Moses, Jews in the eleventh century established a joyful holiday called *Simchat Torah* or "rejoicing in the Torah." One can easily notice a host of allusions to a wedding ceremony because it is the commemoration of God being "married" to the Jewish community through the transformative revelation of the Torah. Candles are lit, wine is drunk, blessings are prayed, and all are encouraged to dance with joyful abandon.

Another festival of singing and dancing is Purim, a minor historical holiday that recounts the story of the salvation of the Jewish exiles in Persia (under King Ahasuerus) during the life of Queen Esther. In addition to the courageous and decisive Esther, the characters of the sagely Mordecai and the evil Haman come to life at this time. Purim is celebrated in a joyous tone as a reminder that life's bitter trials can be overcome through strong faith and patient hope. Because it celebrates the events of a feast (Esth 9:18–28), participants should eat and drink to their heart's content. Interestingly, God is not mentioned in the book of Esther. Perhaps, just as individuals wear masks on this free-wheeling holiday, so God also dons the "mask" of our fellow humans in order to bring redemptive blessings into our midst.

Passover (Pesach) celebrates the liberation of the Jewish people from centuries of bondage and oppression. This explains why some Christians are quick to draw a parallel between Passover and Easter and note that Jesus prepared the Last Supper with the twelve disciples during the Passover Feast. One of the sad consequences of this frequent parallel has been that throughout the centuries of Jewish and Christian interactions, this holiday has been one of the times in the calendar that was particularly filled with outbreaks of anti-Semitism and atrocity. Stories were circulated across medieval Europe and the Russian Empire that Jews used the blood of Christian children for the making of their Passover matzo. Good Friday sermons in the past often charged the Jews with the murder of God in the person of Jesus. The reality, however, is that wine is always (and only) a symbol of joy for Jews, and that, in fact, the consumption of blood is forbidden in many places in the Bible and is the reason for salting and soaking meat as part of the *koshering* (making fit for consumption) process.

In modern Christian-Jewish interactions, it has often been the season of Passover that has led (so-called) "Jewish Christians" to visit churches and perform mock Passover meals in supposed empathy with the Jewish people. One of the lessons of this history of both persecution and appropriation is that the beauty of Passover, and its specific themes, should be examined. One of the major themes of Passover is never to forget where we have come from and how richly God has blessed us with deliverance. The story is commanded to be told from parents to children across the generations. Passover is one of Judaism's most beloved holidays because of the deep connections among family forged during its observance. Passover rings with joyful gratitude for freedom from the bitterness of slavery. One of the messages of Passover is that—even in life's darkest times—we can experience a fresh beginning with devoted expectation. The story of Passover is found in Exodus (12:27–39) and the keeping of the ceremonies surrounding the festival are found in Leviticus (23:5–6). Jews are called to work for the deliverance of others from the grip of injustice as well as to cherish their own freedom.

Hanukkah (חנוכה) is the minor festival of lights that memorializes a victorious battle that the Jewish Maccabees won, with stringent effort and sacrifice, over their Syrian-Greek rulers in 165 B.C.E. It tells the legendary story of how a few faithful believers battled against their many oppressors and were passionate even to the point of death in the cold face of tyranny. The celebration of Hanukkah is also a story of liberation. Phyllis Taylor even compared the Maccabees, who led the revolt against the oppression celebrated in Hanukkah, with the Sandinistas of Nicaragua: "Judas Maccabeus—our Sandino—led the people in a guerilla struggle to liberate our land."[166]

Helping Christians appreciate the vitality of Jewish celebrations allows them to see the dynamism of a lived tradition. The explanation of these holidays also works to confront those Christians who presume that Judaism is a stale religion of dry formalism. Barriers of disrespect diminish, and some Christians even claim that they begin to "envy" their Jewish neighbors for their access to such a rich banquet of celebration and remembrance. There are many other Jewish holidays, and each of these is a teaching tool that also underscores the centrality of memory for the life of the community. Rabbi Kerry Olitzky writes Christians should better appreciate that "there is little distinction between Jewish culture and Jewish religion" because "Jewish religion was the route into Jewish culture."[167] Each celebration reinforces moral values and can be a useful teaching resource to help Christians better appreciate that which is being cherished by Jews.

Rituals of Life

Sometimes the challenges Christians face in appreciating Jewish symbols and rituals is simply an expression of the fact that there is no parallel to these elements within their own tradition. This explains why some Christians claim that what they most envy about Judaism is the many rituals that mark out the unfolding seasons of life. One student, after attending a Shabbat service, stated, "It is so wonderful that a group of people are praying together in the same language that Moses spoke thousands of years ago."[168] Some wish that such traditions were to be found within their own churches.

Despite the generally positive responses that the teaching of Jewish festivals engenders, there remain a few skeptics who have responded by concluding that—although these festivals are wonderful—they are also the sum total of the faith in a pejorative sense, in that Judaism only exists to uphold a shared cultural legacy. After one student visited a Bar Mitzvah, they admitted to struggling with how what they were learning related to their own Christian faith. They wrote, "Since the Bar Mitzvah is such a really important issue in a Jewish boy's life, instead of thinking 'this kid is making a big mistake,' I found myself respecting their traditions even though I strongly believe in my relationship with Christ."[169]

These rites of passage—rituals of birth, coming of age, marriage, and death—serve as an ideal educational resource for Christians as they work to appreciate the family-centered and communitarian nature of Judaism. The Bar or Bat Mitzvah (בר מצוה/בת מצוה) makes a child a son or daughter "of the commandment" and marks their formal entrance into the embracing faith of the family and the larger community. Elaborate marriage rituals also serve to underscore and reaffirm the values of the community and to welcome the hopeful expansion of family. A wedding canopy (*huppah* [חופה]) mirrors the home the couple will build together, and the welcoming openness their home will hopefully have is also reflected in the openness of the wedding canopy. Each couple typically signs a marriage contract (*ketubah* [כתובה]) in front of the family and the entire community that reaffirms its loyalties.

Rituals of faith often begin in the warm context of the home. It is the custom of many Jewish families to place a *mezuzah* (מזוזה) on the doorposts of their home (see Deut 6:4–9; 11:13–21) to publicly identify their own family within the larger Jewish community. Throughout life, women are invited to go to a *mikveh* (מקוה)—a ritual bath. When an individual comes to the end of life, burial and mourning rituals assist the family through their seasons of grief and loss. These rituals sustain the faithful in the times when life feels uncertain and unsteady. They provide a clearly marked pathway to go on with life while also honoring cherished family memories. One tradition that helps Jews remember the loss of loved ones is to commemorate the death of a certain person each year on the anniversary date of their passing. This *Yahrzeit* commemoration is a time for family to recite the Mourners *Kaddish* (קדיש), which keeps the memories of the departed in the forefront.

A synagogue is a sacred space designed to affirm the centrality of family and faith running together. Families are encouraged to go together to the synagogue where they join other families to celebrate, worship, and advance their religious and moral education. The synagogue is at the heart of the Jewish community and is a center for the ongoing training and restoration of God's people as they face life's daily challenges. The synagogue is home to holy scrolls, which are owned by all members of the community and are protected inside the synagogue. Symbolic architecture, such as an Ark at the front of a synagogue, reminds individuals of their connections to the blessings of family and to the larger community of Jews worldwide.

There is one other issue that should be mentioned in a discussion of how rituals and ceremonies can help Christians appreciate the ways that Jewish traditions tighten the fabric of a shared community. Is it not the case that these same rituals and practices, when observed by some Messianic Jews (discussed in the next chapter), threaten the health of a local

Jewish community? Theologian Wolfhart Pannenberg is correct that the subject should not be avoided and that, "sooner or later, Christian-Jewish dialogue will have to take notice of the fact" of the "emergence of Messianic Judaism."[170]

The majority of Messianic Jews claim to be both Jewish and Christian and claim to worship Jesus as the Messiah while also participating in various Jewish rituals and ceremonies. In addition, the historic relationship between the synagogue and the local family faces a unique challenge when it encounters Christians (according to other Jews) who claim that they are Jews while practicing their own distinct version of Judaism. Most Jews cannot accept that the blessings of community can be appropriated by those who seek those blessings while also rejecting a commitment to communitarian cohesion.

Messianic Jews often simply call themselves "Jews" and refer to their gathering places as "synagogues" and, in so doing, cause some Christians, who do not know any better, to become confused about the nature of Judaism and the role of a synagogue. Peter Hocken says that Evangelicals are particularly interested in Messianic Judaism because "Evangelicals are almost the only Christians in modern times to take seriously the Old Testament prophecies concerning the people and the land of Israel."[171] This interest also explains why Evangelicals are the "main Gentile supporters of the Messianic Jewish movement."[172]

Culture or Religion?

Issues of religious identity merit careful consideration. North Americans hear about "Jewish food" and "Jewish humor" and may have trouble equating such things with their own majoritive experience (e.g., "Christian food"). One of the most difficult issues for some Christians to appreciate is the tradition of eating *kosher* foods, which has no parallel within Christianity and, as such, often seems to be an expression of ritual formalism or of unnecessary laws. I (Fuller) go to great lengths to describe the role of kosher foods as a resource, not to inflict empty ritual, but as a wonderful way to cement together the bonds of communal identity.

The term *kosher* (כשר) literally means something that is "ritually correct" or "permissible." It usually refers to foods but also relates to other actions, even behavior. One such prohibition is against the eating of blood or pork (Lev 17:11–16). Certain shellfish are prohibited (Lev

11:12) along with scavengers and other birds (Lev. 11:13–19). Animals must be killed humanely and an animal that has already died cannot be eaten (Deut 14:21). Animals must be slaughtered in such a way as to ensure that their death is as humane and as quick as possible: There are several other guidelines relating to food preparation that are cited in the biblical text.

Where does culture end and religion begin? Issues about the inter-relationship between cultural and religious identity are expressed in a few different ways by various communities. While there may be such a thing as "Christian music," it is identified because of its faith-based lyrics and not in any other specific quality. Some Christians have asked me (Fuller) if the Jewish people are a "race" or a culture as opposed to a "religion." It is neither a "race" nor just a religion; it is a peoplehood. Part of their confusion springs, not from Judaism, but in the varying ways that North Americans sometimes blur the lines between these categories. Even categorical terms used, such as "Latina," "Black," "White," or "Jew," are open to a wide range of stereotypes and varied social meanings.

The word "Jew" derives from the name of Leah's fourth son, Yehuda (יהודה, Judah, meaning "he shall exalt"). This name is interesting because it contains within it the four-letter name of God, YHWH. The Jewish people are often a community of faith committed to the exaltation of God's name and God's greatness in the world. To call yourself a Jew is a conscious self-identification that describes how an individual relates to both a community and to God.

It is instructive to note that one can also be an atheist and a Jew. In the broadest sense, being Jewish means sharing a story and choosing an identity. Jews are a "peoplehood"—a nation that has focused on a specific piece of land and shared a common language, ethos, ancestry and culture. Leo Tolstoy answered the ancient question "what is a Jew?" by declaring:

> The Jew is the emblem of eternity: He whom neither slaughter, nor the tortures of thousands of years could destroy. He whom neither fire nor sword, nor inquisition was able to wipe off from the face of the earth; he who was the first to produce the oracle of God; He who has been for so long the guardian of prophecy and who transmitted it to the rest of the world—a nation of such people cannot be destroyed. The Jew is everlasting as is eternity itself.[173]

Contemporary Jewish communities are focused on finding a balance between celebrating cultural and religious differences while also encouraging their youth to marry other Jews and raise further generations of Jewish families. The blending of worship and an increase in multifaith marriages complicates the challenge of maintaining a faith that eschews all forms of proselytism.

While Jews affirm those within their communities who choose to marry those of other faiths, there is also a hope that such couples will raise their children in an intentionally Jewish context. Assimilation is a force that blurs the distinctives of community. It is not right to overemphasize commonalities while also neglecting those interfaith issues that have dramatic ramifications for those in the minority.

Judaism is obviously made up of a wide diversity of individuals from many cultural and ethnic backgrounds. King David, for example, descended from a Moabite (pagan) convert named Ruth and some Jews feel that the promised Messiah will come from her family of ancestors. Some of the greatest teachers within the tradition are converts from other religions (or from no formal religion at all). What Jews share is a common commitment to a shared community and a sense of a common destiny. It is for this reason that Messianic Jews are not recognized as mainstream Jews. They have chosen to fundamentally identify, as do all converts, to a new religion from the point of their previous adherence.

From one specific angle, Judaism is a religion. It is a faith in the Jewish sense of the term—as a gathering of families together to create a cultural community of shared faith—more than in the historic Christian sense of the term. The way that some Christians use the term "religion" does not parallel all that can be said about the experience of being Jewish. According to William J. Leffler and Paul H. Jones, this difference can best be appreciated in the way that both Jews and Christians structure their religious experiences. Unlike in Christianity, the structure of Jewish worship is "not intended to strengthen the worshipper's faith since it is assumed that the congregant's belief does not need this form of reinforcement. Whether accurate or not, it is taken as a given."[174]

Jews worship because they are born Jewish in the same way that many others in other traditions seem to automatically embrace the faith of their parents. Faith only secures what is already in place. This underscores the claim that Judaism is more than simply the sum of the Jewish people. It is a community of families who come together to celebrate a series of shared ideas, behaviors, and a cherished historical legacy of faith. How can this be best explained? The breadth of nationalities housed within the world's Jewish community discredits the idea that there is a "Jewish race." If an individual can make the decision to convert to becoming Jewish, then it should be clear that it cannot only be a genetic inheritance. A person cannot decide to convert to becoming "Asian," or "Hispanic." Nor is Judaism a nationality: This notion began during the time of the Spanish Inquisition and reached its nadir with the genocidal crimes of Hitler (and other Nazis, fascists, and Stalinists). Sometimes, ironically, obfuscations on such issues have come from, of all places, the Jewish community itself. These questions need to be nuanced for the benefit of those within the majority culture who have different views about how faith relates to personal and corporate identities.

People of all faiths can appreciate that any faith tradition is rooted in a host of cultural specificities. Although some approach religions as a cafeteria-style selection, others simply follow the faith of their parents and do not even consider any other faith tradition. Taking a more global perspective, few people convert to another religion or intentionally choose their own religion. The vast majority come to their faith through accidents of birth or geography. While some may have the notion that they are, in some ways, "free agents," religious identity and cultural location are almost always very closely intertwined. Realizing this fact helps Christians better appreciate how Judaism is both a cultural and religious reality.

Conclusion

An obvious danger arises when ritual becomes the primary fulcrum used to explain Judaism. The fact is that many tens of thousands of North American Jews practice no rituals at all. One rabbi lamented that many Jewish youth received nothing from their Judaism because, "they don't practice it in a disciplined way. But it is meant, obviously, to be practiced that way. There's daily prayer, minute-by-minute practices about eating and how you conduct your business, and even how you conduct yourself sexually."[175]

The fact that some people fail to see this major fact of contemporary Judaism speaks volumes about the extent of "otherization" that is going on in their perceptions. A more nuanced view helps non-Jews appreciate that the non-observance of ritual is just as vital to understanding the story of North American Judaism as is the supposed centrality of ritual practices and festival observances.

There are, on the other side of the coin, many benefits that accrue when non-Jews interact directly as observers/participants at Jewish places of worship. For those learning about Judaism for the first time, however, the gracious hospitality of their Jewish neighbors to allow non-Jews into their midst for the reason of education is quite constructive. In a short period of time such encounters can confront long-held presuppositions about Judaism that are often negative. One student exalted:

> I always had the notion that Jews were very far from God and rather impassionate. I found the very opposite to be true. I think that students could learn a lot from going to the temple. It was also very gratifying to realize that with real living proof, Judaism is not a rule-based "right-and-wrong" type of religion but one that believes in the grace and mercy of God. I really felt the love of God in the synagogue. I left feeling really awakened to his love. I think that Judaism can really help Christians. Of course, I will never reject Jesus, but how they worship is so inspirational and so admirable.[176]

Chapter Nine

Messianic Jewry

No Jew was ever foolish enough to turn Christian—unless he was a clever man.
—Israel Zangwall, 1892

Jews are a people with a deep commitment to their historical past. They have vivid recollections of their ancestors enduring martyrdom rather than abandoning their Jewish faith. Jews have suffered from Christian missionary actions for almost two millennia. They regard the Hebrew Christian movement as but another effort in spiritual genocide, albeit in a more fraudulent form. And they will resist such attempts to wean them away from their ancestral faith, as they have for two thousand years.
—Rabbi Yechiel Eckstein

Considering Auschwitz, any deliberate attempt to convert Jews to Christianity can be seen only as a more subtle form of Hitler's "Final Solution"—the plan to erase Jews from the face of the earth.
—Eva Fleischer

Messianic Jews

FOR CENTURIES, IF A Jew became a Christian, they were eager, by force of necessity, to deny any connection with the Jewish community or any relation with their previous heritage. In the modern era, a new

94

movement—multivalent and multifaceted—has emerged where some Jews have converted to Christianity but have sought to maintain, some connection with the faith that they have chosen to leave. One of the first Messianic Jewish missionaries, A. M. Meyer explained, "Let us not sacrifice our identity. When we profess Christ, we do not cease to be Jews. Paul after his conversion did not cease to be a Jew. We cannot and will not forget the land of our fathers . . . . As Hebrews, as Christians, we feel tied together; and as Hebrew-Christians we desire to be allied more closely to one another."[177]

The groups in this movement call themselves "Messianic Jews," "Hebrew Christians," "Completed Jews," "Jews for Jesus," and a host of other similar terms. David Novak explains, "These Jewish converts to Christianity not only claim to be Jews, they also claim still to be practicing Judaism. Some of them insist that they are indeed practicing the true Judaism, thus implying, if not actually affirming directly, that their practice be accepted as a legitimate form of Judaism."[178] Messianic Jews claim to be in character with the first ethnically Jewish Christians who first believed that Jesus was the Messiah. Messianic Jewish-Christian scholar Lidia Tonoyan claims that after the first century, "it would take another 1600 years before the appearance of a newly articulated Jewish Christianity staked a renewed claim in the continuing drama of Christianity."[179]

There are Messianic Jewish congregations throughout North America, Europe, and, more recently, in the former Soviet Union thanks to extensive Messianic Jewish missionary efforts by evangelists such as the Rochester, New York-based Messianic Jewish Rabbi Jonathan Bernis. Interestingly, many of the members of these congregations have no Jewish ethnic heritage at all but are simply Evangelicals who want to identify with the worldwide Jewish community. Such participants further blur an already murky territory that claims Jewishness is primarily ethnic and allows space for Jews to become Christians and retain their integral Jewish identity. Speaking of his own conversion, Jonathan Bernis explained that "embracing Y'shua was the most Jewish thing that I have ever done."[180]

Messianic Judaism is about the construction of a new identity that claims ancient roots. The hope of Jews who convert to "Hebrew Christianity" is to blend together two distinct religions as if they did not have two distinct histories. Theologically, the movement is a form of Evangelical Protestantism framed in the form of a caricaturized Jewish ritual and ethnic experience. This melding explains why Messianic Judaism is often revivalist, charismatic, and focused on apocalyptic themes, which often focus on themselves as being central to the end of the world and the return of Christ. Theologically, their critique of Judaism in failing to recognize Jesus is fundamentally identical to conservative Christian critiques of Judaism.

Messianic Jews are sometimes critical of other Christians who are seen to be "pagan" for corrupting the true Christianity of Jews with certain practices that are not found in the Bible (e.g., Sunday worship instead of the Sabbath, or participation in holidays such as Halloween, Christmas, or Easter). These positions underscore why some Messianic Jews claim to function as an evangelistic bridge between Christianity and Judaism. Messianic Jews, it can be argued, are less interested in the continuity of a historic group of people—the Jews—than they are in their own desire to identify themselves as they choose: Jews who believe in Jesus as the Son of God or Messiah. This is reflected in the lives of their children and grandchildren, who, studies have shown, often eventually shift into the larger Christian world as any sense of cultural identity is overwhelmed by the faith-orientation of Christianity.[181] Of course, in a free society with religious liberty ensured, anyone has the right to construct any kind of religious identity they want and call themselves whatever they want to call themselves.

Jewish converts to Christianity are a compelling concern for Jewish-Christian dialogue because they have become one of the most common ways that some conservative Christians come to learn anything at all about Judaism. In many North American Evangelical churches, Messianic Jewish speakers have made presentations about the many ways that Christianity and Judaism relate to each other. In addition, many are part of Christian denominations that are active in attempts to convert Jews to Christianity and with groups that support the validity of Messianic Jewish movements. In some Christian churches, it is not unusual that congregants would hear prayers from their preachers that go something like, "Lord, we pray that our Jewish friends will learn the truth about their Messiah."

Many Messianic Jewish organizations are accepted without question by Christian congregations and some of the larger churches may support such groups with substantial financial gifts. Others have read the wildly popular books from the *Left Behind* series, which present the Jewish people as passive pawns in the hands of Satan forced to suffer for their sins until Jesus returns at the rapture after a seven-year period of tribulation to rescue all Jews who now recognize—none too soon—that Jesus is their long-awaited Messiah.

Messianic Jewish groups (such as the Messianic Jewish Alliance –MJA) are public in their practice of a host of Jewish ceremonies, festivals, and ritual practices. The public performance of these rituals is also provocative to Jews who see their enactment as the efforts of play-acting imposters who have coopted cherished symbols for their own evangelistic purposes. Messianic rabbis are seen to be hiding behind a mask of being Jewish while performing a form of deceptive entrapment especially geared towards uneducated Jews (in places such as the former Soviet Union) who are told that such rituals are authentically Jewish.[182]

Of course, biblical rituals are inclusive to all Jews but, in a vital sense, are also exclusive in that they symbolize relationship to the larger community. Religious rituals, however, should not be appropriated by Christians any more than a cherished Christian ceremony such as the taking of the Eucharist should be practiced casually (or even with empathy) by non-Christians. Messianic Jews, and others who carry out Jewish rituals while not being Jewish, are "playing Jewish." Such actions are often seen by Jews as the trivialization of centuries of symbology laden with educational significance.

Christians who describe themselves as Messianic Jews claim they are Jews who have been "completed" by embracing Jesus as the Son of God. This is not a new phenomenon: there have been several instances throughout Christian history where some have sought to foster a more Jewish quality to their lives as Christians. In the modern era, groups such as "Jews for Jesus" have stirred up a hornets' nest of resentment among many members of Jewish communities worldwide for a host of differing reasons. Fellow Christians have also expressed concerns, not only by some of their methodologies, but also in the reticence that some Messianic Jews have expressed in fully identifying themselves as Christians and members of the worldwide church.

This view has not historically been shared by Christians in the inverse: one cannot argue the fact that if a Catholic person, for example, converted to Judaism that the Catholic Church would no longer consider such individuals to be Catholic. A former Baptist or Lutheran who converts to Judaism would not have much traction among their original communities if they referred to themselves as "completed Baptists" or "fulfilled Lutherans." Christians should not be surprised that many Jews find the notion of a Jewish-Christian being a "true Jew" offensive. They certainly should not be expected to serve as a "unique link" between the two communities.

One estimate claimed that there are about 100,000 Messianic Jews worldwide.[183] These "Completed Jews" claim that they have not abandoned their faith but are now practicing Judaism as it actually should be practiced in its "fulfilled" form. Some assert they are simply another denomination of Judaism alongside groups such as the Orthodox, Conservative, or Reform Jews. For many Christians and Jews, however, the question arises as to how one can be both Christian and Jewish at the same time given the distinct claims of both contemporary faith communities.

The Messianic Jewish claim that Jesus is the Son of God means to almost all Christians that they are Christians. At the same time, almost all Jews would agree that this same decision makes them decidedly Christian and not Jewish. Messianic Jews ignore these assumptions because their position is contingent upon a conviction that, in effect, they are gifted by God and chosen to be able to determine exactly what constitutes Judaism. This claim arises although (almost) the entire world's fourteen to fifteen million Jews would emphatically assert that they are not fellow Jews. Jewish leaders worldwide have not claimed that Judaism is an amorphous ethnic stew that can be reorganized at a whim without any reference to millennia of community, doctrine, and tradition.

Jews worldwide have suffered and died to bear witness to the oneness of God and the suggestion that Jesus is God has no place in a traditional or normative expression of Jewish thinking about the oneness of God.[184] To the Jewish world, Messianic Christians have spurned their faith, abandoned their communities, and forfeited any right to claim they are Jewish. Rooted in historical memory, Jews recognize that the goal of any Messianic Jew is to convert them from Judaism into their Jewish-Christian networks. According to all major organizational structures of Judaism, any Jew who accepts Jesus as the Son of God ceases to be Jewish. Even though Messianic Jews use the same terms as Orthodox or Conservative Jews when practicing Jewish rituals, they use these terms in a new context and with a new understanding of their meanings. Messianic Jews, who are Christians, are—it is assumed by Jews—taking Jewish customs out of context and outside of the realm of the larger Jewish community. Many Jews who are offended by their use of Jewish ritual feel that such practices make a mockery of their cherished traditions.

Some Christians have wondered how such practices can be genuinely Christian. Even early church leaders, such as St. Ignatius, wrote that it was "inconsistent to talk of Jesus Christ and to practice Judaism at the same time."[185] Messianic Jews respond to both Christians and Jews by claiming that they are in line with the spirit of first-century Christianity, which began as a Jewish movement. This claim, however, fails to consider that the intervening two thousand years matter in the equation of how Jews and Christians relate to each other.

One of the most visible ways that Messianic Jewry has affected the perceptions of some Christians is through yearly Passover Seder celebrations held across some North American churches. The idea is conveyed that such Passover Seder celebrations are geared to help Christians gain a deeper appreciation of the Jewish tradition. With this guise of tolerant appreciation, what often happens is that individuals with no authority to practice such cherished rituals—both Messianic Jews and Christian pastors (and others)—carry out these rituals in the name of helping church members appreciate how Christ is foretold in every aspect of the Passover meal. Of course, there may be an appropriate place for Christian congregations asking Jews to help them better appreciate the Passover Seder. Such an inquiry, however, should never become a roundabout way to advance an agenda that denigrates the vitality of Judaism by presenting a caricature and through re-representing the meaning of each ritual element.

Why does it seem that many Jews focus on the status of Messianic Jews with such passionate conviction? Counter-missionary organizations such as "Jews for Judaism" have even come into being to expose the efforts of Messianic Jewish groups. It is not because these Jews who oppose Messianic Judaism care about some notion of the purity of definitions within Christianity. Anyone can fully appreciate that individuals are free to believe whatever they want to believe. This is not the issue. It is not even that many Jews are concerned over having "lost" a few more people from their number. One of the basic principles for any level of interfaith dialogue is that each faith community should be able to interpret their own self-definition and affirm their own basic self-understandings (even to construct an identity known as "Messianic Judaism"). Beyond dialogue, what is also at stake with the use of the term "Jewish-Christian" is that it has the potential to generate all kinds of confusing misunderstandings for unaware Jewish and Christian youth. A term such as "Messianic Jew" blurs inarguable distinctions between two faiths through a series of theological and ritual obfuscations. Further, the notion of a person being a Messianic Jew easily provides an obvious staging-ground for some

Christians to proselytize unsuspecting Jews by encouraging them to remain Jewish while also becoming Christian.

These concerns are based on countless interactions with members from such groups who present themselves as being Jewish and, thus, cause all kinds of muddying of the waters. Pamphlets from the organization "Jews for Jesus," for example, were translated into Russian and given to Russian émigrés who had recently arrived in North America through the extensive administrative efforts and financial gifts of a few international Jewish aid organizations. Proselytes have distributed "Jewish calendars" filled with images from Judaism while also promoting their primary message. Christian television and radio stations have aired a weekly program called "The Jewish Voice." Messianic Jews have established synagogues (without crosses) in the name of "Y'shua" (Jesus), and their leaders travel through communities calling themselves rabbis. One can contrast these dynamics with a statement shared by most Jews: "The acceptance of Jesus as the Messiah is not theologically consistent with Jewish belief and therefore Jews who profess to accept Jesus can no longer be considered practicing Jews."[186] One might, of course, challenge this claim in reference to the earlier claim that one can be both an atheist and a Jew.

The high-profile assertions of Messianic Jews should help other Christians appreciate why many Jews look with suspicion at those conservative Christians who support such groups with financial aid or moral support. Since many conservative Christians tend to be sympathetic to Messianic Jewish groups, it should not be difficult for these same Christians to appreciate why some Jews are suspicious (or even unwilling) to enter so-called "dialogues" with those who have "joined the enemy." Interreligious intentions must be transparent. When they are not, one can assume that a host of problems will arise.

At the very least, Christians should reject any approaches to evangelism targeted at Jewish people which are not transparent and straightforward. Evangelicals who want to see Messianic Jewry as a possible link to other Jews can be easily disabused of this fantasy if they only take the time to talk to almost any rabbi in North America. The question of evangelizing Jews is especially central given a stark history of Christian violence and persecution against Jewish communities for centuries. Messianic Judaism, as an irritating source of friction for Jews who seek to relate to Christians, cannot be ignored. All types of Christians and Jews—including Messianic Jews—should talk about these issues and how they relate to the promotion of suspicion and distrust. More than being a threat, in and of themselves, Messianic Jewish groups threaten the basic trust needed for improved Jewish-Christian interactions going forward. Michael Lotker expresses the feelings of many Jews when writing:

> I have a major problem with those Christians who would try to mislead me and other Jews into believing that one can be both Jewish and Christian. It is no more meaningful to be an authentic "Jew for Jesus" than it would to be a "Christian for Muhammad" or a "Muslim for Buddha." The teachings of Christianity as beautiful as they might be are simply inconsistent with Judaism in the same way that the teachings of Islam are inconsistent with Christianity.... I believe that "Messianic Jewish" organizations seek to seduce Jews into believing that they can remain Jewish while accepting Jesus. The critical question that should be asked of such Messianic Jews is the very simple question "Is Jesus God?" As Judaism and Christianity define themselves, no Jew can answer this question in the affirmative and no Christian in the negative.[187]

When a Christian individual converts to another religion, they are an "apostate." Using this same lens, why do some find it difficult to see that a Jew who chooses to become a Christian is also an apostate Jew? Granted, the main issue in Judaism is not a belief-orientation, but even though the reasons are divergent—in this case, a Jew who becomes a Christian is seen as one who is renouncing his/her community—the basic premise is the same.

Perhaps in the first century at the dawn of Christianity, as the Jewish community was progressively moving towards rabbinic Judaism, the argument could be made that someone could think of themselves as not being an apostate while also believing that Jesus is the Messiah. Today, however, there is a clearly defined history and experience of the two distinct faiths which means that a Jew who becomes a Christian has chosen to step outside of the umbrella of the history and tradition of their community.

There remains some discussion among Jews about who is an "active" and who is a "passive" apostate from the faith while continuing to choose to relate to the Jewish community on ethno-cultural terms. Whatever the conclusions of these arguments—which may also include some level of acceptance for Messianic Jews—in the final analysis, what it means to be Jewish should clearly remain within the purview of the Jewish community. It was with this conviction that the Israeli Supreme Court (1989) ruled unanimously that two applicants, Jerry and Shirley Beresford, could apply for Israeli citizenship as Christians (also eligible for citizenship) but not as Jews, even though they claimed to be Messianic Jews.[188] The Messianic Jewish movement in Israel, however interesting, is beyond the scope of this study.[189]

Shoshanah Feher summarizes Messianic Judaism as an Evangelical group that "offers strongly conservative doctrines, personal forms of worship, and the promise of salvation and redemption—in short, a clear identity in a shifting world."[190] They offer a distinctive community with a worldview of what is right and wrong with the world. It is the right of the corporate Jewish community, in its countless forms, to determine that they do not see groups who identify with another faith as being Jewish. Messianic Jews who insist they are still Jewish are Christians telling Jews how they should define Judaism which forces the reactive response against them from the larger Jewish community that, actually, they are the ones who do not understand or embrace the true, corporate meaning of an acceptable Jewish identity.

The questions surrounding this issue are complicated. In response to reading this chapter, renowned New Testament and Jewish Studies scholar, Professor Amy-Jill Levine wrote: "If Jews are a people, a Jew who turns to Jesus is still a Jew. There is no reconversion ceremony. Messianic Jews are more of a problem than you suggest."[191] Internal relationships are very different in their dynamics than external boundaries imposed on large groups from a distance. No one appreciates it when a married person takes off their wedding ring and pretends to be single! As Rabbi Gary Greenbaum of the American Jewish Committee says of Messianic Jews, "If you want to be a Christian, be one. Just don't tell me you are a Jew."[192] It should not be difficult for Christians to appreciate that the evangelistic efforts of Messianic Jews are seen as an unwelcome intrusion into the life of North American Judaism and how Christians might feel if the "shoe were on the other foot."

Evangelizing Jews

Every semester we share with our students a fifteen-minute video aired by ABC's 20/20 (in 2002) about a twelve-year-old Jewish boy named "Zack" from the Dallas-Fort Worth area who was lured into an evangelism service at a Baptist Church called "target night." The video shows a Baptist outreach program aimed at reaching "unsaved" youth.

According to the video, after the church service where the youth leaders staged several enjoyable games for the children and provided them with food and snacks, the mood changed dramatically, and the church youth program became serious. At this point, the twelve-year-old was told if he asked Jesus to forgive him, all his "sins would be erased" in the same way a spot of "mud is removed from dirty clothes." The video shows that when "Zack" went to the front of the church, he told the counselor that he was Jewish. The counselor assured the boy, "that's okay, a lot of Jewish people are both [i.e., are also Christians]."[193] Eventually, the twelve-year-old renounced his decision at that church and returned to his Jewish community in Dallas to warn other Jewish youth about the true nature of the youth-ministry tactics and how these Baptist evangelists had caused him confusion and pain. We show this video in order to discuss questions about whether Christians should seek to convert Jews (or anyone) through such deceptive evangelistic methods.

Featuring prominently in this video is "Zack's" Bar Mitzvah instructor Rivka Arad. Rivka is a close friend (Fuller) and we worked together in the Dallas area. Rivka has agreed to travel to Waco a few times to speak about this experience and give her responses to this event after students see this video and share their own perspectives. Some students noted how she "wore her heart on her sleeve."[194] Some students have felt troubled by her emphatic views about Christians who try to evangelize Jews. Some reported after Rivka's visit that they felt judged and put in an "apologetic mode for an act that they did not take part in."[195] Others stressed that the story of "Zack's" encounter with this church should not be seen as representative of all Christians while others felt that Baptists should continue to do their God-ordained mission work to "target" Jews with their efforts. One student responded,

> Rivka was very strong and seemed very certain. I was fully sympathetic to the plight of the Jewish boy. The Baptist Church did trick him into coming to church by calling it something it was not. However, I believe that Rivka's strong personality intimidated the class into refusing to join in dialogue. Maybe the Christians in the room felt attacked; it's hard not to want to defend your religion even when it is in the wrong. People must feel safe in order to be willing to be vulnerable.[196]

Evangelism is an area with many fascinating implications. The issue comes to the forefront for some Christians because they have been taught throughout their lives—by families and churches—that they are obligated to share the good news of Jesus with anyone, including Jews. One organization, the World Evangelical Fellowship, explained: "Failing to preach the Gospel to the Jewish people would be a form of anti-Semitism."[197] One of the most ardent ideas supporting "targeting" Jews for evangelism, drawn from the New Testament statements of St. Paul in Romans, is that, although he is the apostle to the gentiles, the message of salvation through Jesus that Paul preaches is "for the Jew first." Messianic Christian authors have written a host of books that can easily be found in any Christian bookstores (or in the libraries of their churches and colleges) that teach how to evangelize the chosen people.

Moishe Rosen in his book *Share the New Life with a Jew* encourages Christians "not to be afraid of Jews." Rosen also warns Christians that they should expect to have a tough time in their evangelization efforts because "the Jewish person has years of conditioning to overcome, as well as the natural inclination of man to turn away from God."[198] Rosen suggests that Christians invite Jews to their homes and "never to hesitate to say a table grace before meals when entertaining Jewish friends in your home" because, evidently, Jews who may normally be able to resist proselytizing efforts cannot resist a free meal.[199] At the same time, Rosen warns that one should "never ask an unconverted Jewish person to pray aloud with you," although the author leaves it to our imagination to guess whether it will be a plague of locusts or boils that will descend upon those who make such an egregious error.[200] The main consideration that Christians have to remember, according to Rosen, is that "Jewish people are confused between religious obligations and moral imperatives."[201] The Jews, Rosen explains, may have made a pact with the devil, but Christians must persist in teaching to Jews the true revelation of their own religion: "Satan's lie is that God is through dealing with the Jews and it is no use trying to witness to them because they are predisposed not to listen."[202]

Although the group is far from being monolithic, some Evangelicals have complained that those who complain about evangelistic efforts focused on Jews are being overly protective. Jews should expect to be confronted in the North American context with a message of their benighted spiritual blindness. Further, just because Jews do not evangelize (and even make it difficult for others to convert to Judaism) they should not expect other religions to view things in the same way. Echoing the earlier comment cited from the World Evangelism Crusade, some feel it would be unloving if a Christian did not try to convert Jews to Christianity. One student wrote about the tensions that were felt while watching this video and interacting with Jewish guests in class:

> Evangelism is always something that has confused me because, while I believe in God, I don't know how I can convey this to someone who does not. There's a huge dilemma when it comes to attempting to convert people of another faith. I understand that many evangelists think they are saving souls from the fires of hell and they very well may be. It's just that maybe they aren't, maybe they are just scaring people into believing something they really don't believe as in the story of target night. In converting someone it's as though the converter knows for sure that they are correct. Beside the possibility that they aren't right, it exudes a sense of arrogance and a "we-know-better-than-you" vibe, that is commonly associated with Christianity. When it comes to evangelism, I've heard just to live a good life and others will see and that will lead people to Christ. If someone wanted to come to know Christ, I would be thrilled to help them.[203]

When I (van Gorder) am asked about such issues, I stress the key difference between being a Christian who is a faithful witness to Christ (in words and actions) and being a person who is focused on the individuals around them as prospective "targets" for proselytizing efforts. While Christians are obligated to witness for their faith (Matt 28:18–20), there is no coinciding obligation that such efforts promote interfaith alienation, hostility, resentment, and defensiveness.

There is wide latitude between the worst- and best-case scenarios when it comes to sharing our faith with others. Jews accept and understand that some Christians feel spiritually obligated to seek their conversion. Jews are simply asking that Christians admit that efforts seeking their conversion do not jibe with statements that Judaism is being given a special status of respect. These very efforts imply Judaism (as Jews know it) should be erased. Christians should appreciate that there is a breadth of options available in being a faithful witness of Christ. There are good and bad ways to undertake the relational tasks of evangelism. The specific example of "Zack" in the DVD shows a situation that is both insensitive and deceptive.

In one discussion, I (Fuller) raised the idea that a commitment to tolerance is not the same as genuine, loving respect. At one point in my progression as a resource for this class, I began to ask students what they thought it might feel like to be "loved" by Christians who, theoretically, are doing so out of concern for my soul. I would point out that in a healthy marriage, spouses don't try to change their partners; rather, they accept them unconditionally for who they are. Could they not find a way to "love" me that same, accepting way? I also at times wondered if perhaps the need that some people feel, that they must evangelize Jews (and others), might spring from a feeling of inner emotional or spiritual insecurity. I wondered if the need to denigrate other religions was also not related to an idea that individuals can feel better about themselves because they are right, and others are wrong or on their way to hell. One student wrote, "I know that for myself, I am secure in my faith and don't need to convert others to feel better about myself."[204] Another student explained, "It was an interesting feeling to be the misunderstood one for a change. I am rarely in a place where what I believe is what offends people."[205]

It could be argued that Judaism began as a missionary religion because there was a clear message that people were called to believe. It can also be argued that, especially during the early biblical era, Jewish people and their prophets were called to carry out what Christians would call "evangelism."[206] There are countless citations in rabbinic literature that refer to Father Abraham being a person that one might call a "missionary." Prophets Isaiah (2:2–4) and Micah (4:1–3) speak of gentiles coming to Israel to learn from Jews the truth of God's ways (see also Zech 8:20–23). There are many citations in the Bible of foreigners who convert to Judaism and, even today, some individuals make this decision. In the big picture, however, there is no parallel passage in the Hebrew Bible to the command of Christ that followers should go to the ends of the earth (Matt 28:20). Further, there is no history in Judaism that approximates the missionary history of Orthodox, Catholic, and Protestant Christianity. Judaism has not been missionizing (as in proselytizing) or evangelistic for at least a millennium. Judaism does not teach that one must be Jewish in order to be in right relationship with God. The Torah (Exod 15:11) and the liturgy both say, "*mi chamocha ba'eilim adonay*—who is like You among the gods, Lord?"—acknowledging that other "gods" exist, according to the author of this text, though none are like the Jewish God (see Deut 4:39).

One of the beneficial dimensions of Jewish-Christian conversation is to help people to see how others view faith and religious assumptions.

Many Christians become surprised to learn how their own views (and the views of other Christians) are offensive to Jews. I (Fuller) encourage students to put themselves in "my shoes" and think of what it might be like if they were members of a minority religious tradition in a context where the majority religion was so intent on your conversion. I try to encourage students to see that some Christian views, when rooted in supersessionist values, are seen by some as a threatening form of intellectual and relational "violence." I hope Christians can realize that a Jew cannot become a Christian and remain a Jew, according to most other Jews. Centuries of persecution of Jews at the hands of Christians, along with countless interfaith marriages, underline this claim.

Conservative Christians have rarely considered how evangelism, something they assume is normative, can be so alien to other faith traditions. One student wrote, "When I went to the masjid [mosque], they tried to convert me, so they talked with me for a long time. But the Jews, they never talk."[207] After a lengthy discussion with Rivka Arad and Rabbi Fuller, one student realized for the first time that no Jew in her entire lifetime had ever tried to convert her to Judaism while, in contrast, "as a Christian I have heard my whole life growing up in church that it was my responsibility to witness to everyone."[208] Another student explained,

> I am shocked how little I knew about the feelings that Jews had about this kind of evangelism. As a Christian I have never been encouraged to have a dialogue with a Jewish person unless it was to convert them to Christianity. Churches seem comfortable with the fact that they are going to heaven and everyone else who is an unbeliever is going to hell. The lack of interest that some Christians have in other faiths allows Christians to go through the motions of their religion without any real conviction. . . . After Rivka told the class her opinions, it is easy to see why some Jewish people are so angry with some Christians. I now have a deeper understanding of how some Jewish people view Christians.[209]

As a Christian, I (van Gorder) understand that my faith, without apology, is a story to be shared and the sharing of the gospel message is at the heart of the Christian church. I have heard many Evangelicals say that, while an individual may be born Jewish, there is no such thing as being born a Christian. One can only become a believing Christian through a conscious act of faith. The conviction that many hold that Jesus alone provides salvation needs not be seen to be anti-Jewish (or anti-anybody). It is helpful to link differing views about evangelism to questions of whether efforts of evangelism should be "targeted" specifically to adherents of Jewish communities.

The heart of the issue for this Christian is the idea of aggressive evangelism directed to the Jews. The "targeting" of Jews by the Southern Baptist Convention as described in the ABC 20/20 video has a long history within Christianity. Such efforts were reaffirmed in the Willowbank Declaration of the World Evangelical Fellowship, which announced, "We deny that there is any truth in the widespread notion that evangelizing Jews is needless because they are already in covenant with God through Abraham and Moses and so are already saved despite their rejection of Jesus Christ as Lord and Savior."[210] Such attitudes should be rejected if, for no other reason, that they are bound to be ineffective and seen as disrespectful to a community already under threat. Such views as those expressed by the Willowbank Declaration do nothing but alienate Jewish communities and create further levels of social alienation.

For most of our two-thousand-year shared history, Christians have been fascinated with the idea of trying to convert Jews to the Christian faith. In the modern mission era, one of the first groups founded to convert Jews was the London Society for Promoting Christianity Amongst the Jews (1809). In North America, similar movements have emerged. Leopold Cohn, a Hungarian Jew who immigrated to the United States organized a group called the American Board of Missions to the Jews in 1892. The Messianic Jewish Alliance of America (formerly known as the Hebrew Christian Alliance of America) was formed in 1915, and the Union of Messianic Jewish Alliance of America was founded in 1979. Instructive to note is that "the major goal and driving force of the Hebrew Christian movement was evangelism ... to provide for the Evangelical Christian churches of America a reliable channel on how best to serve the cause of Jewish evangelization."[211]

The notion of "targeting" Jews is, in our opinion, a clear form of anti-Judaism. It is rooted, at its worst, in contempt for Judaism or, at its best, in the assumption that Judaism is fundamentally deficient before God. This view is shared by Eliot Abrams: "Jews should object to proselytization efforts targeted at them in principle, not because in the United States such efforts have been effective but because they display—as they have through the ages—contempt for Judaism."[212] While our argument would appear to some as treading a fine line between "having one's cake and eating it too," I would point to the statement of the Roman Catholic

Church that asserts, "The temptation to create organizations of any kind, especially for education or for social assistance, to 'convert' Jews is to be rejected."[213]

When Christ encountered the woman of Samaria (John 4), Jesus did not talk to her about the common religious views of Samaritans at that time. The same is true when Jesus traveled to the Roman pagan regions of Caesarea Philippi (Matt 16; Mark 8). St. Peter was rebuked for pre-judging the spirituality of Cornelius (Acts 10). When St. Paul preached to the Athenians (Acts 17), he was careful to avoid any traces of pater-nalism or targeted dismissiveness with the people of his day. Whenever Christians share their faith, they should do so with a posture of profound respect for fellow human beings made in God's divine image. Interfaith engagements should have no trace of argumentative or confrontational rejection of what others (even Messianic Jews) hold as truth. Evangelism and witness which honors God is that which also honors all our sisters and brothers.

Therefore I (van Gorder) think Christian support for the evange-listic efforts of organizations such as "Jews for Jesus" is inappropriate if there is any desire that Christians and Jews should relate to each other in ways that honor God's loving-kindness. I agree wholeheartedly with Billy Graham's statement (1973), "Gimmicks, coercion, and intimidation have no place in my evangelistic efforts. I have never felt called to single out the Jews as Jews nor to single out any particular groups, cultural, ethnic, or religious."[214] Messianic Jewish groups unapologetically "target" Jews. Further, the methodologies used by some Messianic Jewish groups often "blur the line" by claiming that they are not actually trying to lure any-one away from their religion but only trying to help them to experience their own religion in a vibrant new way. One organization sponsors a television program called "Jewish Voice" which presents itself as a Jewish organization while also seeking to convert Jews to Jesus, their Messiah. One would think, given our history, that Christians would be the first to grant the Jewish community the right to determine what being Jewish is just as Christians would expect that same right.

Truth in advertising works both in the civic and the religious spheres of society to promote a greater degree of trust. The former editor of *Christianity Today*, D. Kenneth Katzer, has written of the efforts of the Jews for Jesus:

Christians should abhor any deception in seeking to present
Christ to Jews. A small minority of Jewish Christians disguise
their Christianity to attract unsuspecting Jews to accept Christianity. This is deceitful and contrary to the New Testament
teaching. Evangelicals have more reason to oppose this type of
deceptive practice than do Jews, but we have often failed by our
silence.[215]

Other Christians have recognized that such approaches make interfaith
engagement anything but genuine. The Bishops of the Protestant Evangelical Synod in Germany (1980) wrote, "We believe that in their respective callings, both Jews and Christians are witnesses to God before the
world and before each other. Therefore, we are convinced that the church
may not express its witness toward the Jewish people as it does its mission to the people of the world."[216] The leaders of the United Church of
Canada, "reject and repudiate all mission and proselytism seeking to convert Jews to Christianity."[217] The fact that many conservative Christians
might find this statement disturbing provides a compelling starting point
for conversation about the basics of interfaith interactions.

In contrast, the fact that some Christians are becoming more respectful towards Jews and Judaism are welcome by all committed to constructive interfaith relations. Eliot Abrams writes about these changes in
attitude as a revolution,

The immense changes in Christian attitudes towards Jews and
Judaism have been amazingly underreported and underappre-
ciated in the American Jewish community. In most Christian
denominations, a two-thousand-year war against Judaism is being called off and its direct connection to anti-Semitic violence
is being admitted. Contemptuous and hostile attitudes towards
Judaism that date back to the years immediately after the death
of Jesus have been questioned, criticized, and rejected. The
historic role of Judaism has been appreciated and reaffirmed,
and in many cases its ongoing covenant with God has been acknowledged. Efforts to convert Jews to Christianity have been
questioned in some churches and brought under strict control
in others. This is revolutionary.[218]

For many evangelistically minded Christians, however, while Jews may be
"respected" for being moral and devoted, the fact remains that they need
a mediator to gain God's cleansing from their sinful natures. What is vital
to being Jewish is known to these Christians while it remains unknown

to the Jews themselves; without Jesus they can have no spiritual vitality. As "Rabbi" Moishe Rosen, Jews for Jesus founder, explains, the Jews are a "messenger people without a message."[219]

Conclusion

Hitler was intent on creating a "Jew-free" world. Evangelistically minded Christians should admit that a commitment to proselytizing Jews, if successful, ultimately relates to the realization Hitler's sordid agenda for the elimination of Judaism. Darrell Jodock writes, "Christians need to be careful lest vigorous, targeted proselytizing becomes an alternative way to make the world 'Jew-free' and thereby to give Hitler a 'posthumous victory.'"[220] Hubert G. Locke thinks that after the Holocaust "the appropriate stance of the Church in the presence of the Jewish people is that of penitence, not proselytization."[221] Because God promised to make the Jews a blessing to the world, Christians should appreciate the many ways that the Jewish community richly adds to the global community, which speaks of God's goodness, instead of focusing on what they perceive to be a lack within Judaism. Ridding the world of Jews through their ultimate conversion to Christianity would be a tragedy for all (especially for Christians).

In the 1980s, Leighton Ford, a colleague of the evangelist Billy Graham, was asked to participate in a conference of Evangelicals with Jews. His humorous response captures something of the challenges that are related to this issue: "Some of my Jewish friends will suspect the worst; that I am there to evangelize them. And some of my Christian friends will probably also suspect the worst; that I am *not* going to try and evangelize."[222] Ford concluded by reaffirming his commitment to the Great Commission mandate of faithful witness to Christ's gospel while also calling for genuine respect in every encounter when Jews meet Christians. Ford rejected all forms of subtle trickery and manipulative deceit and called on Christians to approach Jews in their full humanity and not framed within stereotypes, preconceptions, or in the framework of their specific and distinct religious identity as Jews. Ford accepts the distrust that some may have to his calling to be an evangelist and admits that many Christians have failed miserably in their interactions with their Jewish neighbors. In one statement of apology to his Jewish friends, Ford lamented, "If you have met insensitive Christians who see Jews only as trophies to be bagged in an evangelistic safari, please don't take them as completely representative."[223] Ford claimed that he had come to the conference to learn how to be more loving and was motivated to learn all that he could from Jews about Judaism because he had a God-given appreciation for Judaism's richness and beauty.

Messianic Jewish (and other) readers may find our analysis in this chapter as being too dismissive and, at times, even disrespectful. Critics might suggest that our logic and tone is inconsistent with our larger calls for mutual recognition and respect. Certainly, it is sometimes difficult to know how to define lines or clarify concepts that are continually changing. Messianic Jewish movements, for example, have continued to adapt to criticisms leveled against them by both Christians and Jews and claim that their communities are misunderstood by all. It is also true, as we have stressed before, that these groups are not monolithic in their approaches or methodologies or even about their ideas about trying to convert Jews to accept Jesus. Messianic Jewish theologians such as Mark Kinzer, however, continue to see that "Jesus is divine within a Judaism not hospitable to the possibility of the divinity and incarnation of the Son of God."[224] Such statements underscore the confusion that such organizations promote among both Jews and Christians. Messianic Jews continue to hope that their unique perspectives—outside of both Jewish and Christian theological reflection—will become accepted as theologically cogent and representative of a new paradigm that is relevant to both traditions.

One of the missions that Christians should take seriously, along with evangelism, is the call to work for the betterment of the Jewish community worldwide. Our shared ethical yoke of the kingdom of God means that Christians and Jews are obligated to honor God by working as spokespeople for each other. We can forge mutual partnerships dedicated to each other's progress as people of faith in the God of Abraham, Isaac, and Jacob. The world is deeply divided and in need of God's healing touch of hope. It is our shared mission as Jews and Christians to be a "kingdom of priests," and "a light to the nations" that brings glory to God by advancing his kingdom—the dominion and presence of God in the world.

Chapter Ten

Anti-Semitism and Anti-Judaism

The Jews rule the world by proxy. They must never think that they are the Chosen People.
—Mohammad Mahathir, Prime Minister of Malaysia, 2003

The Christian kneels before the image of the Jew, wrings his hands before the image of a Jewess; his Apostles, Festivals, and Psalms are Jewish. Only a few can come to terms with this contradiction—most free themselves by anti-Semitism. Obliged to revere a Jew as God, they wreak vengeance upon the rest of the Jews by treating them as devils.
—Rabbi Moritz Guderman, Chief Rabbi of Vienna, 1907

I see it every time I leave the synagogue. On Saturday morning, after services while going home. It is there for me—challenging me. It is the cross of the nearby Church. Why does it disturb me? It comes from the fact that we Jews tend to view the Holocaust as the culmination of their degradation at the hands of persecution and we largely see the Christians as our persecutors.
—Rabbi Leon Klenicki, Interfaith Program Coordinator, Anti-Defamation League, B'nai Brith

Identifying Anti-Semitism

FEW NORTH AMERICANS THINK they are guilty of blatant anti-Semitism. Not surprisingly, many in the majority-culture do not take much effort to learn about other cultures and religions. One student in a class reflected on the verbose anti-Semitism of their grandparents and sought to distance themselves from their statements: "Like many of the other students in the class, I have stereotypes that Jews are bankers, wealthy, and very frugal in my head but those also fit my Dad to a T."[225] Another student wrote,

> When Dr. van Gorder began the class with a series of anti-Jewish quotes from the Christian church leaders I was shocked. I had no idea that so many people hated the Jews. Here at Baylor we have been taught many things about people like Luther—but none of them negative. They have been portrayed as wise and perfect saints; I never even thought to question any of their teachings. I am disappointed to hear that some people, like the Nazis, can have so much hatred in their hearts.[226]

The term "anti-Semitic" simply refers to that which is anti-Jewish. In contrast, some people view anti-Semitism with the strictest possible rendering of the term—as in the acts of Hitler or other violent attacks. Christians almost never identify themselves willingly as anti-Semitic, and it is usually seen as offensive to even suggest that such a loaded term might have any relation to their worldview: they are not anti-Semitic in their own minds and do not relate with anyone who is. The logic proceeds that if any Christian is anti-Semitic it is because they are not truly Christian. One student reasoned, "It seems to me that much of the persecution stemming from the church either comes from not understanding the gospel, God's covenantal promises, or the realities of conversion."[227] If a Christian really loves Jesus, this logic continues, then they cannot hate Jews but will work for their ultimate eternal salvation in Christ. This explains the problem that historic anti-Semitism raises. The solution is that there is nothing intrinsically wrong with Christianity (or its historic institutions) but only in the cruel actions of those who claim to be Christians who do not love Jesus as much as they should.

Anti-Semitism is a key issue for contemporary Jewish-Christian relations. Anti-Semitism makes a Jew a stranger and discourages any curiosity about Judaism on its own terms and independent of inaccurate conjecture. On the other hand, Hannah Arendt claims that "Christian hostility" against Jews has actually served as a "powerful agent for preservation, spiritually as well as politically."[228]

Jews have often come to understand Jew-hatred as rooted in the bold claims of their beliefs about God and creation and their divine election as a chosen people. In the ancient world, Jews were sometimes hated for their confrontation of pagan pantheons and their many gods. It has even been argued that Jewish iconoclasm set the stage for monotheistic Jews being the world's first religiously intolerant people. Some rabbis observe that the Egyptians were the first anti-Semites (see Exod 1:15–22) as they grew resentful of the number of Hebrew slaves in their midst. Whatever its virulent origin, it is apparent through even the most cursory reading of history that the Jewish people have often been perceived as a community who are incomprehensible, insular, and threatening.

In fact, even those who have never even personally known a Jewish individual can carry within themselves passionate chords of anti-Semitism. It is telling to note, for example, that William Shakespeare could write with such passion about Shylock in the *Merchant of Venice* even though the great Bard probably never met a Jewish person, since Jews had been expelled from England three hundred years earlier. Anti-Semitism and anti-Judaism, the teachings of contempt for the Jews, are ancient viruses that have deep roots within humanity's story. In the Bible, the Amalekite prince Haman tried to exterminate all Jews of the Persian Empire and relied on a few unfair accusations to build his case against Mordecai, a righteous Jew (see Esth 3:8–9). The fundamental argument advanced by Haman was that Jews should be killed or exiled because they were different: they were a national problem.

To be anti-Semitic is to despise Jews simply because they exist. One of the first usages of the term "anti-Semitism" came in the writings of the German Wilhelm Marr, who claimed the "Jews as a group were unalterably tainted and racially determined to overrun society and corrupt the pure Aryan German nation."[229] Marr was certain the many, nefarious problems that sprang from the Jewish people were rooted in their corrupted blood; not even conversion to Christianity would rid them of their inherently evil ways.[230] Such convictions were at the vile heart of Hitler's Nazi propaganda machine.

Some Christian perceptions of Judaism hold that the last thing imaginable is that they themselves are anti-Semitic or anti-Jewish. Some even assert one cannot even use the term "Christian" in connection with such ideas because they fundamentally differ from the central teachings of Jesus. Some argue that Hitler should not be equated with Christianity because his overt loyalties were never Christian.

At best, the argument goes, these so-called Christians were nominal. Can one assert that the millions of devout Christians who followed

Hitler were all nominal Christians? Can one call Martin Luther a nominal Christian? Those who make such claims must remember that acts of anti-Semitism throughout history have often been carried out by those who considered themselves just as much a Christian as they themselves. They were members of their churches in good standing and were rarely censured or excommunicated by their priests or pastors for their virulent actions.

In contrast, some believe that an anti-Jewish impulse lies at the very heart of formative Christianity. This argument asserts that anti-Semitism is basic to a movement that rejected Judaism and then proceeded to spread anti-Jewish ideas around the world through political and national Christian civilizations. Often, churches were the primary vehicle to spread anti-Semitic ideas into a European or North American Christian-majority community. While economic, social, political, and cultural resentments add fuel to the fire of anti-Semitism, one should not forget that the virus has always been rooted in passionate religious language. One only must study medieval Christian art, literature, or architecture to see vivid representations of misled, greedy Jews and a spiritually bankrupt Judaism in a most unflattering light.

Is the New Testament Anti-Semitic?

Michael Lotker suggests that the New Testament was written "during a period of maximal competition between Jews and Christians. For Christianity to be correct, Judaism had to be discredited."[231] Lotker reminds us the New Testament is the first place where a narrative emerges which describes two "kinds" of Jews—those wise Jews who immediately followed Jesus and those hostile Jews who bitterly opposed Christ despite prophecies confirming Jesus as the Jewish Messiah. Of course, most Jews living at the time of Jesus never heard about the Galilean teacher or knew anything about the new Christian movement.

Different commentators have cited a host of polarizing passages in the New Testament that could be described as anti-Jewish. Some of the most frequently cited are Luke 23:20–21, where the Jewish crowd stridently demands that Jesus be crucified; Matthew 27:25 where the Jews seem to call down a curse on themselves; John 10:8, which says all who came before Jesus were "thieves and bandits"; Mark 7:6, where Jesus says "Isaiah prophesied rightly about you hypocrites"; and John 20:19, where the author says "the doors of the house where the disciples had met were locked for fear of the Jews." Some cite Paul's statement in 1 Thessalonians 2:14–16, where it says the "Jews" killed Jesus. Another of the most frequently cited passages reinforcing this theme is John 8:44, where Jesus says to Jewish religious leaders, "you are from your father the devil and you choose to do your father's desires."[232]

The writers of the various New Testament books, over time, became increasingly focused on reaching out to non-Jewish audiences. This may help explain why some of the more categorical or generalized passages seem decidedly anti-Jewish. These writers may have been trying to help others appreciate how distinct the bright message of Christianity was from "Judaism"—a term that "refers to an essentializing abstraction that could not have existed in the first century."[233] When Jesus is about to be executed, the Jews in Matthew's Gospel announce: "His blood be upon us and our children" (Matt 27:25), even though the Roman governor of Judea insists that Jesus is innocent (Matt 27:24). These verses have helped some Christians conclude that the Jews have been cursed by God to suffer for all eternity for killing the Christ of God. According to Amy-Jill Levine, however, "The phrase is a technical expression (Lev 20:9, Josh 2:19, 2 Sam 1:16, Jer 28:35, Acts 18:6) for accepting responsibility for someone's death, and the inclusion of offspring in such curses also appears in the early sources (1 Kgs 2:33)."[234]

There are several references in St. John's Gospel about the passion of Christ that refer to a generalized group of individuals—simply referred to as "the Jews"—who were responsible for killing Jesus (see John 5:16, 18; 6:41; 7:1, 13; 8:48; 9:22; 10:31; 19:12; 19:38). This emphasis is challenged by the fact Jesus was crucified—a *Roman* form of execution for political criminals—instead of being stoned to death, which was the Jewish penalty for those who had committed the sin of blasphemy (see Lev 24:10–16). These passages from John's Gospel are often preached from pulpits at Eastertime; usually without the speaker bothering to contextualize such phrases (or taking the time to explain these references, considering the historic damage such statements have brought to Jewish communities). Fred Bratton writes: "To use the generalized term 'the Jews' implies that Jesus was not a Jew."[235] Passages from the Book of Acts refer to a broad and generic group of people: "the Jews" who are intent on attacking righteous Christians (see Acts 9:23; 13:50; 17:5; 20:3). The general usage of this term, intentionally or unintentionally, may open the door for a blanket sense of collective guilt.

Biblical scholars have tried to soften the blunt edge of these assertions by suggesting that the authors were focusing on the geographic
context of these specific incidents. They note Jesus is frequently referred
to as a "Galilean" and that these references to the "Jews" might better
be translated as "Judeans" (in contrast to Galileans). According to Shaye
J. D. Cohen, "Judean" is an "ethnographic term" that "designates members of the ethnic group inhabiting the district of Judea" and, only later,
transitioned to have a more religious meaning.[236] Several modern translations of the Bible into English (such as the TEV and Eugene Peterson's
The Message) have rejected the term "the Jews," to avoid any confusion
about what they perceive as the more neutral, and less malicious, intent
of the original New Testament writers. In contrast, Adele Reinhartz ad-
vises caution, stating a deliberate motive on the part of these authors:
"To be sure, not all of the Gospel's approximately seventy references to
the *Ioudaioi* express an explicitly hostile stance. Sixteen such occurrences
are neutral in the sense that they convey neither a positive nor negative
stance and call forth no emotional response whatsoever."[237]

Jesus is presented as calling collectively all "Jews" the "sons of the
devil" who was a "murderer from the very beginning" (John 8:44). Of this
rhetorical passage that stresses a clear binary opposite, Adele Reinhartz
argues: "The identification of the Jews as the children of the devil" encourages readers to view the Jews "in a negative light and for that reason
to distance themselves from these children of Satan."[238]

Supersessionism takes root in the Christian theological tradition in
the widely asserted argument that the Jews, except those who recognized
Jesus as the Messiah, turned their back on the covenant that God had
made with them. Christians are now the "new Israel" and the Jesus makes
a "new covenant," which replaces the "old" way. Christianity is the new,
and only true, faith for anyone who hopes to win eternal salvation. Paul
"spiritualizes" the notion of being a Jew in reference to the Abrahamic
promise of an eternal blessing and dismisses the fact of biological lineage
when writing, "for he is not a Jew who is one only outwardly . . . but he is
a Jew who is one inwardly" (Rom 2:28, see also Rom 9:6–9). At the same
time, however, St. Paul asserts that the newly blessed and chosen gentiles
must remain humble and recognize that the transforming message of the
gospel came first to "the Jews" (Rom 11:11, 18).

Jewish writers such as Avi Beker claim that St. Paul "conveyed a
deep hatred for the Jews. It was mainly Paul who shifted the guilt for the
crucifixion of Jesus from the Romans to the Jews, leaving behind him

violent anti-Semitic texts."[239] Other scholars, such as Amy-Jill Levine and Warren Carter, have challenged this view as being fundamentally inaccurate and unfair to Paul. They write, "Acts portrays Paul as a faithful, practicing Jew who worships in the Jerusalem Temple, begins his missionary work by preaching in synagogues, does miracles, and speaks in public brilliantly."[240] Supporting this view, Mark Nanos writes, "Paul saw himself wholly within Judaism . . . Paul did not leave Judaism, neither the Jewish way of life, nor Jewish communities."[241]

Christians should look at New Testament passages and discuss what they might have meant to their original readers. An emphasis on the Jewishness of Jesus, of course, goes a long way to showing that any criticisms that Christ may have had about the religious leaders of the time were rooted within the framework of Christ's own commitment to the Jewish tradition and a high regard and love for that tradition.

Translations that offer renderings of problem passages that seem to suggest an anti-Semitic intent might be avoided when careful explication is not possible. Texts that provide such problems should be read "forward" as well as "backwards" to describe for modern listeners how such passages have given rise to historical anti-Jewish feelings. Preachers who rely on stereotypical categorizations of the "Jews" as religious "legalists" should be challenged. The very fact that a Jewish community existed during the time of Jesus stands as a lasting tribute to a people who have remained faithful to God's covenant despite facing tremendous challenges.

This is a controversial issue—best explored with careful and patient deliberation. Even if we cannot agree on its causes, at least we can agree this issue must be addressed before all other interfaith issues between these faiths. Christian theologian Rosemary Radford Reuther and the Anglican James Parkes admit it is hard to ignore that the New Testament is the ultimate source for centuries of Christian anti-Semitism. Reuther stated the anti-Jewish message of the New Testament was "the left hand of Christology" because, to accept that Jesus as Messiah is to accept the bankruptcy of the Jewish tradition.[242]

While we disagree with the following quote, it is instructive to understand the point of reference and to take it into consideration at the relational level of one extreme, but still possible, response to interfaith sharing of scriptures. One of the strongest statements from the Jewish community (and one of the most difficult for many Christians to consider) is the claim made by Eliezer Berkowitz:

> Christianity's New Testament has been the most dangerous anti-Semitic tract in history. Its hatred-charged diatribes against the Pharisees and the Jews have poisoned the hearts and minds of millions and millions of Christians for almost two millennia. No matter what the deeper theological meaning of the hate passages against the Jews might be, in the history of the Jewish people, the New Testament lends its support to oppression, persecution, and mass murder of an intensity and duration that were unparalleled in the entire history of man's degradation. Without Christianity's New Testament, Hitler's *Mein Kampf* could never have been written.[243]

Our purpose in sharing this quote is not to deflate the hopes of anyone committed to interfaith mutual interactions but to use such a statement to emphasize, even more, the need for a profound sense of respect and genuine engagement between Jews and Christians.

Anti-Semitism in the Early Church

Once the canon of Christian scriptures was closed (in 367), the theologians of the early church began to clarify in their declarations the ways that Christianity related to Judaism. Gradually, the church became increasingly gentile and less ethnically Jewish. One of the results of this shift meant that some synagogues were transformed into churches. This transition sometimes resulted in polemic at a "fever pitch" that "testified to the appeal of the synagogue" to some of the newly baptized Jewish Christians.[244] Eventually, fewer accounts emphasized the Jewish heritage of Jesus. Fewer and fewer individuals appreciated the fact that many of the Christian rituals they were practicing had their roots in the Jewish tradition.

Many of the early church fathers promoted ideas that were clearly anti-Semitic. Bishop Melito of Sardis (d. 190) was one of the first to accuse the Jews of "deicide"—the murder of God. One of the earliest critics of the Jews was Origen (185–254), who was generally seen as a tolerant voice and (has even been described by some as) a defender of the Jewish faith. When it came to explain why the Jews had suffered throughout history, however, his views were quite emphatic:

> On account of their unbelief and other insults which they heaped upon Jesus, the Jews will not only suffer more than others in that judgment which is believed to impend over the world

but have even already endured such sufferings. For what nation is in exile from their own metropolis, and from the place sacred to the worship of their fathers save the Jews alone? And these calamities they have suffered because they were a most wicked nation, which, although guilty of many other sins, yet has been punished so severely for none as for those that were committed by the Jews.[245]

St. Justin Martyr explained that the Jews "alone should suffer that which you now justly suffer" because the Jews had murdered "the Just One."[246] One of his disciples, Hippolytus (170–236) wrote a tractate called *The Expository Treatise against the Jews,* where he declared:

> Now, then, incline thine ear to me, and hear my words, and give heed, thou Jew—Many a time does thou boast thyself, in that thou didst condemn Jesus of Nazareth to death, and did give him vinegar and gall to drink; and thou dost vaunt thyself because of this. Come therefore, let us consider together whether perchance thou dost boast unrighteous, O Israel, and whether that small portion of vinegar and gall has not brought down this fearful threatening upon thee and whether this is not the cause of thy present condition involved in these myriad troubles.[247]

Hippolytus goes on to explain that the path of the Jews has been darkened because they are not following the true light of Christ. These same arguments are echoed in the writings of many other fathers of the early church, such as St. Cyprian (200–258), who asserted that the Jews misunderstood their own scriptures; therefore, they were rejected by the God of true revelation. A consensus emerged among these writers that Jesus had come to invalidate the Jewish law and the priesthood and replace it with a superior, clearer truth. Another influential father of the early church was St. Gregory of Nyssa (331–396). He shared the views of his colleagues and claimed that the Jews were:

> Slayers of the Lord, murderers of the prophets, adversaries of God, men who show contempt for the law, foes of grace, enemies of their father's faith, advocates of the Devil, brood of vipers, slanderers, scoffers, men whose minds are in darkness, leaven of the Pharisees, assembly of demons, sinners, wicked men, stoners, and haters of righteousness.[248]

The views of St. Gregory of Nyssa were also held by noted contemporary St. Jerome (340–420), who was a brilliant scholar of Hebrew and

considered to be one of the key translators of the Bible into Latin. St. Jerome called the Jews "haters of men, vipers, and cursers of Christians."[249]

St. John Chrysostom (344–407) is often revered in church history
as the "golden-mouthed" orator who preached with such power that
individuals often wept with newfound love for God. He was also quite
anti-Semitic: For Chrysostom, Jews were deceived and would deceive
the simple-minded with their misguided sophistry. All Jews were consigned to eternal hellfire damnation. Chrysostom's hatred toward Jews—
expressed in his writings—seemed to know no bounds. This saint was
certain:

> The Jews sacrifice their children to Satan, and they are worse
> than beasts. Their synagogue is a brothel, a den of scoundrels,
> the temple of demons devoted to idolatrous cults, a criminal as-
> sembly of Jews, a place of meeting for the assassins of Christ,
> a house of ill-fame, a dwelling of iniquity, a gulf and abyss of
> perdition.[250]

St. Chrysostom believed Jews were cursed because of their cruel murder
of Jesus. Jews were an obstinate people who had fallen to a condition
worse than any wild animal. They were a degenerate race: "I hate the
Jews. I hate the synagogue because it has the Law and the Prophets. It
is the duty of all Christians to hate the Jews."[251] When speaking of Jews,
Chrysostom announced:

> If someone had killed your son could you stand the sight of him
> or the sound of his greeting? Wouldn't you try to get away from
> him as if he were an evil demon, as if he were the devil himself?
> The Jews killed the Son of your Master; . . . will you so dishonor
> Him as to respect and cultivate His murderers—the men who
> crucified Him? . . . The martyrs especially hate the Jews, because
> they love so deeply the one who, by punishment, were those
> who killed Christ. It is because they shed the precious blood that
> there is now no restoration, no mercy anymore, and no defense.
> Therefore, they are being punished worse now than in the past.
> . . . If this were not the case, God would have turned His back on
> them so completely thus, they who have sinned against Him are
> in a state of dishonor and disgrace.[252]

These fathers of the faith are not revered because of these rarely
cited statements but honored despite them. Their anti-Jewish sentiments are rarely known by most Christians. These ideas, however, were
so pervasive that they touched almost every noted theologian of early

Christendom. One of the most revered theologians of the early church was St. Augustine. In *On the Creed: A Sermon for Catechumens,* St. Augustine wrote of Jews:

> The Jews hold Him, the Jews insult Him, the Jews bind Him, crown Him with thorns, dishonor Him, overwhelm Him with their reviling's, hang Him upon the tree, pierce Him with a spear. The Jews killed Him.[253]

For St. Augustine, Jews were the guardians of the Hebrew Bible and were a living affirmation of the fundamental truth of Christianity because they served as a living typology of a bankrupt spirituality. They served as a reminder of what would happen to those who reject God's love. To those who thought Jews should be killed he countered: "Slay them not, lest my people [the Christians] forget; make them wander to and fro (Ps 59:12)."[254] Just as Cain—whose offerings were unacceptable to God because he had killed his brother Abel—so had the Jewish people killed their brother Jesus and made their faith of no account. St. Augustine argued that the Jews were "stranded in useless antiquity" and were willfully blind to the truth of the scriptures because they hated the ultimate message of truth.[255]

Anti-Semitism in Europe

When Christians came to political power in Europe, beginning with the rise of the Holy Roman Empire, it was not uncommon for them to persecute Jews. Perhaps this was because the very physical presence of Jews within their communities was an uncomfortable reminder of a secret they did not want to reveal—that Christ himself was Jewish—as were the foundations of the Christian faith. In this section we will explore how intense persecution of the Jews took an even more violent turn throughout the centuries of the Crusades and during the many inquisitions of the Catholic Church.

It is impossible to ascertain exactly how many Jewish communities were wiped out by their Christian neighbors and rulers. Charges were often made in European villages that Jews had poisoned local wells and had killed Christian children in order to make their Passover meals. Accounts in Europe described how innocent university students who trustingly rented lodgings from scheming Jews (with beards and pointed hats) were lured into lurid sexual immorality and would also mystifyingly find themselves indebted to their Jewish landlords beyond belief.[256]

Medieval paintings from Europe showed Jews as demonic agents of greed, usury, and lust. Illustrated folios dating from the medieval era depict the Jewish "crucifiers of Christ" being turned away from heaven and thrown into hell because of their bloated love of money and their animal lustfulness.[257] Paintings also depicted Jewish sorcerers—in league with the devil—tricking innocent Christian youth into selling their eternal souls to Satan.[258] One painting shows a devilish Jew carrying a striped cat and bags of money while bowing down in prayer to a figure described as the end-times anti-Christ.[259] A few stained-glass windows in European sanctuaries portrayed Jews buying bread designated for the communion table in exchange for bags of gold. Other paintings showed the debauched and "carnal stench" of "publicans, infidels, and all bad people," clearly portrayed as Jews with beards, pointed hats, and distinct Jewish symbols, greedily stealing communion bread and wine for their gluttonous meals.[260]

When Pope Urban II launched the Crusades (1096), the first victims of crusader swords en-route to the Holy Lands were the Jews of the German Rhineland, who were slaughtered *en masse*. Papal Inquisitions in the thirteenth century explored the question of whether the Talmud was a heretical book. In 1215, the Pope decreed Jews should wear a visible "badge of shame" on their clothes in order to be properly identified. In France, the King ruled that Jews had to wear a *rouelle*, a yellow circular patch. Polish Jews were forced to wear a pointed green hat to distinguish them from their neighbors. English Jews were required to wear a strip of cloth resembling the tablets of the law. Jews in Europe were forbidden to own slaves and were often relegated to such unacceptable practices as money-lending.

Some Christians blamed the Jews for the quick and lethal rise of the Black Plague (typhoid) which swept across Europe in the fourteenth century. One Swiss court at the time decreed that all Jews over the age of seven should be killed because of their responsibility for this unhealthy and ferocious scourge.[261] Entire communities of Jews were slaughtered. Jews were also accused of the economic exploitation of the Christian peasants across Europe. European Literature of the medieval period is replete with vivid images showing Jews as greedy and lustful degenerates, forsaken by God and forced to endlessly wander the earth. What is instructive about such negative accounts is that these are largely ignored by non-Jews while these same accounts are widely known among modern Jews.

By the eleventh century in Europe, there is little, if any, concord between Jewish and Christian theological ideas. Some Christians openly persecuted Jews and some Jews responded by writing several pamphlets (such as *Toldot Yeshu*—"The Lineage of Jesus"), which asserted that Jesus was an illegitimate child who learned enough sorcery to convince ignorant people of a certain crafty ability to use miraculous powers. Many other attacks were leveled against the Jews. Texts explained how in synagogues the congregants waited until a black cat "of a marvelous size" came down a rope whereupon the faithful would proceed to "kiss him, . . . some his feet, many under the tail, and very many his private parts."[262] Despised Christian heresies were conflated together with Judaism and were often assumed to have Jewish roots. It was common in the literature of the time to "randomly mention Jews and heretics together" in the same text. Jews were the "original" heretics and their denial of the claims of Jesus illustrated how the Jewish people were seen purely in terms of their relationship with the claims of Christianity.[263]

In response to many of these offenses, Jewish scholars in the Middle Ages studied Christianity and participated in debates to refute the claim Jesus was the Jewish Messiah. Even these accounts, often presented under great duress, must be examined with the recognition that surviving accounts of these encounters have often been handed down to our modern era through Christian sources.

Beginning in the fifteenth century Jews began to be expelled en masse from Spain, England, and France. In Italy, Jews were forced to live together in *ghettos*. Jews in Russia, Poland, and throughout Eastern and Central Europe faced increasing persecutions. Problems became particularly pronounced in Germany where, at the start of the sixteenth century, local governments determined that Jews were lowly "dogs" and not humans and that they should be quarantined into ghettos. In 1507, a German Jew who converted to Christianity, the butcher Johannes Pfefferkorn, claimed that Jews—above all else—cherished books, and, because of that, all Jewish books should be burned because they contained profanities and attacks against the church.[264] In spite of the promising advances of the Renaissance and the Enlightenment era, many communities across Christian Europe saw Jews marginalized and exposed to all kinds of horrific difficulties.

Luther

Martin Luther is one of the most seminal and towering figures in the march of Christian history. This former Augustinian monk is the central hero in the birth of Protestantism, because he is celebrated for liberating the gospel of truth from the corruptions of Roman Catholicism. It can also be argued that Luther was "the father of German nationalism. He had a great influence on German attitudes toward the Jews and his writings were widely quoted by the Nazis."[265] To those who assert anti-Semitism reflected nominal Christianity, what Luther wrote about the Jews is particularly noteworthy.

What exactly did Luther say about the Jews? His writings are filled with many attacks against the Jewish people and Luther even considered German-born Jews to be aliens. He wrote: "The Jews, being foreigners, should possess nothing and what they do possess should be ours."[266] Early in his ministry, Luther penned articles with the hopes of converting German Jews to Christianity. When these efforts failed, however, he explained it is "as easy to convert a Jew as to convert the Devil" because their "hearts are as hard as wood, as iron, as the Devil himself. They are the children of the Devil condemned to the flames of Hell."[267] Some of his declarations defy modern sensibilities and easily affront our imaginations with their fierce denunciations. In one such statement, Luther declared:

> Cursed goy that I am, I cannot understand how they manage to be so skillful, unless I think that when Judas Iscariot hanged himself, his guts burst and emptied. Perhaps the Jews sent their servants with plates of silver and pots of gold to gather up Judas' piss with the other treasures, and then they ate and drank his shit, thereby acquiring eyes so piercing that they discover commentaries in the Scripture not to be found by us cursed *goyim*.

> Know O Adored Christ, and make no mistake, that aside from the Devil, you have no enemy more venomous, more desperate, and bitterer, than a true Jew who truly seeks to be a Jew. Now, whoever wishes to accept venomous serpents, desperate enemies of the Lord, and to honor them, to let him be robbed, pillaged, corrupted, and cursed by them, need only turn to the Jews. O God, my beloved Father, have pity on me who in self-defense must speak so scandously against thy wicked enemies the Devils and the Jews. You know I do so in the ardor of my faith.[268]

Protestants are often shocked when they read these virulent statements and learn, for the first time, what Luther had to say about Jews and the Jewish faith. One student asked a question (writing in bold letters): "I cannot believe that I WAS NEVER TOLD ABOUT THIS SIDE OF LUTHER UNTIL THIS CLASS! I think it was a shame that my Christian schooling since eighth grade has told me how great a man Martin Luther was without ever mentioning what he thought about the Jews. Did my teachers just not know or are teachers of religion still trying to deny that Christians ever do bad things?"[269] Another student wrote that Luther's anti-Semitism raised troubling questions about the spirituality of the father of Protestantism: "How did Luther abandon the protection and softening heart that God so freely gives us?"[270] One student, with a perceptive eye toward present interfaith relations wrote: "Luther believed that he had the moral and legal right to take steps against the Jews because Christians were in the majority in Europe and had legal power. Luther showed a complete lack of respect for the basic rights of Jews as citizens when he suggested the measures to be taken against them."[271] Another student was motivated to see what they had just learned about Luther through the prism of how they hoped to be agents for change going forward: "How dare we Christians set apart the Jews in the opposite direction that God set them apart. What have we done?"[272]

Because Luther is such a prominent figure in the rise of Protestantism, some Protestants develop a Good Luther/Bad Luther version of the fabled Dr. Jekyll and Mr. Hyde legend. This view posits there are really "two Luther's"—one who was a young, sincere revolutionary of the faith and an older version that became corrupted and cynical who came to mercilessly insult the Jews while working for powerful elites. One student explained "Sadly, something happened to this once God-filled man. I have heard that he was supposed to have had some awful disease like syphilis in which case such a change would not be such an unimaginable thing."[273]

The last thought on this discussion should be to encourage Protestants to realize that these views are disavowed by modern Lutheran leaders. In 1983, for example, the Lutheran World Federation emphatically declared: "The sins of Luther's anti-Jewish remarks" and "the violence of his attacks on the Jews must be acknowledged with deep distress."[274]

Notable Responses to Christianity

Christians should learn not only about historic Christian anti-Semitism, but also about how such views were responded to by Jewish religious and intellectual voices throughout history. There have been a wide range of Jewish theological responses to Christianity and one or two of these will be introduced in this very brief section. Some scholars (such as Rabbi Meiri) related to Christians with a more amicable approach. Instead of concluding the doctrine of the Trinity was nothing more than an expression of idol worship (*avodah zarah*), he explained it was a view that was muddled but that it had never intended to undermine the basic unity of God's nature.

Maimonides, and others, focused on the larger idea that Christians claimed at least to be monotheists and were eligible for God's blessings through the Noahic covenant. A trend of increasing sympathy between Jewish and Christian intellectuals marked interfaith relations through the era of the European Enlightenment. One of the main lessons of the French Revolution was a sense of the universal fraternity of all individuals regardless of their religion. This does not mean there were also not countless localities where innocent Jews were viciously marginalized by their anti-Semitic Christian neighbors.

North American Anti-Semitism

Christians should be encouraged to learn more about the anti-Semitism Jewish immigrants faced when coming to North America. For the Jews of the New World, the most pressing issues related to how to avoid assimilating completely into majority cultures without resorting to a tribalist insularity. The story needs to be told that North American Jews also faced instances of persecution. Even when offenses are minor, such as when one student wrote of "getting Jewed when getting ripped off," these attitudes must be addressed.[275]

Some pastors, politicians, and even scholars throughout the history of the United States have described their country as being a "Christian nation." Because of this widespread assumption, many Jewish people, especially those living away from large urban areas on the North American East Coast, experienced varying degrees of marginalization in the workplace, in the housing market, and in the classroom. Business magnate Henry Ford, for example, felt comfortable enough to express his virulent anti-Semitism by providing each of the customers who bought a Ford automobile a copy of the fictitious anti-Semitic tract, originating in Russia, called *The Protocols of the Elders of Zion* (with the new title *The International Jew*).[276] In some parts of the country, some neighborhoods, clubs, local organizations, schools, and universities banned Jews from being members of their groups or living in their communities. Terrorist groups, such as the Ku Klux Klan, committed countless acts of violence against Jews. Decades of offenses led to the formation of the "Anti-Defamation League." Much of the discrimination against modern Jewry is subtle and not usually expressed in overtly violent ways. The Christian faith, once again, becomes central in this issue; the results of one 1986 survey among people who attended church at least once a week showed that 59 percent of individuals polled agreed with the statement "Jews can never be forgiven for what they did to Jesus unless they accept Him as the true Savior."[277] Even if respondents misunderstood the question and meant to support the idea that Jesus was the only source for the forgiveness of sins, the fact that Jewish people could be so marginalized, over twenty years after the Second Vatican Council's declaration absolving the Jews of deicide, speaks of the ways that many Christians compartmentalize their understanding of their faith in relationship to Judaism. To most North Americans, the worst instances of discrimination are distant points of a remote history. Most Christians, even those who articulate supersessionist views, are slow to acknowledge they are anti-Jewish in any way. Most North Americans describe themselves (and society) as tolerant toward others. Some Christians are perplexed at assertions that there are still forces lurking just beneath the surface that would marginalize Jews.

In an ideal world, North American Jews would live as fellow citizens instead of being marked with a sense of exceptionality. Because much of North American society is so committed to pluralism, any segregation that happens, it is claimed, is almost always self-imposed. At the same time, will this successful acculturation result in a "watering-down" of Jewish self-consciousness "to the point of disappearance?"[278] Is David Ben-Gurion accurate in claiming "I still do not believe it is possible to enjoy a full Jewish life outside of Israel"?[279] There are many signs this is not the case. As people reject parochialism, there is every reason to hope all citizens will steer a reasonable course between appreciation of differences and the acceptance of those differences in ways that are not antagonistic, arrogant, or ethnocentric.

Tragically, in 2018 and 2019, attacks against Jewish synagogues continues to rise in North America and around the world. A violent attack against the Tree of Life Synagogue in Pittsburgh on October 27, 2018 left eleven innocent victims dead and another attack in Poway (near San Diego) California in April 27, 2019 resulted in an additional death. Another tragic attack took place in Overland Park, Kansas on April 13, 2014 where three people were killed. The neo-Nazi march in Charlottesville, NC in August of 2017 included vocal anti-Semitic chants. Statistics in the United States show that violent attacks have doubled since then, including cases of assault, harassment, and vandalism. In October of 2019, an attempt was made to attack a synagogue in Halle, Germany which led to the tragic deaths of two bystanders.

Conclusion

Any discussion about anti-Judaism that seeks to move people from historic events to contemporary issues is one fraught with challenges. Lines get blurred as individuals begin to talk about feelings of victimization and the emotional quality of some of these issues does little to foster a sense of objective intellectual reflection. Sometimes people feel defensive in such accusatory conversations and, because of that, it seems hard to detach long enough to see the bigger picture. Most individuals (even the most naïve) are well-intentioned and their relation to these issues is often more about ignorance than it is about a cultivated hatred.

One of the ways that I (Fuller) have sought to generate discussions about stereotypes that exist about Jews is to ask a simple question: How many Jews are in the world today? One student noted: "I felt that there would be many more Jews," after a class discussion where he guessed there were close to a billion Jews in the world instead of only fifteen million.[280] Another student said "the number of Jews was shockingly small. I have only had one Jewish friend and I guess my familiarity with the faith is slim."[281] Over six million followers of Judaism live in the United States, making Jews about 2 percent of the entire population. Even though Judaism is at least 2,500 years old, the percentage of Jews in the world is far below one percent (about 0.02 percent). Jewish missionaries will not be going door to door anytime soon and there are no plans in the works for Jewish television evangelists to hold massive tent crusades at America's cavernous stadiums and sports arenas.

Anti-Semitism and its modern expression among some Christians (anti-Judaism) must be reframed among a new generation of Christians, who are increasingly removed from the stark expressions of anti-Jewish feelings to more subtle (and far fewer) observable expressions. The recasting of the historic blood-guilt myth, for example, in Mel Gibson's 2003 movie *The Passion of the Christ* can be discussed from a Jewish perspective in terms of how it is not only deeply anti-Semitic but also distorts historical reality.[282] In the film, in which nearly all of the characters are Jewish, many of them are depicted in a repulsive and unfavorable manner, while Pontius Pilate, a man responsible for the crucifixion of thousands of people, is presented in a sympathetic light ; shown to have been forced to kill Jesus against his will because of the insistence of enraged Jewish religious leaders. While some students held this film in high regard when it was released, they should have been told that Gibson himself is part of an ultraconservative Catholic group that refutes Vatican II assertions about the chosenness of the Jews; that Gibson's father (Hutton Gibson) is a Holocaust denier; and that Mel Gibson himself asserted, while drunk, that the "f***ing Jews" were "responsible for all the wars in the world."[283] The point is not to defame Gibson's character but to underline the pervasive nature of recent expressions of anti-Semitism not always readily recognizable.

In reference to expressions of anti-Semitism in the United States, another issue to consider are the revival of "passion plays" that show that the Jews were at the heart of the crucifixion of Christ. Of course, many of these religiously-themed programs are without malicious intent, but there are some productions that have raised considerable concern among the Jewish community. One of these is the "Great Passion Play," which was organized by Gerald Smith in Eureka Springs, Arkansas. Smith (who died in 1976) himself had written many anti-Semitic comments throughout his life rooted in his political assumptions about the role of a corrupted national media and the State of Israel. After visiting Eureka Springs, Daniel Radosh shared his perspective on these programs:

> Many passion plays manage to use authentic gospel messages in a manner that distorts what most people accept as the authentic gospel message, not to mention authentic history. These productions emphasize Jewish perfidy and group guilt, downplay or ignore passages that affirm the essential Jewishness of Jesus and the apostles, and exaggerate suggestions that the Roman authorities were doing the bidding of the Jewish leadership.[284]

As issues relating to anti-Semitism are shifted from the theoretical to the lived experiences of modern Jews, there is hope for more meaningful Jewish-Christian dialogues about such topics. Modern forms of anti-Semitism rely upon old, unchallenged myths that can be easily exposed for their rootedness in historic caricature. Jean Paul Sartre talked about the need to humanize those who have been dehumanized. In his book *Anti-Semite and Jew,* he wrote that what the French should realize is that "the fate of the Jews is *his* fate. Not one Frenchman will be free so long as the Jews do not enjoy the fullness of their rights. Not one Frenchman will be secure so long as a single Jew in France—or in the world at large—can fear for his life."[285]

Chapter Eleven

Teaching the Holocaust

O the Chimneys / On the ingloriously devised habitations of death / When Israel's body drifted as smoke through the air / Was welcomed by a star, a chimney sweep, / A Star turned black / Or was it the rays of sun?
—*O the Chimneys,* Nelly Sachs

Here in this carload / I am Eve / with Abel my son / if you see my other son / Cain, son of man / tell him that I . . .
—*Written in Pencil in the Sealed Railway Car,* Dan Pagis

You who live secure / In your warm houses, / Who return at evening to find / Hot food and friendly faces: / Consider whether this is a man, / Who labors in the mud / Who knows no peace / Who fights for a crust of bread / Who dies at a yes or a no / Consider whether this is a woman, / Without hair or name / With no more strength to remember / Eyes empty and womb cold / as a frog in winter / Consider that this has been / I commend these words to you / Engrave them on your hearts / When you are in your house, when you walk on the way, / When you go to bed, when you rise. Repeat them to your children / or may your house crumble, / Disease render you powerless, / your offspring avert their faces from you.
—*Shema,* Primo Levi, January 10, 1946

Judaism and Christianity do not merely tell of God's love for humanity. They also stand or fall on their fundamental claim that the human being is of ultimate and absolute value. The

133

> *Holocaust poses the most radical counter-testimony to both Juda-
> ism and Christianity. No statement, theological or otherwise,
> should be made that would not be credible in the presence of
> burning children.*
> —Rabbi Irving Greenberg, *What Can We Say?*

The Unteachable

DAVID WEISS HALIVNI STATED that, in Jewish history, "there have
been two major theological events, revelation at Sinai and revelation at
Auschwitz."[286] The challenge facing the educator is how to communicate
the interrelationships and tensions that exists between these two revelations. North Americans have probably read several books (or seen a few
movies) about the Holocaust (*Shoah*) before they come to university;
these narratives, however, rarely focus on the religious components of
the Holocaust. Invariably, individuals from any religious tradition recoil
in revulsion when forced to confront the facts of the Nazi-inspired genocide of the Jews. A student commiserated: "It makes me sick to think how
Hitler could think and do all of these horrible things to people."[287] When
Rabbi Moti Rotem, formerly Waco's Reform Rabbi of Temple Rodef Sho-
lom, visited our class to speak about the *Shoah*, one student, responding
wrote: "Wow! You guys really suffered a lot."[288]

Discussions about the Holocaust invite unique and daunting challenges. It is often poorly portrayed in the generalized dynamics of many
dramatic movies or testimonial books. When we confront the *Shoah*, we
are doing much more than simply participating in a remote and objective
statistical analysis of historical events. When harsh facts about the *Shoah*
are softened by distancing conceptualities and generalized abstractions,
it becomes far easier to avoid underlying issues such as culpability or the
ways that such atrocities continue to revisit humanity.

No one should come away from considering the *Shoah* by concluding that the primary fulcrum of the Jewish experience is that Jews are
consigned by God to suffer. Even in the darkest hells of anti-Semitism,
victims often rose in the full-throat of human dignity and scorned the
inhumanity of their oppressors. Even in Auschwitz, Birkenau, Dachau,
and in countless other camps, the people of God were always more than
simply silent victims. Small victories won through art, music, and acts
of decency were generated by individual loving-kindness in the face of

horror and revealed expressions of human strength and the power of hearts that look to God for ultimate justice. Those who survived present to all an eternal testament to their indomitable will.

Shock and Awe

On May 1, 1978, President Jimmy Carter established the "President's Commission on the Holocaust," a fifteen-member panel dedicated to memorializing the events of the *Shoah* (שואה) (the Hebrew term for "burning") for future generations. The Holocaust Memorial Museum in Washington, DC was the principle legacy of this study. Local municipalities across the nation—including Harrisburg, Pennsylvania, and Waco, Texas—hold yearly commemoration services where reverential songs are sung, sobering texts are read, and inspirational candles are lit. Rabbi Jeffrey Wohlberg of Temple Beth El was one of the first rabbis in Harrisburg to organize such a program; many others have followed since those first services of commemoration.[289] In towns across North America, the dead of Ponar, Auschwitz, Babi Yar, Chelmo, Buchenwald, Belzec, Terezien, Treblinka, Dachau, Sobribor, Mauthausen, Maidanek (and many other places) are remembered in measured reflection.

How should we encourage non-Jews to think about issues of historic culpability? The cold iron gates of Auschwitz must never become a whipping board against those who are innocent. Fostering a sense of guilt does not help anyone to progress with insight or promote efforts of reconciliation. While it is true that few Christians fully appreciate the role that co-opted Christianity played in the Holocaust, such issues should be contextualized. All people of faith should be humble in the face of atrocity, but the *Shoah* should not become simply a way to prove the ways one (or all) religions are fundamentally deficient. The sufferings of millions should not assume an instrumentality that advances agendas. At the same time, overly sensitive concerns about such issues can become a distraction. The goal is not to invite resentment, which only cheapens the suffering of victims. We must never forget, nor should we remember in a way that is partial, manipulative, or self-serving.

We can become anesthetized to the events of the *Shoah* or we can retreat into an emotional clamshell, saying that it makes us feel overwhelmed. One student confessed after a lecture on the *Shoah*: "I realized quickly my own callousness and cynicism. My own viewpoint is like those who say the Jewish people and the rest of the world should just move past the Holocaust. It happened so long ago."[290] Another wrote: "In the Old Testament the Jews were looking for something in the future. I don't want to discredit the importance of the Holocaust for the Jewish people, but this active looking back at the Holocaust is one of the main reasons I see Jews looking to the past and not to the future."[291] This response returns blame to the Jewish people for their suffering and, in effect, states that the Holocaust is something that people have to "get over."

The *Shoah* has become a one-dimensional made-for-television event where famous actors convey a range of compelling emotions with complex ramifications. This can be both good and bad: Movie-goers munch on mountains of buttered popcorn and gulp down liters of Coca-Cola while watching Holocaust-themed movies in cushy seats and air-conditioned comfort. North American schoolchildren often read compelling narratives such as *The Diary of Anne Frank* or Elie Wiesel's *Night*. Such books should be taught. What is also vital is that such introductions should serve as starting points to a life-long reflection on the many historic, cultural, economic, political, and religious factors that contributed to the *Shoah*. When too much is shouted in an emphatic tone, key lessons can be lost and cascades of words can promote sensitivity fatigue. Some Americans admit they no longer watch anything about the *Shoah* because it is too difficult to focus on such disturbing accounts. We can become detached and numb; providing fertile soil for denialist questions of unquestionable facts.

A balance between analytical reason and stark trepidation mark constructive discussions about the *Shoah*. Terror leaves us speechless in the same way the High Priest Aaron was struck dumb when told his two sons died suddenly (Lev 10:1-3). While we must speak, our speaking must be accompanied by thoughtful silence in the same way that, when Moses approached God on Mount Sinai, he removed his shoes and proceeded with caution because he was on holy ground (Exod 3:5). The "blood that cries from the ground" (Gen 4:10) calls for discussions framed with measured reverence.

Divine Punishment

Questions of faith merit exploration: How did the Jewish community go forward after the *Shoah*? How can one be optimistic about ideals concerning universal brotherhood after the Holocaust? Why do some Christians ask Jews for forgiveness for events that happened decades earlier?

But one question perplexes many: what was God's "plan" in allowing the Holocaust? The history of anti-Semitism has been marked by accusations that the suffering of the Jews was a result of God's curse for denying that Jesus was their Christ. One student wondered: "Has God been following through on his promise to curse those who curse Abraham and Isaac? If they are God's people, then why did God not intercede on their behalf in the Holocaust?"[292] Foundational to the worldview of some Christians is the conviction that nothing happens without God's foreknowledge (or approval), which means that whatever happens is part of a larger plan. This view is at the heart of John Hagee's argument that God had sent "Hitler as a hunter of the Jews" so the divine plan for the restoration of Israel could eventually unfold.[293] Such Christians conclude that the *Shoah* was part of a larger design. One student wrote, "So why did God allow the Holocaust? You don't know why God does these things. I don't know why God does these things."[294]

How can anyone suggest that suffering comes because of an individual's sin if that individual is a Jewish child (Deut 8:19–20; 28:15–68; Jer 16:10–14; 22:9; Amos 3:2)? After the *Shoah*, the Reform Book of Prayer eliminated the statement found in some liturgies (from Deut 11:13–21) that explained: "Because of our sins we have been exiled from our land." Such causalities are too shrill when related to children sent to crematoria alongside parents and grandparents. What is appropriate about those who have taken as their stance the (perhaps poorly translated) words of Job: "though God slays me, yet will I trust God" (Job 13:15)?

In what sense is every member of the Jewish community a "survivor of the Holocaust"? Is there any larger, moral message to be found in post-Holocaust Judaism? How can a believer in a loving God continue to say: "will not the judge of all the earth do right?" (Gen 18:25). The most basic question is also the one hardest to fathom: "Where was God?"

As vast as these questions are, the *Shoah* should never be appropriated as part of some universalizing metanarrative to assert the validity of generic moralizations. Jews were killed in a systematic way using the most advanced technology. Bureaucrats carefully recorded each murder in ordered ledger books. The perpetrators were often respected villagers and educated technicians, intellectuals, and professionals—fathers and sons. European Jews were slaughtered simply because of their ethnicity.

The idea of "Jewish blood" reduced individuals to being accursed inhuman souls. At some visceral level, any sermonizing is as meaningless as it is disrespectful. Notions of an idealized, universal brotherhood are conclusively exposed as fraudulent by the *Shoah*.

At the same time, there are a few common threads between the suffering of the *Shoah* and the victimization of the Armenians or the tragic events of Rwanda, Bosnia, or Cambodia. It is not constructive to argue about whether the deaths of one group are qualitatively different while agreeing that quantative numbers do not lessen the force of evil. We can proceed across this tightrope of sensibilities by stressing the uniqueness of each story without losing sight of greater issues.

Christian and Jewish interactions proceed considering the events of history; how historic Christian anti-Semitism has had fatal implications for the Jews. Elie Wiesel is correct that "past tragedies do not cancel each other out as they succeed one another. On the contrary they accumulate, becoming more unjust with every blow."[295] This cumulative, instead of episodic, response to waves of persecution will cause us to face complex questions. The *Shoah* challenges both Jews and Christians to confront the ways faith responds to such unimaginable atrocities. How can one talk about the tender mercies of God and the *Shoah* in the same breath? How can any sense of divine chosenness—or divine will—remain after Dr. Mengele's selections at the gates of Auschwitz? How can individuals talk about the inherent goodness of humanity after the Holocaust? Does it not seem that God was silent? Jewish theologian David Novak states that "the only people to whom the Holocaust belongs are the Nazi murderers. They alone are responsible for it by their own freely chosen ideas."[296]

Holocaust Education

Survivor and scholar Emil Fackenheim stated that the 614th commandment for Jews was to "survive and not grant Hitler a posthumous victory."[297] Beyond survival, some have hoped that interreligious dialogue can diminish prospects for future waves of anti-Semitism. What can Jews and Christians do to build bridges of mutuality that both remember the horrors of the past and lay the groundwork for improved interactions? What role does the remembrance of the Holocaust play in constructive interfaith interactions?

Interfaith conversations about the *Shoah* bring certain risks as well as rewards. Just as Abraham left the security of home in obedience to God, the modern believer sets out on a path without the confidences of all that is familiar. Israel was he who "struggled with God and prevailed" (Gen 32:28-29); teaching the Holocaust is very much a journey without maps.

In 1987, some Jews became angry when a Polish Roman Catholic nunnery very close to Auschwitz displayed visible signs of the cross. The Mother Superior, Sister Teresa Madiera, responded to criticisms by remonstrating: "Why do the Jews expect special treatment in Auschwitz only for themselves? Do they still consider themselves the Chosen People?"[298] The controversy surrounding this clash of sensibilities is compelling. From one Christian perspective, one interfaith consideration might be found in the symbol of the cross—a source of consolation for Christians but a symbol that evokes centuries of confrontation between Christianity and Judaism. The symbol of love for Christians is also a symbol of betrayal for some. The cross of Jesus accurately conveys all those things within itself and, as such, becomes a symbol with many meanings but, like all symbols, it should be used with caution in public contexts. Places of suffering, such as a cross for execution or a gas chamber for genocide, should never become mere symbols that minimize the power of their sordid reality.

Righteous Gentiles

Israel established a Holocaust Memorial in Jerusalem called *Yad Vashem.* Visitors walk down a peaceful "Avenue of the Righteous," a tree-lined walkway that honors the many Christians and others—including Muslims—who rescued Jews from death during the Nazi terror. An intellectual walk down this street is a good place for students to begin ensuring that they will not assume that all non-Jews persecuted Jews during that chapter of history. Nazism was not a Christian movement. In fact, Nazism, while it worked with Christian organizations for political reasons, had always been implicitly anti-Christian from its inception. This fact is confirmed by those few Christians who were persecuted as they tried to save Jews and others from Nazi programs of murder.

Common ground for interfaith contexts that confronts the *Shoah* comes from those who stood against evil and helped their fellow human beings in hellish times. The stories of Pastor Andre Trocme and the other French Protestants of Le Chambon-sur-Lignone; Father Kolbe, the King (and the people) of Denmark, Christian X, who—a story a later shown to be inaccurate—chose to wear a yellow star; and the accounts of many other "righteous gentiles" should be linked with other stories that accurately note that the vast majority of Christians in Europe were complicitous in the face of Nazi anti-Semitism.[299]

Some Christians have only focused their attention on the few Christians in Europe who risked their lives for righteousness. The story of the greatest tragedy imaginable has sometimes been recast as a testament to the goodness of the very few. In the face of horrific barbarism, there were a few people who acted with kindness and goodness. An inspiring movie was made entitled *The Hiding Place* (1975) which celebrated the actions of Dutch seamstress Corrie ten Boom. Many Catholics remind their congregations of Father Maximillian Kolbe, but fail to remind these same congregations of the ways that the Catholic Church and the Pope at the time collaborated with fascist attempts to persecute Jews.

Many Protestants in North America and Europe have stressed the opposition to Hitler by the Lutheran Pastor Dietrich Bonhoeffer even though the famed *Barmen Confession* of 1934 that he championed, while opposing Nazism, said nothing about the plight of the Jews. The efforts of Pastor Andre Trocme, Pastor Édouard Theiry, educator Roger Darsiac, and others in a southwestern French village provide us with vivid examples of those who stood up to injustice. When asked by the Vichy Nazi authorities to produce a list of Jews in the village, Trocme replied: "We do not know what a Jew is. We only know what a human is."[300] These agents for good should challenge us to higher levels of moral courage. Malka Drucker states that these individuals "goad us" as much as they inspire us.[301] They were not larger than life heroes but common people.

Stories of resistance to Nazism often ignore troubling realities. In the case of Bonhoeffer, for example, one can find ample quotations that frame his views of the Jews within the predictable confines of a narrow German Lutheran perspective. In 1939, for example, Bonhoeffer repeated the ancient notion that the Jewish people were cursed for killing the Christ: "The church of Christ has never lost sight of the thought that the chosen people, who nailed the redeemer of the world to the cross, must bear the curse for its actions through a long history of suffering."[302]

Many have complained that those who have compared the *Shoah* with other atrocities create an abstraction out of the lives of real women,

men, and children. One student made one such a statement when comparing the victims of the *Shoah* with accounts she had heard throughout her education about the persecution of fellow Christians. This student concluded by creating a ranking of suffering: "I guess the Holocaust is right up there with the enslavement of African Americans in my knowledge of oppressed peoples."[303]

While educators need to affirm the uniqueness of the Holocaust, they also need to stress that the Holocaust was not inevitable. The revealed Torah, and not the *Shoah*, is the inevitable inheritance (*morashah*) of the Jews as described in Deuteronomy 33:4. The agony that individuals experienced during the Holocaust was not some rational divine morality play about divine judgment. What happened cannot be accepted and future inhumane tragedies should not be assumed. The *Shoah* must stand alone. There must also be a sense of insistence expressed in talking about the Holocaust that the disturbing theological and moral reasoning that engendered these unique atrocities should be recognized in contemporary (and far more subtle) anti-Jewish incarnations.

Road to Auschwitz

Had Jesus lived in Nazi Germany, the founder of Christianity would have been shot at the edge of a huge pit or sent in a cattle car to an extermination camp. At the same time, many Christians tend to view themselves as "outsiders" when it comes to the events of the *Shoah*. Throughout the Middle Ages, the "Jewish problem" was dealt with by officials and clergy insisting that Jews convert to the Christian church. This is the same final solution offered by some Evangelicals today. Over time in Europe, a more radical solution was sought as fascists began embracing notions of Social Darwinism, which claimed that racial purity was compromised by intermarriages and other social interactions. The logic of the Nazi utopian eugenics program led to the conviction that Europe needed to be cleansed of "Jewish filth." All such views emerged among cultures that, at the time, claimed to be devoutly Christian. It cannot be sidestepped that "the massive failure of the churches at this time calls into question the moral and spiritual credibility of Christianity."[304]

Christians, in an era after these horrors, should confront the facts that many of their leaders and the messages that their clergy preached set the stage, even if only in small ways, for the *Shoah*. While Nazism was not a Christian movement, Nazis successfully manipulated Christian communities and blurred the moral horror of their actions in the name of competing demands. This interplay is often avoided altogether. One student explained in response to this assertion: "I am ashamed that it is members and founding fathers of my own faith that are largely responsible for the anti-Semitism that grew into the terrible atrocity of the Holocaust."[305] Lucy Dawidowicz states that European Christians told the Jews that they had no right to live as impure Jews in their midst. Over time, secularist Europeans adapted this message to assert that Jews had no intellectual grounds to hold on to their ancient superstitions. This cycle of progressive denigration culminated in Hitler's lambast that no Jew had any right to live in modern Europe.[306]

Other events of history are far clearer in their relation between the church and anti-Semitic actions. In a quest for purity, the church-sponsored Spanish Inquisition, for example, established that Jews should, on penalty of exile or death, wear easily identifiable yellow stars on their clothes and face a whole host of other indignities because, as a people, the Jews were responsible for the death of Christ. Seeking purity, the church—and not the S.S.—was the first to consign Jews to ghettoes and organize the burning of Jewish-authored books. As mentioned earlier, Martin Luther, in a book entitled *Of the Jews and Their Lies* (1543), declared, long before Hitler, that sober-minded Germans should have no compassion for Jews within their midst:

> Their synagogues should be set on fire, and whatever that does not burn up should be covered or spread over with dirt so that no one may ever be able to see a cinder or stone of it. And this ought to be done for the honor of God and of Christianity . . . . Secondly, their homes should likewise be broken down and destroyed, for they perpetuate the same things there that they do in their synagogues. For this reason, they ought to be put under one roof or in stables, like gypsies.[307]

If German Christians were only "following orders," as some claim, could it not be argued that these orders came from the highest pulpits of their most prominent churches? While Luther sought the conversion of the Jews and Hitler sought their destruction, it is also clear that, for both, what Jews believed about their faith was of no consequence. European anti-Semitism was a widely embraced tradition rooted in historic Christianity that allowed Jews to become despised as impure *untermenschen* ("under," "lower," or "lesser" people). Nazi anti-Semitism built on a historic Christian groundwork of dismissal to create a distinctly race-based (as opposed to religion-based) attack against the Jews of Europe.

Teaching about the Holocaust can commence with describing how widespread anti-Semitism was through the annals of Christian history and how that bias was reflected in various forms of political fascism that culminated against the Jewish people under the religious leadership in place when the Nazi political movement came to power in Germany (1933). After the rise of Hitler, with few exceptions, German Lutherans and Roman Catholics said little or nothing in the face of rabid Nazi anti-Semitic propaganda. Furthermore, Pope Pius XII (Eugenio Pacelli) did not excommunicate the "Catholic Hitler" (or any other European Catholic in any country) for pouring out hate-filled attacks against Jews.[308] Furthermore, when the Vichy French government contacted the Vatican in 1941 to see if anti-Jewish laws in France would be challenged by the Pope, he received this response: "In principle, there is nothing in these measures which the Holy See finds necessary to criticize."[309] Historian John Cornwell, no advocate of recent efforts to beatify Pope Pius XII, is correct that Pacelli's "complicity in the Final Solution through failure to register appropriate condemnation was compounded by a retrospective attempt to portray himself as an outspoken defender of the Jewish people."[310] Cornwell's indictment is that Pope Pius XII was "not only the ideal Pope for the Nazi's Final Solution, but (also) a hypocrite."[311]

German Christian communities either openly supported Hitler or, when they opposed him, did so on tentative grounds other than his hateful statements about the Jews. In 1932, with the urging of the National Socialists, a group of Christian leaders founded the German Christian movement. Doris L. Bergen explains that a group was formed to "build a church that would exclude all those impure and embrace all *true* Germans."[313] Hitler's speeches were cited in Sunday morning services and prayers of thanks were offered that God had given the German people such a strong leader. The Nazis were God's emissaries on the earth and their work a modern-day divine revelation. Members of the movement believed that there was a God-ordained link between church and state. German Christians spoke out against all forms of intermarriage between Christians and Jews and any forms of interfaith dialogue. German Christians should keep the "race" pure, just as earlier Christians had striven for social and religious purity by excluding the impurity of the Jews. One of the founding statements of the German Christian Movement announced: "As long as the Jews possess the right to citizenship and there is thereby the danger of racial camouflage and bastardization, we repudiate a mission to the Jews in Germany. Holy Scripture is also able to speak about a holy wrath and a refusal to love."[314]

Hitler proclaimed that the Aryan people were God's true chosen people and mocked the caricature of Jews who claimed that they had been chosen by God. Because many Christians saw Jews as demons who needed to be cast out and not as true humans made in the image of God, the story of Cain killing his brother Abel was of no restraining moral value to German Christians in the years leading up to the sordid events of the *Shoah*. Years of scornful degradation of the Jews laid the sure foundation for the Holocaust. Even though a small handful of German Christians protested when Hitler began killing the physically and mentally challenged, there was no similar protest when Jews were rounded up to be killed in cold blood. It was European Christians that taught that government authorities should not be questioned and that injustices should be met with wishful words of spiritual hope. There was little interfaith goodwill to be found when such forces were needed as never before.

Hitler did not act alone in killing three million Polish Jews and three million Jews from the other nations of Europe. The Führer came to power in a democratic election and his ideas about the Jews were openly popular in many countries, appealing to nationalist pride. Hitler exulted: "The struggle for world domination will be fought entirely between us, between the Germans and the Jews. There cannot be two Chosen People. We are God's People."[315] Tens of thousands of Germans were enlisted in the work of killing Jews; most had no problem in carrying out their God-given duties.

When confronted with a mountain of facts describing the role played by Christians in centuries of anti-Semitism, some Christians become defensive and resort, as mentioned earlier, to the good Christian/bad Christian model that claims that those Christians who were anti-Semitic were tepid believers and totally unlike their own honorable variety. One student explained: "From my standpoint, Christians are not evil, and I would like to say that Hitler was not a Christian. However, it would be difficult to say if Hitler was or was not a Christian."[316] Even more shockingly, one student—and obviously, all students only represent themselves—actually expressed the twisted view that there might be good Hitler/bad Hitler perspectives: "Wasn't Hitler doing good things for Germany—minus killing all those people? I mean, wasn't the unemployment rate going down and wasn't he fixing up the roads and other things within the country?"[317]

Franklin Littell asserts: "This monstrous crime was committed by baptized Catholics, Protestants, and Orthodox Christians, none of them rebuked, let alone excommunicated."[318] There are hosts of disturbing dynamics at play in the story of Judaism and Christianity that eventually led to the Holocaust. Leaving aside those of other nationalities or political views, the Nobel Prize winner Elie Wiesel framed the events of the *Shoah* in stark terms: the world has been "struck by a harsh truth: in Auschwitz all the victims were Jews; all the killers were Christians."[319] Marc H. Ellis explains that "to admit culpability is to enter into the realm of confession and vulnerability."[320] False justifications and tepid rationalizations must be swept aside.

"Never Again"

Russian Nobel Prize winning author Alexander Solzhenitsyn warned that "the salvation of humanity will depend on everyone becoming concerned about the welfare of everybody everywhere."[321] Christians and Jews should remain ever vigilant to ensure that such idealizations do not emerge again in any form. As mentioned earlier, the 2007 rants of the Reverend John Hagee of San Antonio, Texas, that explained that God had "sent" Hitler to be a "hunter" in order to eventually establish the nation of Israel is one such example. One should never suggest—even indirectly—that the suffering of the *Shoah* was somehow meaningful in relation to a broader Christian metanarrative about the return of Christ as it relates to the founding of the State of Israel.

Discussions about *Shoah* education are rooted in the identity of the parties considering the events; it is personal. Stephen Smith writes that the memory of the Holocaust is a "dangerous one" that "accuses on the one hand and confuses and disrupts on the other."[322] It is a deeply disturbing story with long-term consequences for how individuals view intercultural relations and their own role in the world. Decades later, we are still forging fresh ways of learning from the *Shoah*.

Holocaust education is forward-looking in that it challenges everyone to see themselves in the events of others. Healthy Jewish and Christian interactions will proceed only in reference to the inarguable facts of the *Shoah* that demand our own response. One student, while trying to come to terms with how her own views on salvation related to the potential for denigrating others, said: "I am struggling with a fascinating and disturbing question and while I am wrestling, I cannot seem to find an answer. If we hold to the idea that the Jewish people are not saved as we are all saying, are we allowing their lives to be devalued because of their so-called denial of Christ?"[323] The devaluation of life is one of the key messages to be emphasized in Holocaust education. The devaluation of life is on display in those who are sure that Jews who do not accept Jesus are damned to hell because their religion, and thus their identity, is ineffective and deficient.

Evangelical author Ted Dekker wrote a novel called *Obsessed*, which was set during the Holocaust and which told of a Jew at the Stutthof Concentration Camp in Poland becoming a Christian in the camp after hearing a gospel message from a rabbi who also believed that Jesus was the Messiah. This book, and others like it, turns the *Shoah* into an exotic background to preach a Christian message. In so doing, it affronts victims and survivors. Responding to this book, Daniel Radosh wrote, "You can see how a book that proposes that the lesson of the Holocaust is to become a Christian would be somewhat upsetting—even if you call it Messianic Judaism."[324] From a Jewish perspective, many Jews embrace the conviction, mentioned earlier, that the 614th commandment is "do not grant Hitler posthumous victories," and that consequently Jews had to live *as Jews* in order to thwart the Führer's ultimate mission.

Fundamentally, it is impossible to "use" the event of the *Shoah* to teach people about anything besides the lives of the victims themselves. What do we mean by that? We must teach facts: the Auschwitz death machine was only one such factory, but it was obligated to reach a "production" quota of at least ten thousand murders per day. Women who carried children were always assigned to the line for the crematorium. It was simpler that way to keep everything quiet and moving smoothly. It was only when the mothers and children reached the crematorium that they were separated from each other. This was done to pack in the adults more efficiently. At this point, the children were either "thrown straight into crematorium furnaces or, if it was more convenient, the babies were simply "thrown in over the heads of the adults once the chamber was packed."[325]

Facts and details, vital as they are, can only take us so far. Educators talking about the *Shoah* should eschew reductionistic, generalizing conclusions. When God spoke to Job out of the whirlwind, the divine presence unleashed a litany of questions beyond response. The Holocaust offers a similar whirlwind of unexplainable mysteries. Just as Job had no defiant answer to the statements of God beyond a reaffirmation of his faith, so believers today are humbled in the face of the unbridgeable chasm created by the Holocaust. The *Shoah* is a place of mystery that no one should ever think can be contained in cold concepts or lifeless words. The incomprehensibility of the *Shoah* is its primary revelation about the nature of God and the nature of humanity. Just as one should never utter God's name in vain one should never speak of individuals who died as remote concepts or abstract lessons. The men, women, and children who died are elusive and wandering ghosts with six million different names. These six million men, women, and children—two out of every three Jews in Europe at that time—populate their own kingdom of ghosts; they invite us to know their names and learn their stories.

Chapter Twelve

Zionism and Israel

The word Palestine always brought to my mind a vague sugges-
tion of a country as large as the United States. I do not know
why, but such was the case. I suppose it was because I could not
conceive of such a small country having so large a history.
—Mark Twain, *The Innocents Abroad*, 1869

In Israel, in order to be a realist, you must believe in miracles.
—David Ben Gurion, October 5, 1956

Israel is a newborn child whose womb is thousands of years old.
—Yahya Rabah

JUDAISM HAS LONG HELD a conviction that Israel is a holy land reserved
by God for the Jewish people. The city of Jerusalem is a holy city for three
world religions. Israel is a rough and arid land and is surprisingly insignif-
icant in terms of total acreage. Speaking of this geography, Martin Buber
states, "This land is a small, humiliated land—yet the hope of the world
is contained within it."[326] For centuries, the lands of Palestine have been
the focus of devotional prayers and emotional longings for many people.

Some of the 613 holy commandments that God gave to the Jewish
people can only be fulfilled in the land of Israel, and what happens to
the residents of Israel has a direct emotional impact on Jews worldwide.
These passions have also resulted in contested centuries of conflicts over
the control of the region that simmers into the present. On May 14, 1948,
the dream for a renewed State of Israel became reality once again after
millennia of Jews living without their own political homeland.

Christians and Jews in the United States seem more passionate about the State of Israel (*Medinat-Israel* [מדינת ישראל]) than citizens of any other countries of the world. This term *Israel* refers (at the same time) to the biblical name for the Hebrew people and the land that God is claimed to have given the sons of Abraham, Isaac, and Jacob for an eternal inheritance. Yet, Israel is also the religious and political focus of many Christians throughout the world. Marc Saperstein explains that this love for Israel, and the number of Christian tourists that go to the country, is more about the "love of Israel as a doctrine" than it is about "Israel as a reality."[327] It is not uncommon among some Christians to display bumper stickers asking passersby to "pray for the peace of Jerusalem." Millenarian preachers such as William Blackstone (1841–1933) advocated that Christians should support statehood for Israel in order to quicken the return of Christ. Anglican chaplain William Hechler of Vienna supported Zionist leader Theodor Herzl and claimed that Herzl's work was divinely ordained as a preface to the end of time. British Evangelical politicians such as Arthur Balfour and David Lloyd George—to name just a few—actively promoted their biblical vision for a restored Jewish homeland with their political efforts.

Since Israel's declaration of statehood, the nation has become a central factor in Jewish and Christian interactions. German Evangelical Basilea Schlink wrote that the land of Israel was "promised to them by God," while Billy Graham announced that God had been "delivering His promise to return the Jews to His Land."[328] Evangelist John Wilkinson teaches that "God has chosen Palestine as the geographical center of the world. Israel is destined in the revealed purpose of God to be an instrument of blessing to all the nations of the earth."[329] Evangelical Jerry Falwell established a "Christian Embassy" in Jerusalem. Falwell explained: "Israel is moving to the front and center of God's prophetic stage" and exults that "the very existence of a thriving, worldwide, present-day Jewish community can be accounted for solely based on the Old Testament promises of God to preserve Israel forever."[330]

Countless eschatological studies have been written by Christians who see the future of Bible prophecy coming to a dramatic end-time conclusion in the nation of Israel. Pastor John Bray preaches that, at the end of time, Jews will be the focus of a coming God-ordained season of "vengeance and devastating persecution" that will exceed the extent of the Holocaust; "their [the Jews] judgment will be more severe than those who have not heard the word of God as they have."[331] Conservative

Christians often teach that after Christ returns to the earth in the "rapture," the Messiah will establish a kingdom for a thousand years that is centered in Israel. John Walvoord explains that all Jews will accept Christ as their Messiah and then will be "allowed to enter the Promised Land (Israel) as the first citizens of Christ's new kingdom on the earth. Their hour of persecution will be finished forever, and they will receive all the blessings that have been promised to the children of Israel since the time of Abraham (see Gen 14:14 -17; Rom 11:26–27)."[332]

Texas televangelist John Hagee wrote dozens of books that taught his audiences that the Jews "are the apple of God's eye, and the family of God. If you bless the Jews, God will bless you. And if you curse them, the judgment of God will come upon you."[333] Hagee warned fellow Christians to "stop praising the dead Jews of the past . . . while hating the Goldbergs across the street."[334] The preacher was certain that the United States has a God-ordained destiny to protect the modern-day State of Israel. America would be materially blessed, it is claimed by Hagee, if America materially supported Israel, and would be cursed if they do not.

Discussing the many varying views that Jews and Christians have about the role of Israel in Jewish-Christian relations cannot be avoided. A vast number of the Christians who visit Israel are either devoted Catholics or Evangelicals who travel to the "Holy Land" for a spiritual pilgrimage. Many of these pilgrims return home with strong opinions about the present political challenges of that nation. Ironically, many progressive/liberal Protestants and Catholics are often those Christians who are also most supportive of the plight of the Palestinian people and, thus, are the most likely of Christians to criticize the policies of present Israeli governments. On the other side, the strongest Christian supporters of Israel are politically and religiously conservative and often espouse a dizzying mess of odd claims that eventually all Jews will convert to Christianity. It is not unusual for pastors in some Christian churches to call on members to financially and politically support Israel. These same pastors explain to their congregations that a day will eventually come when all Jews will come to accept Jesus Christ as their own Messiah. The preservation of Israel is vital to their vision of the unfolding end-time work of God because Israel will be the stage for the final battle of Armageddon and the long-promised return of Jesus.

What are the grounds for such views? How should Jews respond to notions that inevitably lead to the assumption that all Jews will eventually become Christians? Elliot Abrams explains that Evangelical support springs from "Christian theological interpretations that see the creation of the State of Israel and the settlement of the Jews in Israel as part of a New Testament prophecy about the Second Coming of Jesus."[335] Is it true, as Meir Kahane asserts, that conservative Christians are "the most potent weapon that Israel has within the United States"?[336] While many Jews appreciate such support from the "Evangelical Right," it is easy to understand that there are also concerns about their underlying motives and how any partnerships can avoid becoming contexts for Christian attempts to convert Jews to Christianity. While many conservative and Orthodox Jews (such as members of the Rabbinic Alliance of America) find consonance with those Christians of the Evangelical Right who are alarmed at levels of moral decay or social breakdown in American civic society, there are others who are concerned about the ways that conservative Christians are increasingly engaged in political activities and wonder where such efforts might eventually lead as it relates to issues of the separation of church and state; a tradition deeply cherished by North American Jewry.

Some liberal Jews (such as those in the Union for Reform Judaism movement, or URJ) encourage Jews to steer clear of entering into partnerships with political and religious organizations such as Jerry Falwell's Moral Majority. Many in the middle of the left and right political divide are grateful for any support that fellow Americans offer for Israel even though they are "loved" as Jews because they are targets for evangelistic concern. They recognize that for many in the Evangelical Right what is being "loved" is not the actual State of Israel (or the Jewish people), but rather the theoretical *idea* of Jewishness and the State of Israel, which plays a definitive role in their foretold end-time drama.

One religio-cultural movement that should be mentioned in this context is often referred to as "Christian Zionism," which espoused an idea that came to be known as "British Israelism." This faction began when some British Evangelicals in the nineteenth century identified their own experiences with the plight of the Jews. It was a theological movement that expressed itself in the political support for the founding of the State of Israel. Some of the leaders of this group (such as Foreign Secretary Henry John Temple, Lord Palmerston and Anthony Ashley Cooper, Lord Shaftesbury) used their considerable influence in the Victorian Age to call for the Jews to be granted a homeland in the ancient lands of the Bible. While their motives were mixed, their political agitations decades before the twentieth century laid the foundations for the announcement of the Balfour Declaration of 1919.

On the other hand, some Christians have asserted that the Jewish rejection of Jesus means that Jews today have no religious claim to live in the land of Israel. These Christians sometimes cite the story in which Jesus tells the Samaritan woman that a time is coming when no land or mountain will be holy (John 4:21–23). Scorn is given by some to the notion of Zionism, which equates the ancient boundaries of Israel to the modern political situation. Scholars from the Presbyterian Church in America (not to be confused with the PCUSA, the founding organization that it left in 1975) gathered at Knox Theological Seminary in 2002 and issued a statement that asserted:

> The entitlement of any one ethnic or religious group to territory in the Middle East called the "Holy Land" cannot be supported by Scripture. In fact, the land promises specific to Israel were fulfilled under Joshua. The New Testament speaks clearly and prophetically about the destruction of the Second Temple in A.D. 70. No New Testament writer foresees a re-gathering of ethnic Israel in the land, as did the prophets of the Old Testament after the destruction of the First Temple in 586 B.C. Moreover, the land promises of the Old Covenant are deliberately expanded in the New Testament to show the universal dominion of Jesus.[337]

Such views relate with supersessionist ideas that overlook such passages as Exodus 32:13, which says that God will give the land of Israel to the descendants of Abraham to "possess forever."

It may be difficult for some to appreciate the deep bonds that Jews have with the land that God gave to Joshua as a land of promise thousands of years ago. Rabbi Harold Kushner observes: "Over the years, I have found that the issue that puzzles non-Jews the most about Judaism is the role that Israel plays in our minds and souls. It has no analogue in the Christian world."[338] Many non-Jews have failed to appreciate the relationship between contemporary Judaism and the State of Israel. For many Jews, issues about Israel are often at the heart of interactions with non-Jews; especially those who are critical of the policies of the State of Israel. Zionism is an historical attempt to translate these ancient aspirations and zealous passions into concrete, political realities. It may be challenging for some Christians, raised in a context that valorizes the idea of the separation of church and state, to appreciate that support for Israel is seen as a religious and historical obligation as well as a function of a political sensibility. Jews worldwide often see the State of Israel as a "bridge-link" to the dynamic hopes of their historic tradition; this is a sentiment with no parallel among most non-Jewish students.[339] Israel is also the center of worldwide Judaism and is the "ultimate melting-pot" with Jews coming to it from over 130 different nations.[340]

When Christians go on pilgrimage to the Holy Land, they admire many biblical sites and may be emotionally moved, but rarely identify with Israel as their homeland. In contrast, as Leffler and Jones explain, "To the Jew, this geography and this State are part of who he/she is as a Jew; to the Christian the antiquities he wants to see relate to Christ, and the modern things pertain to citizens of another country with whom he feels no personal connection or identity" on a religious level.[341]

There is no parallel "Christian people" in the same way that it is argued by some that there is a "Jewish people." This becomes evident when thinking about the role of Israel and its relation to contemporary Judaism. Aside from the Vatican (which is revered only by Roman Catholics), there is no political entity in the world that claims to be a distinctly and completely "Christian nation." Even European or American countries where Christians are the religious majorities, the claim is not directly made that God is the sole author of their existence and that citizens exist to fulfill a divine mission. Another factor that contributes to a sense of difference between many Jews and most Christians is the issue of language. There are no such things as a distinctly "Christian language" while Judaism cherishes both Hebrew and Yiddish and, to a much smaller degree, "Ladino."[342] Jews are dependent on the Hebrew language to appreciate the many nuances of the biblical text far more (for better or worse) than are most Christians. Leffler and Jones explain: "Because a people can have languages, Judaism has languages. Because there are no Christian 'people' per se, Christianity does not have any indigenous religious language."[343] The only possible exception to this observation might be the use of Church Slavonic or the use of Latin historically within the Catholic Church. In Israel, biblical Hebrew was revised from ancient texts and revitalized as the modern language of the nation-state in the early 20th century.

Jews use different names to describe the Holy Land of Israel; one of the most common is simply *ha-aretz* (הארץ), which can be translated as "the land." There is also an intimate attachment to the geography of Israel that has no religious parallel for most Christians. In almost every traditional Jewish wedding, a glass is shattered to momentarily remember the historic destruction of the temple even during a celebration of joy. Centuries of Jews have pleaded at every Passover table that, perhaps next year, they would celebrate their Seder in Jerusalem—*le-shannah ha-baʾah b'Yerushalayim!* (לשנה הבאה בירושלם). Jews through the ages have looked to the promise that God would "take the people of Israel from the nations . . . and bring them to their own land" (Ezek 37:21). Israel is the same land that God told Abraham would be given as a divine gift in order that the people of the land would bless all the world (Gen 12:2–3). God gave the land to the people of Israel (Gen 15:18) as an "everlasting possession" (Gen 17:7–8). According to a specific reading of the Bible, Israel rightfully belongs, both religiously and geopolitically, to all descendants of the Jewish nation (Gen 35:12); the land where Abraham, Isaac, Sarah, Rachael, Leah, and Jacob are buried. It is a homeland that will experience a future messianic era (Isa 27:12–13).

The first reference to the land comes in the covenant that God offers with Abraham (Gen 12:1–5) and is referred to numerous times throughout the Torah. For Jews, the land of Israel is part of the covenant with God, albeit conditionally; just as God judges the seven native Canaanite tribes for their immoral behavior by having Israel vanquish them in warfare, so too is Israel warned: "do not let the land spit you out" (Lev 18:26-28). The land of Israel, then, is not only included in the covenant independent of the people, but it is also an active partner who has a moral obligation to remove the Jewish people if those people fail to follow the path of God's commands; thus, breaching their obligations under the covenant. In Rabbinic literature (Babylonian Talmud Yoma, 9b), the reason for the destruction of both temples and the subsequent exiles of the Jewish people from the land of Israel is their own behavior: idolatry and immorality (in the case of the First Temple) and baseless hatred toward their fellow Jews (in the case of the Second Temple). The dream of *Shivat Tziyon* (שיבת ציון)—a return to Zion—is found throughout prophetic literature, and a return to the land has been a focus of Jewish prayer for almost two thousand years.

The dream of nationhood moved to political activism with the Zionism of Theodor Herzl and began as a political lobby whose primary goal was to establish a homeland for Jews throughout the world. In the mid-nineteenth century, a group of Jewish intellectuals led by Leon Pinsker, Moses Hess, and, later, by the Viennese journalist Theodor Herzl, launched the Zionist movement and published a book in 1896 entitled *The Jewish State* that called for a specific plans of action. The main Zionist idea, in its simplest form, was that if the Jews had a "house" of their own on the street like all the other nations, anti-Semitism would become a thing of the past.

Because the land of Palestine was under Ottoman control at that time some early Zionists considered establishing a uniquely Jewish state in part of Argentina. An organization grew that finally gained some support through the 1917 Balfour Declaration, an official statement by the British government that spoke of an eventual Jewish homeland in Palestine after the fall of the Ottoman Empire. Jews began to immigrate to Palestine and encountered opposition from aggressive Arab nationalists who resented their presence. Finally, on November 29, 1947, the United Nations approved the creation of both a Jewish and an Arab state within five months—ironically, a "two state solution", with Israel for the Jews and Transjordan for the Arabs. The British left Palestine on May 14, 1948; the modern State of Israel was born that day with their Declaration of Independence.

Although the Jewish people have long nurtured a deep aversion to violent conflict, the lessons of history, especially illustrated in the Holocaust, provide ample reminders that the Jewish people must have some protection so as not to find themselves as defenseless targets against enemies who seek their ruin. The State of Israel is many things: One of these is a living testament to the determination of Jews worldwide to take a greater degree of control in charting their own destiny. Centuries of martyrdom have shown that passivity in the face of injustice provides no shelter. The State of Israel is directly tied to the future of the Jewish people worldwide and a sense of Jewish identity. Some cite the passage, "For Zion's sake I will not keep silent, and for Jerusalem's sake, I will not rest" (Isa 62:1), as theological underpinnings for such convictions. Others feel that the re-birth of Israel is nothing less than a divinely orchestrated miracle that signals the phoenix-like rise of a people out of the ashes of a European crematoria. It is as if the dry bones of the valley have finally come to life again after centuries of silence (Ezek 37). At the risk of being misunderstood, one could assert that Jews cannot now turn their backs on Israel any more than they can turn their backs on God.

This love for Israel is framed within specific political and military realities that cannot be ignored. Within ten minutes after the birth of the new nation, the United States recognized the legitimacy of the State of Israel. The Hebrew language became one official language (along with English and Arabic) and a new government was set in place. The Arab nations surrounding Israel, however, declared war and their populations outnumbered the Jews of Israel by over twenty to one. The surrounding Arab-majority governments told their fellow Arabs to move to "temporary camps" while their armies "pushed the Jews into the sea." The plan was for these refugees to then return and take everything that belonged to their Jewish neighbors. With the promised victory never delivered, many Arab Palestinians referred to this time as the *nakbah* (disaster) and they were basically abandoned by their Arab non-Palestinian neighbors to fend for themselves. Despite these odds, Israel drove away her many aggressive attackers. Those Arabs who stayed within the boundaries of the new State of Israel and swore loyalty and allegiance to its constitution became Israeli citizens and their families attend universities, vote, and hold office to this day. The Knesset, Israel's parliamentary body, has always had a number Arab members, and the Supreme Court has had Muslim justices through the years. Unfortunately, many of those who went in the "temporary" camps remain there today, never helped, supported, nor absorbed by any of the other Arab nations around them. They and their descendants are today's Palestinian refugees, who certainly deserve a home of their own.

Another war broke out in 1956 when Israel attacked Egypt to gain its shipping rights back in the Straits of Tiran after Egypt closed the Suez Canal as well as the Straits. With French and British support (though not public at first), the three countries were able to achieve their strategic goals. U.S. and Russian pressure, however, prompted restoring control of the Suez Canal to Egypt and its dictator, Gamal Abdel Nasser, as part of the armistice agreement.

In 1967, Egypt and its allies were again massing troops on Israel's borders. Israel once more began a pre-emptive strike against Egypt for closing its shipping channels (such closure is considered an act of war by international law). The Israeli air force was able to completely defeat the Egyptian air force while it was still on the ground. At the same time, Israel's defense forces were able to push the Syrian and Jordanian armies away from their borders, and from the high points and crossings they controlled. This swift Israeli victory became known as "The Six Day War."

In 1973, Egypt and Syria launched a surprise attack on Israel on Yom Kippur, the Jewish Day of Atonement. Golda Meir, Israel's prime minister at the time, never imagined these enemies would attack on the Jews' holiest day of the year, so she chose not to call up Israel's reserves. Her mistake nearly cost Israel its existence as the invaders enjoyed success for the first few days. Once called up, the reserves were able to rebuff the attacks and return to the post Six Day War borders by the time a ceasefire was attained. Prime Minister Meir never sought public office again after the Yom Kippur War.

Thanks to the courage and foresight of Egyptian President Anwar Sadat, Israel and Egypt reached a comprehensive peace settlement in 1977. Sadat traveled to Jerusalem and met with Israeli Prime Minister Menachem Begin to negotiate the peace settlement. Egypt achieved return of the Sinai Peninsula in this "land for peace" deal accepted by Israel. Sadat was assassinated back home in Egypt for his efforts. Though considered a "cold peace", it has endured for over forty years. In 1994, King Hussein of Jordan also signed a peace treaty with Israel.

In the peace treaty between Israel and Egypt, signed in 1978, there was no provision for returning the Gaza Strip to Egypt. Similarly, Jordan's peace did not include the return of any of the West Bank of the Jordan River, which had been under Jordanian control prior to 1967. Those two areas, the Gaza Strip and the West Bank, have been territories where, in addition to refugee camps, the Palestinians have built thriving cities. To be sure, there are many tensions that have arisen without reprieve within the last fifty years as unresolved issues between Palestinians and Israelis have continued to fester without resolution. While mistakes and missteps continue to be made by both sides, all people of goodwill hold out hope for a peaceful resolution within our lifetimes.

Some describe the nation of Israel as having a "Masada complex" because many Jews seem ready to sacrifice their lives, for the sake of the nation's existence. Critics have assumed that Israel has been unnecessarily oppressive in their treatment of Palestinians while failing to consider a proven history of extensive efforts to murder as many Israelis as possible in the name of Palestinian liberation. A case in point is the barrier Israel built between itself and the West Bank to prevent the terrorist attacks occurring regularly during the first (beginning in 1987, ending with the Oslo Accords of 1993) and second (beginning in 2000) "intifadas". The barrier reduced hundreds of annual deaths of Israeli citizens to near zero.

These issues are far too complicated to be bandied about in academic contexts with glib bumper-sticker assertions. The fact remains that many North American Jews have called on the United States to provide weapons to Israel to aid in its very survival. Such a posture, especially by religious communities, invites the scorn from those who enjoy the luxury of being immune from serious threats against their own security.

It should be noted, however, that ever since the time of King Saul and King David, Jews have closely tied political power to religious practices. People of faith have moral responsibilities that are rooted in political realities. Political power is a necessity in Israel but the leaders of the nation, such as Golda Meir—and others—have always called on the Jewish people to recognize some of the potential dangers of relating spiritual practices with political and military power.

Some Christians (and some Jews) have criticized the way that an American-Israel lobby has intruded into some Jewish and Christian interactions. Many of these same critics are some of the most active voices in supporting the plight of the Palestinians against their Israeli opponents.

While it is entirely appropriate to deal with moral issues in an inter-religious context—such as concerns for the people of Palestine—students also need to appreciate the many complexities of Palestinian-Israeli tensions that defy simplistic generalizations and blanket assumptions about who is right and who is wrong in every situation. It is constructive to help Christians appreciate a range of opinions, including those within the Jewish diaspora, as well as to help them see that "Israeli society is made up of a very variegated continuum of possibilities," which includes a seemingly infinite number of views about Palestinian-Israeli relations.[344] A focus on the political nature of Palestinian-Israeli relations will help Christians better appreciate why some Jews bitterly oppose those who advocate for the cause of the Palestinians in a way that ignores larger issues of how Israeli statehood is a fragile reality established on a host of tenuous political and military factors.

One should not conclude that those who question the political or military actions of the State of Israel should automatically be labeled as anti-Semitic. At the same time, no government or organization is beyond criticism and no political organization should be above the challenges of those who question certain actions or statements. Israel stands among all other nations and should be judged for its actions and declarations as are all countries. What cannot be denied, however, is that some attacks against the State of Israel may also sometimes actually be veiled expressions of contempt against all Jewish peoples, reflective of lingering anti-Jewish resentments. There should be no room for blanket vilifications against all Israeli policies that go along with broader attempts by Israel's enemies to delegitimize Israel's place among the nations. It is the view of the Catholic theologian Jacques Maritain that being "anti-Israel is not better than anti-Semitism . . . the anti-Zionist propaganda at work today, and of which the political origins are easily discernible, is in actual fact, well-orchestrated anti-Semitic propaganda."[345] One cannot, in all cases, separate the State of Israel from the political loyalty and feelings of many Jews worldwide. Attacks about "Zionism" from some regions of the world conflate facts and emphasize injustices to such a degree that they begin to support centuries of insidious stereotypes articulated by anti-Zionists and anti-Semites.

Although it cannot be denied that some major injustices have taken place over time in Israel—including at times unfair and punitive policies against Palestinian communities—the State of Israel, even with all its many imperfections and failings, remains for many the most promising hope for Jews worldwide to survive a modern era where anti-Semitism has often been given unfettered support.

Conclusion—Healing the World

Religion has two children—love and hatred.
—Russian Proverb

We confess being confounded, the co-responsibility and guilt of German Christianity for the Holocaust. We believe in the continuing election of the Jewish people as the people of God and we recognize that the Church was brought through Jesus Christ into the covenant of God with His people. We believe that Jews and Christians in their respective vocations are witnesses to the world and to each other. We are therefore convinced that the Church cannot fulfill her witness to the Jewish people in the same way as she fulfills her mission to the nations of the world.
—Resolution, Synod of the Protestant Church of the Rhineland, 1971

The righteous of all nations are worthy of immortality.
—Talmud

SOME CHRISTIANS WEAR ARM bracelets which bear the inspirational message—WWJD ("What would Jesus do?"). It is a thought-provoking question in the context of centuries of painful Jewish-Christian interactions. How might Jesus, the Jew, have engaged in Jewish-Christian interactions if he lived in modern North America? There is a story told of a young man who exulted to his rabbi that he loved the rabbi dearly. The response to the youth was that he could not possibly claim to love his rabbi if he did not know how he suffered in pain or if he did not know where and how his teacher was hurting. We cannot claim to appreciate each other while, at the same time, removing ourselves from each other's lives. Even though mistakes may transpire along the way, it is this sense of respectful engagement that opens the way for deeper currents of meaningful interfaith mutuality.

Education provides the best hope for transforming unacknowledged Christian anti-Judaism into an informed awareness of contemporary Judaism as it actually exists. Intolerant Christian triumphalism can be supplanted by equipping Christians with a more accurate perspective of how they are often perceived by many of their Jewish friends and neighbors. Christians can be encouraged to foster an appreciation of those from other spiritualities that focuses on being sympathetic in their deportment, and compassionate in their interrelationships. American civil society supports the call for a general sense of mutual coexistence, which in no way should be a compromise of an individual's faith-convictions. Christians can appreciate a greater sense of the meaningfulness of their own tradition when they see it being capable of relating with the views of others in a way that fosters mutual respect. One student wrote, "I am becoming more and more intrigued with the study of Judaism and what it means for me as a Christian. I have honestly been challenged to reexamine my own personal beliefs. One that I am really having trouble grasping is the whole trinity subject."[346] The study of other faiths is quite capable of meaningfully enhancing one's own commitment to one's own faith: this has been our experience.

Father Padraig O'Hare shifts the focus of Jewish-Christian engagement when asking: "Can Jews revere Christians?" Adherents of both faith traditions should initiate steps toward individual and communitarian appreciation of the other. For both Jews and Christians, theological interpreters will be necessary in the promotion of profoundly secure shared affection. The theological smugness of supersessionism, for example, will be challenged when Christians are encouraged to appreciate Judaism independent of any straight-jacketing presuppositions about its inherent inferiority. Christians can be encouraged to recognize that they sometimes bring to discussions with Jews a perceived sense of inherited (or seemingly inevitable) oppositionality because of stated convictions of a superior faith.

One resource for consideration among Protestant traditions is Anabaptism. Anabaptist theological themes of non-violence (also present in other forms of Christianity), can confront a sense of conservative Christian entrenched oppositionalism. The incarnational commitment to the Christian faith expressed in relational and loving action causes the theoretical to be translated into a proactive sense of relational engagement toward the individual members of a given Jewish community. This will invariably lead Christians away from any confrontational sense of distance that might be created by an overt sense of theological dismissiveness. The living practice of an engaged , relational faith encourages a follower of Jesus, a devout first-century Jewish rabbi, to be both a listener and a learner. The silent years of Jesus—years of seeming inactivity— might be a prescient point of reference to help Christians appreciate how it might sometimes be God's will for their lives to do nothing more than to listen and prepare for what might eventually be the most effective and mature contribution in the advance of constructive and healing interfaith interactions. Further, the past nature of Jewish-Christian relations should be studied because it holds valuable lessons about the reasons behind past relational mistakes.

Christian historic responses to Judaism, rooted in a call to be faithful evangelists, are far from monolithic. Anabaptist Christians often have a unique approach to the issues of interfaith evangelism and how best to relate to other faith traditions. Anabaptism is a Protestant movement that arose in the sixteenth century by preaching that Christians should maintain a strict separation of church and state and should stress personal discipleship expressed in ethical and moral support for peace and justice. Anabaptists often stress that Christians should see themselves as wandering pilgrims in this life and that faith development is a gradual process that proceeds from both individual and communitarian experiences with God. While Anabaptists (along with many other Christians) believe that conversion may bring an initial "experience" of salvation, the long and winding life of Christian discipleship is where that initial seed takes firm root in an ethic of expressed love and mutual respect. In the context of Jewish and Christian relations, such a humble and progressive perspective can address the toxicity and the volatility of assertions that alienate many Jews as they relate to some of their Christian neighbors. Anabaptist theology joins with Jewish assertions that the relational realms of ethical engagement cannot be left at the purely spiritual and "other-worldly" level. Believers bring to the world an engaged presence instead of simply longing to leave this world for an idyllic world-to-come. Worldly justice is forever linked to divine worship while the avoidance of confronting evil is, according to the biblical revelation, a form of self-indulgence; a distorted expression of morality that cannot bring honor to God.

Pedagogical strategies need to be explored in helping Christians confront what many would categorize as latent (or blatant) anti-Jewish assumptions. Issues of textual and communitarian authority should be confronted in the process. This offers a heuristic educational challenge that can be rewarding. One reason why effective educators often rely upon stories, proverbs, poems, and visual images—modern and ancient—is that inherently aggressive assumptions can be disarmed through the aesthetic, poetic, and the familiar. Because many Christians already embrace the idea that faith in an unseen God is experienced in a world of mystery and allusion, they may be open to more creative approaches than a straightforward presentation that might unwittingly underscore the exotic differences of the "other." Because the faith of any individual is a multifaceted jewel that defies simplistic generalizations, multifaith discussions should be patiently approached through varying methodologies. A story or a poem, for example, allows a listener to be "in the middle" of a given situation without needing to have any concordant sense of ownership. Stories can be powerful interpretative tools; folk traditions can humanize that which is viewed as being conceptual. In this way, the ancientness of Judaism can spring to life in more relevant expressions for non-Jewish students. Guardedness on the part of some Christians can be replaced by interest through an indirect story with a message that has potential to lodge questions in the minds of those already fully persuaded.

In the quest to appreciate the spirituality of an individual from another faith tradition, Christians are sometimes being asked to do something that they may have never done before (or needed to have done) in their lives. In the words of Diana Eck, some have never become "alerted to the possibility of beauty and spiritual depth in traditions other than our own."[347] Through listening and learning, the perception of a faith tradition (and its relationship with other traditions) can become increasingly valorized without a correspondent need to weaken one's own faith. It is a powerful experience for an individual from an insular faith context (who may have eschewed multifaith interactions) to experience—perhaps for the first time—answers to universal (and common) questions that come from other traditions, and for these answers to "make sense" and even to "sound Christian."

Christians can be asked to gain something of a Jewish perspective on issues of faith. Sometimes this will call for either glamorized or negative stereotypes about the Judaism that they think they already understand. Christians can be encouraged to think in ecumenical and interfaith ways about the statement of St. Paul to "bear each other's burdens and so fulfill the law of Christ" (Gal 6:2) in terms of how this command relates to their Jewish neighbors. This message of Paul to enter deeper dimensions of identification and appreciation reminds me of a West African proverb that I (van Gorder) once heard: "Perhaps you do not understand me because you do not love me."

Christians can be encouraged to consider the words of Jesus: "judge not lest ye also be judged" (Matt 7:1) in the context of exploring the many fascinating avenues of interfaith encounters. While Christians should always be encouraged to remain passionate about their own convictions of faith, including the need for evangelization and mission, they should also recognize how these cherished passions can sometimes be misunderstood by those within other faiths as being non-relationally judgmental and condescending about the validity of faith of others. Fortunately, when a sincere individual in the middle of a multifaith interaction takes on the posture of a learner, the potential for such dismissive misunderstandings declines appreciably.

Conservative Christians should not be expected to "swallow the elephant whole" and reconcile thousands of years of Jewish-Christian acrimony within the scope of their own singular experience. They can, however, confront their own preconceptions from another perspective and examine their misconceptions about Judaism that they may have unintentionally embraced. Christians can see their study of the "other" (and their coinciding interactions with the "other") as a process of beginnings.

It is difficult to overstate the centrality of addressing the misconceptions and preconceptions that we have described throughout this book. One of the challenges we have experienced in presenting the basics of Judaism in a predominantly conservative Christian context has been the recognition that such an effort provides serious challenges to long-held assumptions about how the superiority of Christianity relates to the inherent inferiority of other faiths. It is fundamentally problematic for some Christians to approach the study of another religion from a neutral perspective if such an approach is seen to bring a potential compromise to their own treasured convictions that their way of seeing things is the one and only God-given truth for all of humanity.

How can one embark upon a comparative perspective when one brings to such a study the assumption that there is nothing to discover about that which is true about God's plan of salvation for the world? While it is inevitable that there will be a host of comparisons that some will make, it is necessary to move some Christians away from the limiting shackles of simplistic comparisons and reductionistic arguments in order to begin to look at the vitality of the Jewish tradition with a new sense of relational engagement. A more non-comparative model will encourage conservative Christians to be less defensive as they learn about Judaism.

This book has introduced some of the seemingly insurmountable tensions at the relational heart of Jewish and Christian interactions throughout history. We have discussed how some Christians have described the church as the "new Israel" and have assumed that the historic Jewish rejection of Jesus means that the Jews are no longer the "chosen people." The faith of contemporary Jews is something that is fundamentally flawed because it is rooted in a tradition that was designed by God to serve as a temporary theological preface (and a moral preparation) for the more liberating truths of God-given Christian revelation of Jesus as Messiah. Some Jews have also held negative, categorical views of conservative Christianity that are neither charitable nor sympathetic. Some Jewish apologists have seen fit to dismissively castigate Christianity and have "presented the Christian church as founded on false prophecies" and functioning as the "new home for forces promoting old anti-Jewish persecution."[348]

Remnants of such confrontative views remain as some Christians remain stridently committed to converting Jews to embrace their own convictions about Jesus as the only Messiah for the Jewish people. Those who undertake a supposed "dialogue" with the "other," but still have an agenda to proselytize, are making such "dialogue" self-defeating. Instead, they devolve into a reassuring monologue and thereby avoid any challenging counterarguments. At the same time, many Jews and Christians have come to recognize potentially fundamental theological barriers with careful responses that offer fresh interpretations that are true to the respective traditions but far less confrontational in their relational expression.

Jews and Christians in genuine interfaith dialogue have often shifted the tone of their interactions by changing the goal of their encounters to a more relational sense of civic engagement. While these paradigm shifts need to be introduced, it may be even more vital to help those already committed to multifaith interactions to find increased common ground. A desire to appreciate others will set a tone that will encourage genuine respect.

Some see interfaith interactions as inherently threatening to the core of an individual's faith identity. There is no need to insist that Judaism and

Christianity are identical faith traditions using different terms and with different constituencies. We can agree to disagree about many issues. When we meet, there is no need to compromise anything of our core beliefs (even about mission or evangelism) or alter the viewpoints of our cherished faith communities. Theological compromises of longstanding doctrines do nothing to advance substantive interfaith interactions that accurately reflect the various traditions. The countless points of ethical and moral agreement already shared among Jews and Christians provide ample ground for the sturdy foundations of constructive and respectful interactions. This is where we should begin as we work to strengthen healthy interfaith friendships and build sturdy levels of trust between each other.

Jews and Christians agree that God is a God of love who calls for covenantal relationship. The God worshipped by both Moses and Jesus is a God who cares deeply about social justice on earth as well as individual salvation in a world to come. Christians and Jews share—among other things—a common ethic, a hope for a redeemed world, and a commitment to progress every day in prayer and devotion to God's divine love. Jeff Levin summarizes this idea in his claim that "Divine Love is at the core of the world's great religious traditions."[349] Jews and Christians also often share a theological belief that God exists in distinct personality. According to Jacob Neusner, "Judaism sees God and man as consubstantial, sharing the same emotional traits. God has three major character traits: power, love, and justice."[350]

In the area of social justice, Christians and Jews can agree to work together with a determination that will build mutual trust and respect. Both Jewish and Christian ethics to bring healing to the world are rooted in the revelation of the Bible. When we work together, we will face each other—standing side by side as friends, sisters, and brothers. Jesus said that those who claimed to love the message of the gospel but refuse to feed the poor—or consider the plight of the orphan and the widow—would find no place in the coming kingdom of God that Christ would establish. Jesus warned that "not everyone who calls out to me, 'Lord! Lord!' will enter the Kingdom of Heaven" (Matt 7:21), because of their prideful rebellion and willful negligence to love others with hearts of gracious compassion. Prophet Micah was unambiguous when stating that the Lord required that all who claim to worship God should: "Do justice, love mercy, and walk humbly" (Mic 6:8). Rabbi Hillel once answered a question about the central message of Judaism by saying that one could stand on one foot and simply say "what is hateful to you do not do to another" and in so doing would capture the heart of the tradition. Rabbi Akiba's thought on the essence of the whole Torah is that it can be summed up as "Love your neighbor as yourself."

Both Christians and Jews are concerned with healing and constructive interrelationships in the conviction that God has created all of us in divine image and that God seeks intimate and individual relationship with the created order. Both traditions affirm that humans are called to relate with God and express that relationship in loving interactions with others. Both traditions call for believers to pray and to study God's revelations (Deut 10:12; 2 Tim 2:15). Both traditions promise that the faithful can enjoy the benefits that come through following God's law (Zech 14:9; Eph 6:2–3). Both traditions affirm that individuals must first understand themselves and their relationship to their creator before they can reach their full potential as people (see Gen 1:27–28; John 1:10–13). Both traditions emphasize that God is glorified whenever believers foster healthy interrelationships among different individuals in a shared commitment to an inclusive community before God (Deut 6:18; 1 Cor 1:10). Both traditions call for a respectful and healthy relationship between individuals and the natural world where people of faith should live with courage (Gen 15:1) rooted in a sense of confident relation with God. Both traditions call on the faithful to show concern towards those who are strangers in their midst. Jesus tells the parable of the "Good Samaritan" (Luke 10:30–37) and warns that blessings will come on the final Day of Judgement to those who show mercy to the poor and the alien (Matt 25:34–35). The views of Jesus are rooted in the commands of the Torah to show love towards strangers (Exod 22:20–23) and to reach out to those in need by loving our neighbors even as we love ourselves (Lev 19:18). Christians and Jews can find common ground in working to bring healing to a world broken by the evils of sin.

Christians and Jews meeting together cannot avoid confronting the troubling nature of our historical interfaith interactions. How have Jews throughout history interacted with Christians?[351] Early in Jewish-Christian relations there are few resources to answer the question of what Jewish attitudes toward the first Christians were. This is because most early sources on this question are written from a Christian perspective and by individuals with a polemical interest in asserting their own views. If some Jews did write about Christians, these writings may have been suppressed (or even destroyed) over the centuries. When Jewish comments are made about Jesus and about Christianity, it is often the case that hosts of polemics were already well-established. It is enough to agree that Jesus was a Jew leading a reform movement and was killed by the Romans along with countless other political dissidents. In that sense, writing serious responses to Christianity may have been seen as giving unwarranted legitimacy.

It is not simply enough to grasp how others have promoted anti-Jewish ideas. What about *our own* possible areas of culpability? While a posture of repentance (or regret) is a welcome step beyond shrill dismissiveness, each of us needs to take concrete, specific actions to confront anti-Jewish sentiment within our own lives. There are no such thing as "harmless" anti-Jewish attitudes. Anti-Jewish assumptions often sneak into people's minds subtly; such sentiments gain ground slowly over time.

Blatantly shocking anti-Semitic acts (such as those of Hitler) were end-products that arose across centuries of unchecked, virulent disdain. We should set the record straight: it is necessary to condemn any and all who, either directly or indirectly, promote ideas that encourage contemporary expressions of anti-Judaism. Christian pulpits should become contexts where active support for the Jewish people is voiced instead of contexts where anti-Jewish ideas go unchallenged.

After the Holocaust, several Christian denominations have been shaken awake by the realization of their own complicity in centuries of anti-Jewish sentiment. This is a hopeful development. One of the most central documents of the Catholic Church on interfaith dialogue, *Nostrae Aetete* (written between 1963 and 1965), unambiguously acknowledges the many ways that the church has been party to the promotion of anti-Judaism. This document, and others, offers a constructive pathway forward for Christians to work to foster a genuine spirit of reconciliation with their Jewish sisters and brothers. In a similar action, the World Council of Churches issued a statement in 1967 that affirmed that the best way to relate to Jews was not through words but through acts of loving respect. Presbyterians (PCUSA), in 1987, declared that "Christians have not replaced the Jews" because "Jews are already in a covenantal relationship with God."[352] Similar declarations have been made by the United Methodist Church and the United Church of Christ, stating: "Judaism has not been superseded by Christianity. God's covenant with the Jewish people has not been abrogated."[353] As latent vestiges of anti-Jewish imagery become exposed, many Christians are beginning to seek to become the best friends possible with their Jewish neighbors.

The question of Christian attempts to convert Jews cannot be swept under the rug. Some Christians, in the name of loving their Jewish neighbors, have often loved the Jews—literally—to death. Christians are commanded by Christ to "be witnesses" and to "teach" the message of Christ—in loving interrelationships—to all individuals worldwide. This relational, missionary mandate, however, does not equate with what often happens in the name of some forms of evangelism directed by those conservative Christians who assertively (and sometimes indirectly and deceptively) target the Jewish people with their efforts. There is a powerful difference between faithful witness rooted in love and crass proselytism, which is often manipulative and equivocal in its expression. I (van Gorder) would agree with Joseph Estes, former Southern Baptist missionary, who explained: "Compulsive individuals, churches, and church organizations, may do—and often have done—violence to the true mission of Christ's church." Any witness for Christ should be gracious, sincere, non-coercive, and sensitive to issues that a given individual might bring to our multi-faith interactions. Faithful and relational Christian witness is a clear and direct presentation, without any veiled conditions, of what a believer has come to realize within her or his own life, and experience about the transforming life and message of Jesus.

While the core of the Christian faith is unapologetically missionistic, there is no reason that evangelism should be expressed in a non-relational, or offensively confrontative manner. The surest way to be ineffective in attempting to fulfill that same Great Commission mandate is to be predatory in a narrow focus that seeks the conversion of the Jews to Christianity instead of a relational posture of commitment that seeks to help and care for each other in loving, mutual respect. Faithful Christian witness among Jewish communities will walk in lockstep with the goal of Jewish preservation and with a profound sense of our fundamental interrelatedness as believers in the one true God of Abraham.

Our relational actions should speak louder than our words. It is disingenuous to say such things and to support any programmatic efforts that seek to convert individual Jews from the warmth of their families and faith communities into joining Christian churches. Christians can listen closely to Jewish arguments that such non-relationally sensitive efforts are nothing more than religious expressions of anti-Judaism, rooted in the core assumption that Judaism is fundamentally lacking as a religion in its ability to bring eternal and salvific blessings from the one true God. Abraham Joshua Heschel stated:

> The mission to the Jews is a call to individual Jews to betray the
> fellowship, the dignity, and the sacred history of their people.
> Very few Christians seem to comprehend what is morally and
> spiritually involved in supporting such activities. We are Jews as
> we are men. The alternative to our existence as Jews is spiritual
> suicide, extinction. It is not a change into something else. Juda-
> ism has allies but not substitutes.[354]

Christians who insist that Jews cannot reach heaven apart from becoming Christians should, at the very least, acknowledge that such a view
comes from one specific interpretation of the Christian scriptures that is
not common among the larger Christian community today. It would be
hoped that these same advocates would at least accept that some Christians disagree with their views—and believe that the Almighty promised
an eternal blessing for all Jews. As a Christian, I (van Gorder) take the
Bible seriously and literally when it says—in no uncertain terms—that
God has made an everlasting covenant with the Jewish people that cannot—and will never be—revoked.

Karl Barth's specific theological assumption of Jewish-Christian
interactions was that "it is incontestable that this people, as such, are
the holy people of God."[355] Reinhold Niebuhr's view was that Jesus is a
way for the *gentiles* to come to God but that the Jews *already* have an
eternal covenant with the Divine. Franz Rosenzweig's starting point in
this discussion was that Christianity and Judaism are "two religions with
one center, worshipping the same God, but with Christianity serving the
purpose of carrying the prophetic message to the Gentile world."[356] The
scriptures proclaim that the "LORD will not forsake His people or will
not abandon His heritage" (Ps 94:14). St. Paul asks "has God repudiated
His people? No, indeed . . . for God's gifts of grace and God's calling are
irrevocable" (Rom 11:1, 29).

Christians who hold on to assumptions that are fundamentally anti-
Jewish are also contradicting the teachings of scripture. I (van Gorder)
do not hold such views merely to be conciliatory. God's works and ways
are mysterious, and a mature posture of sensitive humility is appropriate
when relating to how God will deal with the Jews particularly and with
individuals from other faith traditions generally. Before I should judge
others—or dismiss their views—I should show them in words and actions the merciful, redemptive love of God as I have experienced it in the
person of Jesus Christ. It is my hope that my life and my words will be able
to bless others and be a source of healing and encouragement. Such views

are rooted in biblical revelation and spring from the life of a modern universal church post-Holocaust. Certainly, Jewish-Christian interactions throughout history have been abysmal. The fruit of these relations has often been marked by deep valleys of enmity. Ignorance of the "other" has often taken root and blossomed into weeds of zealous hate supported by simple, isolating stereotypes and misunderstandings. It would be difficult to say that most Christian dealings with Jews throughout history have brought honor to God. Our interactions with each other have often been divisive and harmful.

Contemporary multifaith interactions hold promise but also face clamoring challenges. The more that we can learn about each other and our views, the more likely it will be that future multifaith interactions will be less problematic than the insularity of past dealings. We have tried everything else. Now it is time to begin appreciating each other based on our own terms and not on the foundations of sand that come from tired preconceptions and shop-worn misrepresentations. Jews and Christians celebrate faith traditions springing from similar ethical and moral perspectives. This is grounds for levels of shared social justice partnerships that can be expressed in a wide range of creative ways. Christianity arises from Judaism, and this fact of history offers a refreshing hope for improved interactions going forward. Some Christians seek dialogue with Jews to address their own needs for coming to terms with personal or historic instances of anti-Semitism. Jews, for their part, may participate in multifaith conversations in hopes of fostering a more tolerant civic society for future generations. For many, the promotion of respectful dialogue is a sacred duty as well as a delight and becomes yet another way to advance God's holy work of reconciliation in a broken world.

Pope John Paul II visited the Great Synagogue in Rome early in his papacy; then, later, paid his respects at the Western Wall in Jerusalem. Critics saw these visits as woefully shallow given the legacy of previous popes in history who refused to take a stand against tides of anti-Semitism. While these gestures can be dismissed as being merely symbolic, they also mirror changes among those Christians who hope to reinvigorate conversations with Jews in ways that are respectful. Pope John Paul II was seeking to take a few small steps forward based on a deep respect that he had for the Jewish people. His actions were rooted in a sanctified character marked by prayerful patience and concern for his neighbor. They set the tone for future positive improvements in Jewish-Christian interactions. During his life, Pope John Paul II repeatedly called fellow Christians to listen to their Jewish neighbors:

> Drawing upon the riches of our respective religious traditions, we must spread awareness that today's problems will not be solved if we remain ignorant of one another and isolated from one another. . . . We must do all that we can to turn awareness of past offenses and sins into a firm resolve to build a new future in which there will be nothing but respectful and fruitful cooperation between us. Dialogue is not an attempt to impose our views on others. What it demands of all of us is that, holding to what we believe, we listen respectfully to one another, seek to discern all that is good and holy in each other's teachings, and cooperate in supporting everything that favors mutual understanding and peace.[357]

Pope John Paul II's perspective on Judaism was summarized in his statement (1987) that "Jews are partners in a covenant of eternal love which was never revoked."[358] This affirmation of the message of an eternal covenant (see Rom 11:29) as affirmed by the Pope was repeated throughout the ministry of Pope Benedict XVI. While still Cardinal Ratzinger he wrote, "God's providence has obviously given Israel a particular mission in this time of the Gentiles. Thus, the church's mission no longer includes the wish to absorb the Jewish faith into Christianity and so end the distinctive witness of Jews to God in human history . . . . Jews already dwell in a saving covenant with God."[359] Pope Benedict XVI carried the vision of John Paul II forward and was the first Pope to visit a synagogue in both Germany and the United States. After Benedict, Pope Francis (born Jorge Mario Bergoglio; 17 December 1936) expressed similar views and, as the Cardinal in Argentina, had even co-authored a book with Rabbi (and biophysicist) Abraham Skorka on the need for healthy, healing Jewish-Christian relations. Rabbi Eric Greenberg has stated that Pope Francis has also been instrumental in boldly advancing "Jewish-Christian relations to the next level."[360]

Countless positive contexts for constructive Jewish-Christian interactions have been launched within recent decades by both Jews and Christians. The Institute for Islamic, Christian, and Jewish Studies (based in Baltimore), for example, convened a series of consultations (since the early 1990s) that resulted in a joint statement published in the *New York Times* and many other venues.[361] Critics saw these documents as presenting a partial view of God and a generalizing view about both religions in hopes of forging artificial grounds for agreement. One critic, Jon Levenson, a renowned Hebrew Bible and the Albert A. List Jewish Studies Scholar at the Harvard Divinity School, claimed that the document chose to "neglect rather than reassess the historic points of discord."[362]

Sadly, conservative Christians sometimes perceive no need for dialogue with Jews because they are certain that Jews have nothing to offer when it comes to an accurate understanding of God's ultimate, saving truth. As the passion of an insecure faith intensifies, the idea of certainty, even in contexts of obvious belief (and not knowledge), leads to the replacement of knowledge with assertiveness. The biblical mandate to struggle with God (and with truth) is replaced by a struggle with others who hold different views. It is not enough to embrace a God who declares: "I shall be what I shall be" (Exod 3:14, there are variant translations of this key phrase); it is vital that God should not be fully contained and grasped safely within the confines of one specific religious narrative. Some are not content, as was Moses, to accept that they cannot see the divine face and live (Exod 33:20); they feel the need to recast faith into fact and truth beyond question. The world is purely categorical and safely black and white (and right and wrong) without any murky shadows of lingering doubt.

It is only when we are certain who the "other" is that we can dismiss them (or even kill them if we "know" that the "other" is a "terrorist" or an enemy). Narrow sectarianism dismisses others because sectarian faith provides its own self-conveyed confirmation. Exclusivists cannot really take the stubborn, hard-hearted, and blind adherents of other traditions seriously apart from a stated desire to convert them to their own views (which, then, affirms those views). This perspective is a polite rendering of the harsh German proverb: "If you will not be my brother then I will have to bash in your skull" (*Und willst du nicht mein Bruder sein; so schlag ich dir den Schadel ein*). Division, distrust, and deeply rooted alienation are the interrelational results of simplistic assertions and confrontative, exclusivist postures. Many Christians seem comfortable with the categorical logic of John Chrysostom: "The truth of one religion is dependent on the invalidity of the other."[363] Such aggressive qualities, expressed by some Christians intent on converting Jews to Christianity, are at the heart of the challenges between Jews and Christians. Modern Orthodox Rabbi and North American Scholar Irving Greenberg offers a Jewish perspective on this relationship when writing: "If the doctrines of the Incarnation and Resurrection of Jesus lead to Christian triumphalism, to persecution, and idolatry, then Christianity proves itself to be false. If it leads to deeper compassion and understanding and a grasp of human realities and human needs and motivated covenantal action, then it validates itself as a channel of the divine."[364]

As we listen to each other with patient and mutual respect, interfaith interactions hold rich potential to become fascinating contexts for spiritual growth and intellectual discovery. Anglican Bishop and Oxford scholar Kenneth Cragg noted that "alertness to the perennial crisis of our shared humanity fosters a will to appreciate, by mutual discovery, what we legitimately possess in common."[365] Listening with sensitivity and sincerity is an expression of selfless patience. It even may take a measure of courage to listen to others who have fundamentally different views than our own. Artificial barriers rooted in presuppositions can fall when confronted by shared experiences. After a student visited a synagogue service and had some animated discussions afterwards, the student was moved by the experience to admit: "I really didn't know what to think after the service because I had just assumed that anyone who is not a Christian would have a void in their lives that needed to be filled by Christ."[366] Another student observed: "I think as Christians we are all too quick to judge and too slow to accept and this is one of the most important things that I have learned this semester."[367] Focused and careful interfaith education can become a helpful tools in improving the long-term quality of constructive future Jewish and Christian interactions. Multifaith encounters can become vigorous contexts for mutual respect and friendship as we learn about others as well as learning more about ourselves while also changing the world by fighting social injustices and strife. There is "give and take" in any interfaith friendship: when we can acknowledge that we embrace two distinct traditions (with often widely different perspectives on several issues) then we can agree to respectfully disagree.

This book has offered a brief overview of only a few issues raised during various Jewish-Christian interactions that we have had with students who come from mostly conservative Christian backgrounds. Many issues have, inevitably (and necessarily), remained unexplored. For example, it is instructive to consider how some Christians have seemed to disregard an emphasis on the separation of church and state and have seemed increasingly to embrace a view that religion can be actively political and sectarian. How will such views affect future Jewish and Christian interactions in social, cultural, and political terms? Elliot Abrams, a noted American diplomat, is one scholar who is concerned that America's long history of being largely tolerant and liberal towards Judaism is threatened. Abrams is committed to the Jeffersonian non-sectarian separation between church and state, and warns it "is on a collision course with some Evangelical Christians" who, are beginning to pursue a more strident posture of bringing their faith with intolerance into the public sphere. Perhaps Abrams' claim is overly alarmist about the extent that some conservative Christians will conflate political and religious distinctions. Even if he is not entirely on track, however, the future may be marked by increased tensions on such issues.

Despite such potential fissures, logic mandates that conservative Christians and Jews have little choice but to foster joint coalitions for mutual understanding and social justice that are neither patronizing nor dismissive of each other. One hopeful model for partnership might be found in the work of Dr. Martin Luther King, Jr., who enlisted people from all faiths in his extensive work for social justice, or in recent initiatives by Christians such as Jim Wallis (and many others such as Tony Campolo, Dorothy Day, Peter Marin, Bishop Romero, Cardinal Arinze, Joel Hunter, and William J. Barber II), who have worked across religious barriers to promote shared social justice initiatives.

Constructive partnerships between Christians and Jews will be forced to consider the grim truths of history as they relate to historic Christian anti-Semitism. At the same time, it should also be noted that most North American and European models for cultural tolerance are rooted in the Christian heritage; the proverbial baby should not be thrown out with the bath water. While it may be true that "many Jews understandably associate conservative Christians with anti-Semitism," such a view is too narrow.[368] It may be true that some conservative Christians view Judaism as a "desiccated religion of fanatical formalism" but this is not the entire picture across the broad spectrum of the Christian community.[369] Tensions between Jews and Christians can be lessened when broad generalizations are replaced by thorough discussions about how specific faith communities are also rooted in a host of political, cultural, or regional dynamics that have little (or nothing) to do with organized religion.

While North American Christian colleges may not be concise replications of Plato's Academy, they are often contexts where there is a stated commitment to furthering education rooted in shared Jewish and Christian moral values. While assumptions are made that such places may be hostile to basic religious differences, it is also the case that Christian colleges and universities are able to provide a unique context for a constructive discussion of the ways that our cherished faiths impact social realities. Such institutions, whatever else can be said about them, offer students a specific religious point of reference, which also encourages a measure of a shared commitment to mature, civic responsibility. This is not the same as those decisively sectarian contexts that are more about glib propaganda than open intellectual exploration. In fact, academics in contexts of Christian and Jewish higher education can serve as ideal interlocutors for those within the Jewish and Christian communities who are interested in reanimating spirited discussions about civic society in the context of religious conviction.

One of the results of our decade together teaching Judaism among students has been the observation that few of these students take much time to understand Judaism (or, to be fair, most other faith traditions). Some have gained their scattered arsenal of information from those who assume the worst about the "other." True education, rooted in respectful listening, should be the process of encouraging individuals to be "converted" to understanding the faith of the "other." Students should be invited to appreciate what is already cherished within a given tradition. While some Christians may gain a historical view of contemporary Judaism from sources such as Sunday school curricula or from various Messianic Jewish movements, some Jews may also unhelpfully assume that to be a conservative Christian is only to be an anti-abortion, pro-Trump Republican, xenophobic, and myopic person who is intent on winning their heathen Jewish souls from hellfire. Such starting points explain why many interfaith initiatives stall without ever getting off the runway. Misunderstandings are deeply rooted in both directions and our conversations are often far too limited. When all that some know about post-biblical Judaism comes from watching "Fiddler on the Roof," or all that some people know about conservative Christians come from the pages of Sinclair Lewis, Erskine Caldwell, Theodore Dreiser, Margaret Atwood, or by watching a half-hour of Benny Hinn, Joel Osteen, or Pat Robertson on television, then we have a long way to go. Recent sexual and financial scandals—whether they involve the Reverend Jimmy Swaggert, Jim Baker, Jeffrey Epstein, Howard Weinstein, or Bernie Madoff—have reawakened old stereotypes. For some modern American cultural observers, the nation is awash with a "great swarm of sex-ridden Bible-thumping caricatures who continue to exert pervasive power."[370]

How can those working for interfaith respect, to use the phrase by Dr. King, "carve a monument to hope out of a mountain of despair"? We have worked in our interactions to promote a positive attitude toward multifaith engagement (including towards Messianic Judaism) as much as to teach a host of unrelated facts about modern Judaism. When individuals can learn to celebrate the dynamic religious engagements of their fellow Americans who are Jewish, we are taking a helpful first step.

While the Irish proverb may be true that the "road is better than the Inn," it is also hoped that what we have begun in our communities will slowly result in a change to thinking that is more accepting, open, and pluralistic in its direction. At times, we have been forced to laugh at the absurd and weep at the myopic; all the while, however, we have sought to bring a few notes of hopeful joy to the process of our efforts. Effective interfaith engagement must begin where people are and encourage them to progress as far as they find themselves comfortable without feeling too threatened, which may result in some becoming defensive or reacting by becoming insular. One student wrote: "As I have studied Judaism, I have come to realize just how Christian my thinking really was."[371] Another student at Messiah College, after spending hours talking with the brilliant Dr. Howard Kenig explained: "My eyes are just now being opened. I am learning anew about the relationships between Jews and Christians and my understanding of the details of Judaism is being greatly enhanced. I am excited to continue my reading and listening. I am learning to step back from my own biases so that I can truly learn the intimacy of the religion."[372]

There is an often-unappreciated anti-Jewish sentiment at the heart of some conservative Christians in their exclusivist and supersessionist views. This foundational argument will probably be vehemently denied by some of our readers. Others may suggest that we are calling on conservative Christians to deny their own valued traditions (including calls for evangelism and mission): We reject that argument. Anne Michaels, in a book entitled *Fugitive Pieces*, wrote that the first step in the Nazi goal of ultimately destroying the Jewish people was to systematically transform Jews into "non-real" and "wooden non-human" cartoon caricatures. This mindset laid the groundwork for their eventual systematic attacks. Before the Jews could be killed, they first had to be made "the other" without any question about their inherent inferiority. Over time, in the same way, the good Christian Protestants and Catholics of Germany came to believe that they had no other patriotic choice but to rid their beloved home-lands of the cancerous and immoral presence of the Jews.

Christian supersessionism is rooted in this same process of mar-ginalization, even when veiled in terms of a theological interpretation of God's revelation. Therefore, both of us are committed to doing all that we can to help conservative Christians come to see Jews as more than exotic and remotely inaccessible figures who participate in an arcane and mys-terious religious tradition. We hope to encourage Christians to appreciate Judaism through a fresh encounter with Jewish people within their own communities. If interfaith meetings are not launched by conservative Christians, a sense of emotional and relational "killing," which questions the viability of the Jewish experience, will continue. When individuals assert that those within another religion have no saving truth available to them within their own tradition, then the groundwork remains for continued marginalization at worst or paternalistic sympathies at best. Some Christians must first admit that they believe that Judaism has no intrinsic value for this process to begin. If Jews continue to wear bright "Star of David" labels within the imaginations of some Christians, then the advance of subtle anti-Jewish defamation will continue to bring social discord and misunderstanding. This is not the end of the story; through education, people's perspectives can slowly become more accepting and trusting of those who are not like them.

Another book might explore how North American Jewish students come to perceive conservative Christians. This book, however, has fo-cused on how modern forms of Judaism might best be taught in conser-vative Christian contexts. Fortunately, while many Christians are naïve about Judaism, they also often express a profound respect for Judaism and for the Jewish people. This is a tension that is helpful to remember. Many of our students have written that they have cried while attending services at the synagogue for a host of reasons, many of which, admit-tedly, are problematic. Another student wrote that she was moved to tears when listening to the liturgy. The tears of any person, however, should never be denigrated. We have written this book in the hopes of helping the very students we have been attempting to teach together for the last ten years.

Anglican Bishop Stephen Neill writes of his Jewish neighbors living among Christians by observing: "To the world, the Jews are a political or a social problem—or a menace as the interpretations may go. To the Christian they are also a theological problem."[373] While claiming that the

Jews have never really been properly introduced to the Messiah of God, Neill affirms that they will always be God's people and should never be disrespected. It is vital for Neill that Jesus was a Jew; Neill explains that his own life is given to the reverence of this same Jewish Jesus. In God's design, Jesus of Nazareth lived and died as a faithful Jew. Although Bishop Neill concludes that no one individual can "understand the purposes of God for His ancient people," it is also true that "we must rest in the absolute assurance that the faithfulness of Israel is precious in the sight of God and will in time receive its reward."[374]

After centuries of Jewish and Christian relations rooted in anachronistic criticisms of Judaism as a failed religion, a dramatic change is beginning to take place across the wide spectrum of multifaith relations, which has resulted in the promotion of increased mutual respect. Roman Catholic, Orthodox, and most large Protestant denominations have made public statements lamenting past Christian anti-Jewish actions and rhetoric. These statements have also expressed the conviction that Christians must acknowledge that God has made an everlasting and irrevocable covenant with the Jewish people. Many Christians who have come to the foot of Christ on the cross have felt a call to love all of those whom God loves. Such expressions of personal piety will go a long way in calming fears that some have that they are being targeted and disrespected. Conservative Christians are some of the last Christians to enter this larger ethos of empathetic interreligious change.

Our teaching together has been challenging as we have reworked a host of ideas for the sake of clearer interactions with our students. At the same time, we are aware that few Christians (and not all Jews) are even interested in interfaith education. What is needed is a vital interfaith engagement that, as Jacques Dupuis describes, is "constitutive and relational" instead of self-absorbed postures that are fundamentally alienating, arrogant, un-relational, and dismissive.[375] A dialogue of communities is what is needed before one can launch a dialogue of individuals. We are encouraged to see that many Jews and Christians recognize that we worship the same God and ascribe authority to the (somewhat) same book—the Bible. Many Jews and Christians also feel that it is a sacred obligation to heal the wounds between our two communities.

Adherents of both traditions accept that many interfaith differences cannot fully be resolved until God redeems the entire world as promised in the Bible. What is needed until that time is that, in the words of David Novak, Jews "respect Christian faithfulness to their revelation just as we expect Christians to respect our faithfulness to our revelation. Neither Jew nor Christian should be pressed into affirming the teaching of the other community."[376] Jews and Christians can look beyond our differences without engendering confusion or disloyalty. We have much to learn from each other—even about ourselves. While our differences are clear, there are ample opportunities for us to work together for constructive social justice initiatives that lessen the misery so rampant in the world. We face a host of common enemies with a shared desire to advance God's purposes. In humility, people of both traditions share the vision of the prophet Isaiah that as we go to the "mountain of the LORD," God will "teach us His ways and we will walk in His paths" (Isa 2:2–3).

Some possible solutions to promote constructive multifaith interactions are as simple as they are unlikely. One of the best ways to confront anti-Semitism among Christian educational contexts would be to have students take courses on Judaism from mainstream Jewish professors. The fact that Jews are forbidden to work in many contexts (such as the Baylor Religion Department) is rooted in the notion that such a logical and hospitable inclusion might in some way compromise the student learning experience. In some sense, these decisions reflect an archaic and restrictive narrative of exclusion.

Mutual discoveries continue to unfold between Jews and Christians as they have for centuries across a vast spectrum of distinct multifaith interactions. Unexplored pathways for engagement may offer fresh insights for present challenges. The religion of Jesus was a Judaism that no longer exists and the Christianity that emerged from the first Jewish Christians also no longer exists. Geza Vermes claimed that it was unjustified to "represent Jesus, the Jew, as the establisher of the Christian Church. For, if Christ meant and believed what he preached—namely that the eternal Kingdom of God was at hand, he simply could not have entertained the idea of founding and setting in motion an organized society intended to endure for ages to come."[377]

It is constructive to keep in mind the fundamental problems that emerge when individuals conflate theoretical renderings of the past to address the challenges of contemporary Jewish-Christian relations. Past rivalries should not define the future of Jewish and Christian relations. In our era, a more ordered civil society, based on mutual respect and civic tolerance, allows Jews and Christians to meet in new ways. The Gospels teach that God's Holy Spirit blows like a wind wherever God wills (John 3:8); this is now being expressed through fresh pathways for constructive multifaith engagement. Jews and Christians passionately committed to beneficial multifaith interactions should prepare for countless twists and turns in the long road ahead. What is needed is a passion to proceed in the face of conformist or reductionistic forces that are blindly committed to a "zero-sum" game in which the works of God are anything but mysterious and are revealed as clearly visible in a simple, black-and-white world.

T. S. Eliot once wrote that "what we call the beginning is often the end and to make an end is to make a beginning. The end is where we start from." In the Jewish tradition, there is a delightful story about how passion relates to knowledge. In one *shtetl* (village) in Poland, a group of fine Hasidic musicians gathered at an inn to lead a wedding celebration for two young Jewish people who were admired by everyone in the village. The music of these accomplished musicians was resonant, warm, inspiring, exultant, and delightful; soon everyone had risen to their feet and was dancing with enthusiasm and reckless abandon. At about the same time a deaf man passed by the scene at the inn and looked through the window and saw the crowd of his neighbors wildly jumping up and down. All the deaf man could say was, "Madmen! All madmen!" Only those who can hear the music of the soul can appreciate the melodies of the heart.

God's Word pronounces in exultant tones: "How good and precious it is when brothers and sisters dwell together in unity" (Ps 133). The prayer that all Jews and Christians share for each other is that in our shared dialogues of life and action each of us will go "from faith to faith" (Rom 1:17) and "strength to strength" until each of us finally "appears before the God of Zion" (Ps 84:7–8).

Endnotes

1   Student Response, L (F). All student paper responses are from Messiah College (and designated) or Baylor University (undesignated). At Baylor, students are taking a course entitled REL3345—World Religions. Names are withheld in recognition that these quotations from classroom assignments might have been written differently had students known that their opinions might be made public. Invented initials and genders of the respondents is provided in order to give the reader a sense of the diversity of students represented in these responses.

2   An ideal resource for examining the different ways that various Christian communities have formally responded to Judaism can be found in a compilation by Helga Croner entitled, *Stepping Stones to Further Jewish-Christian Relations: An Unabridged Collection of Christian Documents*. The book includes statements made in Europe and North America by Catholic and Protestant religious organizations. In an interesting introduction to the book, Edward A. Synan quotes Karl Barth as saying, "The Ecumenical movement is driven by the Spirit of the Lord. But do not forget, there is only one important question: Our relationship with Israel," cited on page xii.

3   Walter, "Contemporary Christians and Israel's Ancient Scriptures," 116.

4   According to the *World Christian Encyclopedia* there are at least 34,000 different Protestant denominations; it is daunting to generalize when speaking of such a wide range of experiences. We recognize that our observations are rooted in our own specific context.

5   Wilson, "An Evangelical Perspective on Judaism," 3. Marc Tannenbaum was the National Interreligious Affairs Director of the American Jewish Committee and summarized his views of Messianic Judaism by saying: "Judaism is incompatible with any belief in the divinity of a human being."

6   Class discussion, Baylor University, REL3345 class, October 11, 2011.

7   Student Response, J (M), 2001—Messiah College. Along with Dr. Howard Kenig I taught a semester-long course at Messiah College (for six years before coming to Baylor University) entitled "An Introduction to Judaism." Although the class was mostly co-taught by Dr. Kenig, the chair at the time of the Jewish Community Relations Council, visitors to the class also included Rabbi Chaim Schertz of Kesher Israel Congregation, Rabbi Carl Choper of the Reconstructionist movement, Rabbi Daniel Weiner, and Holocaust survivor Kurt Moses. It was at Messiah College that Dr. Kenig and I began to collect response papers. I found that many of the responses that students had at Messiah paralleled the same ideas that I have heard about Judaism since coming to Baylor University. At the same time, I appreciate that there are many

differences between the two contexts, not the least of which is that a student on the East Coast, and only two hours away from Philadelphia, will probably have had much more interaction with larger Jewish communities. It should also be noted that a yearly conference of Messianic Christian groups was held on the Messiah College campus throughout the years that I was teaching the course. It is not difficult to imagine how such a conference raised tensions between the college and the local Jewish community in Harrisburg. President Rodney Sawatsky of Messiah College worked to improve these relations while I was teaching at the College: One of Dr. Sawatsky's initiatives were to invite noted Holocaust scholar Jack Fischell from Millersville University to teach a course on the *Shoah* at Messiah College, which he began to teach in 2003. Dr. Sawatsky also held several meetings with Rabbis Carl Choper and Chaim Schertz along with Dr. Howard Kenig to address these points of tension. President Kim Phipps carried on this legacy after the untimely death of Dr. Sawatsky in 2005. Dr. Robin Collins and other scholars at Messiah have worked with Dr. Kenig with energy to assist students in helping them to learn more about the Jewish tradition from a Jewish perspective. Any time a student response from my six years of teaching at Messiah College is used; such citations will be followed by the notation—"Messiah College."

8   Student Response, A (F).

9   White, "Israel within Jewish-Christian Relations," 126.

10   Student Response, G (M).

11   Student Response, C (F).

12   Student Response, S (F).

13   Student Response, T (F).

14   Student Response, W (F).

15   Student Response, K (F).

16   Student Response, H (F).

17   Abrams, *Faith or Fear?* 87.

18   Student Response, F (F), Messiah College.

19   Student Response, B (M).

20   Catalano and Sandmel, "Speaking Theologically Together," 1.

21   Pettit, "Covenants Old and New," 27.

22   Levenson, "Judaism, Christianity, and Islam in their Contemporary Encounters," 581.

23   Michael Lotker claims that between a third and a half of all marriages involving a Jewish person is an interfaith marriage. He notes that this rate is some ten times higher than it was in 1960. It is an especially troubling trend because many of the children of such marriages do not openly identify themselves as being Jewish. Lotker, *A Christian's Guide to Judaism*, 93.

24   Heinz, "Contempt for the Jews and Disregard for the Old Testament," 441.

25   I (van Gorder) mention Yunnan specifically because while I lived in China (1989–96), I was told by my Chinese colleagues at the Yunnan University about a group of Jews who had been called the "Blue Mohammedans" in Kunming. These were Jews whom others assumed were Muslims. The Jews of Kunming, in the nineteenth century, deliberately told their neighbors that they were Seventh Day Adventist Christians because the practices of these Christians were known and perhaps the thought was that it would be easier to live with their neighbors if they were seen to be Christians. An extensive study of the story of Judaism in China is Michael Pollak's, *Mandarins, Jews, and Missionaries*.

26   Rousmaniere, *A Bridge to Dialogue*, 81.

27   Raphael, *Profiles of American Judaism*, 106.

28   Student Response, R (M).

29   Neusner and Chilton. *Jewish-Christian Debates*, 55.

30   Student Response, AA (M).

31   Student Response, CC (F).

32   Student Response, DD (M).

33   Student Response, CM (M) Messiah College.

34   Student Response, M (F).

35   The movement was partially supported by Richard Rubenstein but was not seen as primarily a "Jewish problem." One of the first proponents, Gabriel Vahanian, wrote an article in 1961 entitled *The Death of God*. Other leading Christian exponents were Thomas J. J. Alitzer, William Hamilton, and Paul van Buren. Alitzer wrote: "It is a radical Christian proclamation of the death of God which liberates the Christian from every alien and lifeless image of Christ. . . . When the Christian bets that God is dead, he is betting upon the real and actual presence of the fully incarnate Christ. Thus, the Christian wager upon the death of God is a wager upon the presence of the living Christ, a bet that Christ is now at least potentially present in a new and total form. Cited in Leffler and Jones, *The Structure of Religion*, 57.

36   Leffler and Jones, *The Structure of Religion*, 32.

37 DeLange, *An Introduction to Judaism*, 81.

38 Leffler and Jones, *The Structure of Religion*, 32.

39 Leffler and Jones, *The Structure of Religion*, 36.

40 Ellenson, "A Jewish View of the Christian God," 75–76.

41 Sandmel, *Judaism and Christian Beginnings*, 168.

42 Neusner and Chilton, *Jewish-Christian Debates*, 54.

43 Maimonides, quoted in Lazowski, *Understanding Your Neighbor's Faith*, 61.

44 Dorff and Newman, *Contemporary Jewish Theology*, 28.

45 Rosenzweig, quoted in Dorff and Newman, *Contemporary Jewish Theology*, 53.

46 Student Response, CB (M) Messiah College.

47 Student Response, JG (M).

48 Eckstein, *What Christians Should Know about Jews and Judaism*, 64.

49 Eckstein, *What Christians Should Know about Jews and Judaism*, 65.

50 Lotker, *A Christian's Guide to Judaism*, 41.

51 Knight, *Jews and Christians*, 132.

52 Neusner, "Judaic Social Teaching in Christian and Pagan Context," 31.

53 Knight, *Jews and Christians*, 134.

54 Lotker, *A Christian's Guide to Judaism*, 16.

55 Pawlikowski, "The Challenge of *Tikkun Olam* for Jews and Christians," 233.

56 Student Response, AA (F).

57 Buber, *I and Thou*, 127.

58 Leffler and Jones, *The Structure of Religion*, 4.

59 Student Response, MM (F).

60 Student Response, NN (M), Messiah College.

61   Student Response, JJ (F).

62   Levine and Brettler, *Jewish Annotated New Testament*, 185–86.

63   Williams, "The Universal Significance of Christ," 141.

64   Yoder, Cartwright, and Ochs, *The Jewish-Christian Schism Revisited*, 245.

65   Student Response, OO (M), Messiah College.

66   Student Response, RR (M).

67   Student Response, OO (F).

68   Student Response, FF (F), Messiah College.

69   Cited in Tannenbaum, Wilson, and Rudin, *Evangelicals and Jews in Conversation on Scripture, Theology, and History*, 10.

70   Dorff and Newman, *Contemporary Jewish Theology*, 223.

71   Levine and Brettler, *Jewish Annotated New Testament*, 276.

72   H. Taylor, *World Hope in the Middle East*, 25.

73   Student Response, TT (F), Messiah College.

74   Student Response, EE (M), Messiah College.

75   Student Response, KK (F), Messiah College.

76   Cook, "The New Testament," 55.

77   Levine, *The Misunderstood Jew*, 20.

78   Levine, *The Misunderstood Jew*, 51.

79   Student Response, AB (F).

80   Student Response, LH (F).

81   Levine, *The Misunderstood Jew*, 80.

82   Leaman, *Faith Roots*, 21.

83   Student Response, JC (M).

84   Bratton, *The Crime of Christendom*, 51.

85   Levine, *The Misunderstood Jew*, 85–86.

86   Levine, *The Misunderstood Jew*, 69.

87   Levine and Brettler, *Jewish Annotated New Testament*, 338.

88   Cragg, *To Meet and Greet*, 97.

89   Ernst, *Discovering our Jewish Roots*, 9.

90   Beker, *The Chosen*, 41.

91   Beker, *The Chosen*, 39.

92   The relationship between Judaism and Islam is outside the focus of this book. Important Qur'anic references that speak about Judaism include Qur'an 2:13, 47–50, 122; 3:63–71; 4:46; 5:12, 20–21; 7:167; 10:93; 14:6; 17:104. Noted Jewish-perspective scholarship on Jewish-Muslim relations include Bat Ye'or's *Islam and Dhimmitude-Where Civilizations Collide* (2002); Youssef Bogdarsky's *Islamic Anti-Semitism as a Political Instrument* (1999); Mark R. Cohen's *Under Crescent and Cross—The Jews of the Middle Ages* (1994); Norman A. Stillman's *The Jews of Arab Lands: A History and Sourcebook* (1979); Bernard Lewis's *The Jews of Islam* (1987); Abraham Geiger's *Judaism and Islam* (1970); and *Judaism and Islam—Biblical and Talmudic Background of the Koran and It's Commentaries* (1957) to name just a few (written in English).

93   Scholem, *The Messianic Idea in Judaism*, 1.

94   Scholem, *The Messianic Idea in Judaism*, 1.

95   Student Response, MR (F).

96   Student Response, AM (F).

97   Student Response, MC (M).

98   Student Response, CW (F), Messiah College.

99   Schoen, *What I Wish My Christian Friends Knew about Judaism*, 11.

100   Midrash Lamentations Rabah 1:57, cited in Lazowski, *Understanding Your Neighbor's Faith*, 84.

101   Levine, *The Misunderstood Jew*, 56.

102   Levine, *The Misunderstood Jew*, 30.

103   Bonhoeffer, Dietrich. *The Cost of Discipleship.* Translated by Reginald H. Fuller. New York: Touchstone, 1996.

104   Student Response, CB (M), Messiah College.

105   Radosh, *Rapture Ready,* 85

106   Radosh, *Rapture Ready,* 85.

107   Saperstein, "Jews Facing Christians," 25.

108   Kogan, *Opening the Covenant,* 243.

109   Student Response, RRR (F), Messiah College

110   Kogan, *Opening the Covenant,* 37.

111   Kogan, *Opening the Covenant,* 37.

112   Neusner and Chilton, *Jewish-Christian Debates,* 217,

113   Student Response, CC (M).

114   Lotker, *A Christian's Guide to Judaism,* 43.

115   Student Response, LB (F).

116   Lazowski, *Understanding Your Neighbor's Faith,* 93.

117   Lazowski, *Understanding Your Neighbor's Faith,* 91.

118   Lazowski, *Understanding Your Neighbor's Faith,* 93.

119   Student Response, DV (M).

120   Student Response, CC (M).

121   Student Response, KG (F).

122   Student Response, WWW (M).

123   Student Response, JC (M).

124   Student Response, LB (F).

125   Student Response, BK (M).

126   Student Response, NC (F).

127 Student Response, AW (F).

128 Student Response, CL (M).

129 Student Response, GM (M).

130 Student Response, TD (M).

131 Student Response, EVH (M).

132 Student Response, CF (F).

133 Student Response, LB (F).

134 Radosh, *Rapture Ready*, 27.

135 Levenson, "Judaism, Christianity, and Islam in their Contemporary Encounters," 591.

136 Neusner and Chilton, *Jewish-Christian Debates*, 92.

137 Student Response, EK (F).

138 Christopher M. Leighton and Daniel Lehman, "Jewish Christian Relations in Historical Perspective" in Sandmel, Catalano, and Leighton, eds., *Irreconcilable Differences?* 24.

139 Kogan, *Opening the Covenant*, 193.

140 Kogan, *Opening the Covenant*, 193.

141 Student Response, VM (F) Messiah College.

142 Tannenbaum, Wilson, and Rubin, *Evangelicals and Jews in Conversation on Scripture, Theology, and History*, 9.

143 Levenson, "Judaism, Christianity, and Islam in their Contemporary Encounters," 593.

144 Pessah, Meyer, and Leighton, "How Do Jews and Christians Read the Bible," 54.

145 Kierk cited in Kogan, *Opening the Covenant*, 187.

146 Neusner and Chilton, *Jewish-Christian Debates*, 98.

147 Heschel, *God in Search of Man*, 245.

148   Student Response, TTT (M), Messiah College.

149   Student Response, PPP (F).

150   Student Response, TTT (M), Messiah College.

151   Student Response, RRR (F), Messiah College.

152   Student Response, JC (F), Messiah College.

153   Student Response, KF (F), Messiah College.

154   Student Response, CW (F) Messiah College.

155   Student Response, QQQ (M), Messiah College.

156   Student Response, JC (F), Messiah College.

157   Student Response, MC (M).

158   Eckstein, *What Christians Should Know about Jews and Judaism*, 12.

159   Buber, *The Eclipse of God*, 126.

160   Student Response, MS (M) Messiah College.

161   Lazowski, *Understanding Your Neighbor's Faith*, 38.

162   Olitzky and Judson, *Jewish Holidays*, 127.

163   Buber, *Moses: The Revelation and the Covenant*, 82.

164   Ben Shea, *Jacob the Baker*, 86.

165   Student Response, NNN (M), Messiah College.

166   P. Taylor, "A Jewish Journey through Nicaragua," 70.

167   Olitzky, *Introducing My Faith and My Community*, 59.

168   Student Response, MMM (M).

169   Student Response, YY (F), Messiah College.

170   Levenson, "Judaism, Christianity, and Islam in their Contemporary Encounters," 606. The author is citing an article written by Wolfhart Pannenberg and published in *Pro Ecclesia* 11.1 (2002).

171 Hocken, *The Challenges of the Pentecostal, Charismatic, and Messianic Jewish Movements*, 103. Hocken also writes that Messianic Jews reject the idea that they are a subset of Evangelicalism because most Evangelicals do not have a high regard for ritual and feel that tradition is synonymous with ritualistic formalism. Messianic congregations, according to Hocken, tend to become more liturgical over time to assert their fundamental Jewishness.

172 Hocken, *The Challenges of the Pentecostal, Charismatic, and Messianic Jewish Movements*, 103.

173 Lazowski, *Understanding Your Neighbor's Faith*, 98.

174 Leffler and Jones, *The Structure of Religion*, 17.

175 Schiffman, *Generation J*, 43.

176 Student Response, CW (F), Messiah College.

177 Rausch, *Messianic Judaism*, 26.

178 Novak, *Talking with Christians*, 218.

179 Tonoyan, "Messianic Judaism in Ukraine," 14.

180 Bernis, *A Rabbi Looks at Jesus of Nazareth*, 217. Bernis travelled throughout the Ukraine (after the demise of the Soviet Union in the mid-1990s) holding "Festivals of Jewish Music and Dance" that saw tens of thousands of Ukrainians listening to what they thought was Jewish music followed by dancing programs which were followed by Christian evangelistic messages. More than 40,000 people attended the 1995 and 1997 programs in Donetsk, Kiev, and Odessa sponsored by Bernis's organization; "Shema Israel." This organization was instrumental in launching the Messianic Jewish Bible Institute (MJBI) in Odessa, Ukraine in 1995 where students are trained to do evangelism among Russia's Jewish communities. Bernis also promotes his message on television and radio through an organization called "Jewish Voice Ministries International."

181 This issue is discussed at length in several books including a study written by Rabbi Carol Harris-Shapiro called *Messianic Judaism*. Boston: Beacon, 1999. Messianic Jewish perspectives on their own movement have also been written—including Daniel Juster and Peter Hoken's *The Messianic Jewish Movement: An Introduction*. One of the key arguments of this book is that Hebrew Christian missionary efforts should not be synonymous with the Messianic Jewish movement.

182 See Feldman, "How to Reply When the Doorbell Rings."

183 Eckstein, *What Christians Should Know about Jews and Judaism*, 294.

184 While this may seem to conflict with earlier statements about Moses Maimonides (and others) acknowledging that Christians also consider themselves to be

monotheists, this does not mean that Maimonides (or any other Jewish theologian) could accept the Christian theological formulation of the Trinitarian nature of God revealed in Jesus Christ.

185 Eckstein, *What Christians Should Know about Jews and Judaism*, 295.

186 Lazowski, *Understanding Your Neighbor's Faith*, 11.

187 Lotker, *A Christian's Guide to Judaism*, 35.

188 Jerry and Shirley Beresford had originally petitioned for Israeli citizenship as Jews under the "Law of Return" (*hoq ha-shevut*), which guarantees immediate Jewish citizenship to every Jew. This law specifically states that people who also relate to other religious traditions will not be eligible for consideration under these terms. In 1962, a similar petition was filed by Oscar Rufeisen, who was raised Jewish but who had become a Roman Catholic monk and who had assumed the name "Brother Daniel."

189 See Wasserman, *Messianic Jewish Congregations*. One source (Levi Ahim) cited by Jeffrey S. Wasserman claims that there are as many as 20,000 Messianic Jews living in Israel (56) although this number cannot be supported by any other research (that we are familiar with)and seems quite high. Wasserman claims that there are at least 6,000 Messianic Jews in Israel (145). Most of these converts, according to Wasserman, came from North American mission efforts and are often converts who had originally come from the nations of the former Soviet Union. Wasserman dedicates an entire chapter of his book to the question of Messianic Jews in modern Israel (113–51).

190 Feher, *Passing over Easter*, 137.

191 Amy-Jill Levine, personal email correspondence to the authors, received April 8, 2019.

192 Feher, *Passing over Easter*, 32.

193 ABC 20/20 with Barbara Walters first aired May 1999.

194 Student Response, VV (M).

195 Student Response, HHH (F).

196 Student Response, LLL (F).

197 Abrams, *Faith or Fear?* 78.

198 Rosen and Rosen, *Share the New Life with a Jew*, 79. It is important to remember that the "Jews for Jesus" group is one specific West Coast-based evangelistic mission at the Hebrew Christian end of the spectrum of totally assimilated Jews. David Rausch believes: "Moishe Rosen and *Jews for Jesus* thrive on confrontation with Jews, and they often publicize the confrontation they receive because it shows their

Christian backers that they are accomplishing something and, in turn, generates Christian funding of their organization (Rausch, *Messianic Judaism*, 89)." The group is a major point of discussion among the various and ever-changing Messianic Jewish groups. Each group has their own distinct history with their own distinct assertions on such questions as those that relate to evangelism. A long-standing dynamic among these various groups is that some groups are "too Jewish" while other groups are seen as "not Jewish enough."

199   Rosen and Rosen, *Share the New Life with a Jew*, 69.

200   Rosen and Rosen, *Share the New Life with a Jew*, 69.

201   Rosen and Rosen, *Share the New Life with a Jew*, 18.

202   Rosen and Rosen, *Share the New Life with a Jew*, 9.

203   Student Response, UU (M).

204   Student Response, GGG (F).

205   Student Response, HHH (F).

206   In an article by Shaye J. D. Cohen "Did Ancient Jews Missionize" (*Bible Review*, August 2003) this argument is contested. Cohen says that Judaism has never been a missionary religion with the singular exception of the second-century B.C.E. Maccabean period. Cohen notes that one of the few references to Jewish missionaries is Matthew 23:15, which were written by those within the new Christian community who were committed to promoting the idea of mission.

207   Student Response, EEE (M), Messiah College.

208   Student Response, DDD (F).

209   Student Response, CCC (F).

210   Abrams, *Faith or Fear?* 78. The Willowbank Declaration was drafted in 1989.

211   Rausch, *Messianic Judaism*, 31. The statement comes from Article II of the Constitution of the Hebrew Christian movement which was organized in 1915. It is important to understand contemporary movements, such as groups like the Jews for Jesus, considering these historical organizations and the development of the two major American Hebrew Christian organizations. Later groups have sometimes dismissed these earlier efforts as not actually being Jewish but more rooted within the Christian tradition.

212   Abrams, *Faith or Fear?* 96.

213   Abrams, *Faith or Fear?* 80.

214   Feher, *Passing over Easter*, 37.

215   Abrams, *Faith or Fear?* 84.

216   Abrams, *Faith or Fear?* 58.

217   Cunningham, "Covenant and Conversion," 152.

218   Abrams, *Faith or Fear?* 61.

219   Rosen and Rosen, *Share the New Life with a Jew*, 8.

220   Jodock, "Christians and Jews in the Context of World Religions," 140.

221   Locke, "On Christian Mission to the Jews," 206.

222   Tannenbaum, Wilson, and Rudin, *Evangelicals and Jews in Conversation on Scripture, Theology, and History*, 300.

223   Tannenbaum, Wilson, and Rudin, *Evangelicals and Jews in Conversation on Scripture, Theology, and History*, 306.

224   Harvey, *Mapping Messianic Jewish Theology*, 266.

225   Student Response, CCC (F).

226   Student Response, BBB (F).

227   Student Response, AAA (M), Messiah College.

228   Arendt, *Anti-Semitism: The Origins of Totalitarianism* (Part I), 7.

229   Eckstein, *What Christians Should Know about Jews and Judaism*, 270.

230   During the Crusades or the Spanish Inquisition, the life of a Jew could be spared if they converted to Christianity. This was also true during Russian pogroms of the nineteenth and early twentieth centuries.

231   Lotker, *A Christian's Guide to Judaism*, 50.

232   The earliest (and most reliable) manuscripts of the Christian church, as well as other ancient witnesses, do not include John 7:53—8:11. Some early manuscripts do have a version of this story, but it is placed after Luke 21:38. It is also entirely possible that the story may indeed be authentic.

233   Reinhartz, *Cast out of the Covenant*, xv.

234 Levine, *The Social and Ethnic Dimensions of Matthean Salvation History*, 268.

235 Bratton, *The Crime of Christendom*, 27.

236 S. Cohen, "Judaism and Jewishness," 513.

237 Reinhartz, *Cast out of the Covenant*, 68.

238 Reinhartz, *Cast out of the Covenant*, 77–78.

239 Beker, *The Chosen*, 43.

240 Carter and Levine, *The New Testament: Methods and Meanings*, 13.

241 Nanos, "Paul and Judaism," 552.

242 Forward, "Jewish-Christian Relations in the Interfaith Encounter," 229.

243 Forward, "Jewish-Christian Relations in the Interfaith Encounter," 229.

244 Saperstein, *Moments of Crisis in Jewish-Christian Relations*, 7.

245 Bratton, *The Crime of Christendom*, 80–81.

246 Eckstein, *What Christians Should Know about Jews and Judaism*, 277.

247 Bratton, *The Crime of Christendom*, 81.

248 Bratton, *The Crime of Christendom*, 83.

249 Bratton, *The Crime of Christendom*, 83.

250 Bratton, *The Crime of Christendom*, 84.

251 Bratton, *The Crime of Christendom*, 85. All the above citations are from St. Chrysostom's *Eight Homilies against the Jews*.

252 Eckstein, *What Christians Should Know about Jews and Judaism*, 277.

253 Bratton, *The Crime of Christendom*, 86.

254 Saperstein, *Moments of Crisis in Jewish-Christian Relations*, 9–10.

255 Pettit and Townsend, "In Every Generation," 97.

256 Lipton, *Images of Intolerance*.

257 Lipton, *Images of Intolerance*, 119.

258   Lipton, *Images of Intolerance*, 92.

259   Lipton, *Images of Intolerance*, 121.

260   Lipton, *Images of Intolerance*, 107.

261   Children under the age of seven were forcibly baptized as Christians and raised in Christian homes. There were a host of massacres, including 3,000 Jews killed in Prague. The entire Jewish community of Berlitz was burned alive in 1243.

262   Lipton, *Images of Intolerance*, 89.

263   Lipton, *Images of Intolerance*, 84–85.

264   Reuchlin, *Recommendation Whether to Confiscate, Destroy and Burn All Jewish Books*, 1.

265   Beker, *The Chosen*, 44.

266   Bratton, *The Crime of Christendom*, 175.

267   Bratton, *The Crime of Christendom*, 176.

268   Bratton, *The Crime of Christendom*, 175.

269   Student Response, LL (M), Messiah College.

270   Student Response, FF (M), Messiah College.

271   Student Response, PP (M), Messiah College.

272   Student Response, LL (M), Messiah College.

273   Student Response, YY (F), Messiah College.

274   Sherman, "The Road to Reconciliation," 243.

275   Student Response, VV (M).

276   Ford also distributed this article through his newspaper (*Dearborn Independent*). In total, Ford distributed tens of millions of copies of this pamphlet. The *Protocols of the Elders of Zion* was proven a forgery by the *London Times* as early as 1921. The *Protocols* was used by Hitler and republished in the 1960s by President Gamal Abdel Nasser of Egypt. King Faisal of Saudi Arabia also published and distributed copies of this tract in the 1970s.

277   Rousmaniere, *A Bridge to Dialogue*, 89.

278   Bratton, *The Crime of Christendom*, 209.

279   Bratton, *The Crime of Christendom*, 209.

280   Student Response, UU (M).

281   Student Response, GG (M).

282   See the article written by Giles Fraser, "Crucified by Empire," in *The Guardian* newspaper, February 7, 2004.

283   Beker, *The Chosen*, 45.

284   Radosh, *Rapture Ready*, 46. Smith in one fundraising letter (1970) explained "the enemies of Christ are in possession of the Holy Land" (Radosh, *Rapture Ready*, 46), and called the media "a Jew-controlled propaganda machine" (Radosh *Rapture Ready*, 45) and he referred to FDR as "Franklin D. Jewsevelt" (45). Radosh cites other similar quotes in his book.

285   Sartre, *Anti-Semite and Jew*, 153.

286   Halivini, *Breaking the Tablets: Jewish Theology after the Shoah*, 107.

287   Student Response, ZZ (F), Messiah College.

288   Student Response, UU (M).

289   Rabbi Jeffrey Wohlberg was the Rabbi of Temple Beth El when he led a commemorative service on the steps of the Capitol Building of the State of Pennsylvania on March 25, 1980. At that service the Messiah College Choir participated by singing "The Butterfly Song."

290   Student Response, CO (M).

291   Student Response, XX (F).

292   Student Response, UU (M).

293   www.huffingtonpost.com/.../mccain-backer-hagee-said-n-10298html.

294   Student Response, BE (F), Messiah College.

295   Wiesel, *Messengers of God*, 221.

296   Novak, *Talking with Christians*, 150.

297   Eckstein, *What Christians Should Know about Jews and Judaism*, 200.

298   Beker, *The Chosen*, 109.

299   Despite the wide currency of this account, it is probably the case that King Christian X did not actually wear a yellow star. In fact, the Jews of Denmark were not even required to wear the star because the Nazi order, toward that end ,was rescinded because of the resistance to the idea raised by King Christian X and others.

300   Andre Trocme was born on April 7, 1901 and died on June 5, 1971. Along with his wife Magda, his ministry assistant, Édouard Theiry, and the public-school Principal Roger Darsiac, Trocme was able to save at least 5,000 Jews from certain death. Trocme was a Huguenot pastor and ordained in the French Reformed Church. This church, along with the Quakers, the Salvation Army, and the American Congregation of Paris were leaders in the church-based resistance to Nazi anti-Semitism during the Vichy era.

301   Block and Drucker, *Rescuers*, 279.

302   Bonhoeffer, *No Rusty Swords*, 226.

303   Student Response, ZZ (F), Messiah College.

304   Sandmel, Catalano, and Leighton, *Irreconcilable Differences?* 27.

305   Student Response, UU (M).

306   Dawidowicz, *The War against the Jews*, 33.

307   Levenson, "Judaism, Christianity, and Islam in their Contemporary Encounters," 585.

308   Rabbi David G. Dalin, in his book, *The Myth of Hitler's Pope: How Pope Pius XII Rescued Jews from Nazis*, argues that while the Pope publicly seemed to support fascism he was privately working for their protection.

309   Fleischner, "The *Shoah* and Jewish Christian Relations," 8.

310   Cornwell, *Hitler's Pope*, 297

311   Cornwell, *Hitler's Pope*, 297.

312   Rousmaniere, *A Bridge to Dialogue*, 119.

313   Bergen, *Twisted Cross*, 4.

314   Rousmaniere, *A Bridge to Dialogue*, 118.

315   Beker, *The Chosen*, 109.

316 Student Response, ZZ (F), Messiah College.

317 Student Response, YY (F), Messiah College.

318 Eckstein, *What Christians Should Know about Jews and Judaism*, 279.

319 Wiesel, *A Jew Today*, 13.

320 Ellis, "Jews, Christians, and Liberation Theology: A Response," 149.

321 Tannenbaum, Wilson, and Rudin, *Evangelicals and Jews in Conversation on Scripture, Theology, and History*, 231.

322 Smith, "The Effects of the Holocaust on Jewish-Christian Relations," 139.

323 Student Response, RR (F).

324 Radosh, *Rapture Ready*, 100.

325 Lotker, *A Christian's Guide to Judaism*, 60.

326 Buber, *On Zion*, 107.

327 Saperstein, *Moments of Crisis in Jewish-Christian Relations*, 57.

328 Beker, *The Chosen*, 144–45.

329 Wilkinson, *God's Plan for the Jew*, 88.

330 Simon, *Jerry Falwell and the Jews*, 9, 21–22.

331 Bray, *Israel in Bible Prophecy*, 75.

332 Walvoord, *Armageddon, Oil, and the Middle East Crisis*, 197.

333 Hagee, *Day of Deception*, 99.

334 Hagee, *Day of Deception*, 99.

335 Abrams, *Faith or Fear?* 63.

336 Tannenbaum, Wilson, and Rudin, *Evangelicals and Jews in Conversation on Scripture, Theology, and History*, 22.

337 Levenson, "Judaism, Christianity, and Islam in their Contemporary Encounters," 599.

338   McGarry, "The Land of Israel in the Cauldron of the Middle East," 220.

339   The term "bridge-link" comes from Leffler and Jones; first introduced in their book on page 19.

340   Lotker, *A Christian's Guide to Judaism*, 13.

341   Leffler and Jones, *The Structure of Religion*, 33.

342   Some might argue that the Latin language serves this purpose, but Latin existed before the rise of the church. The fact that mass can be said around the world in any language is proof that the Catholic Church does not consider Latin essential to the ideal functioning of a given ritual. While most Orthodox traditions have remained with their ceremonies in their native languages, this is seen more as a link to one's heritage of faith as much as it is to the affirmation of a distinctly religious identity. This becomes enhanced by the fact that any Orthodox or Catholic Christian knows that the language of the original church and of Jesus was not Latin or Greek.

343   Leffler and Jones, *The Structure of Religion*, 34.

344   A. Cohen and Susser, "Reform Judaism in Israel," 29.

345   Eckstein, *What Christians Should Know about Jews and Judaism*, 283.

346   Student Response, ZZ (F), Messiah College.

347   Eck, *Encountering God*, 167.

348   Levenson, "Judaism, Christianity, and Islam in their Contemporary Encounters," 581.

349   Levin, "Divine Love in the World's Religious Traditions," 19.

350   Neusner, "Divine Love in Classical Judaism," 81.

351   A valuable internet resource for the promotion of improved interfaith education between Jews and Christians is found at http://www.jcrelations.net/en/indExodphp.

352   Saperstein, *Moments of Crisis in Jewish-Christian Relations*, 62.

353   Saperstein, *Moments of Crisis in Jewish-Christian Relations*, 62.

354   Talmage, *Disputation and Dialogue*, 335.

355   Barth, *Church Dogmatics*, 287.

356   Eckstein, *What Christians Should Know about Jews and Judaism*, 293.

357   Pope John Paul II, Address at Jerusalem Interreligious Meeting, March 23, 2000, cited in Boys, *Seeing Judaism Anew*, 161.

358   Boys, "The Enduring Covenant," 23.

359   Kogan, *Opening the Covenant*, 181.

360   Eric Greenberg, *Nostra Aetete* on the website www.usccb.org/beliefs-and-teachings/how-we-teach/cathecesis/cathetical-sunday/human-dignity/nostra-aetete/greenberg.

361   The document, *Dabru Emet* ("Speaking the Truth") was written, affirmed, and signed by hundreds of scholars. Many of the ideas in the statement later became part of a supporting volume to the conference entitled *Christianity in Jewish Terms* (2000). The four primary authors were Tivka Frymer-Kensky, David Novak, Peter Ochs, and Michael Signer. It consisted of eight statements summarized in one sentence followed by an explanatory paragraph. These statements were 1. Jews and Christians worship the same God, 2. Jews and Christians seek authority from the same book—the Bible, 3. Christians can respect the claim of the Jewish people upon the land of Israel, 4. Jews and Christians accept the moral principles of Torah, 5. Nazism was not a Christian phenomenon, 6. The humanly irreconcilable difference between Jews and Christians will not be settled until God redeems the entire world as promised in Scripture, 7. A new relationship between Jews and Christians will not weaken Jewish practice, 8. Jews and Christians must work together for justice and peace. On this last point Levenson sarcastically observed that it was wonderful that the authors had been so bold to confront those many critics who are seeking to discourage Jews and Christians for working together for social justice.

362   Levenson, "Judaism, Christianity, and Islam in their Contemporary Encounters," 591.

363   Wilken, *John Chrysostom and the Jews*, 148.

364   Greenburg "Judaism and Christianity," 24.

365   Cragg, *To Meet and Greet*, 3.

366   Student Response, JJ (F), Messiah College.

367   Student Response, HH (F).

368   Abrams, *Faith or Fear?* 63.

369   Abrams, *Faith or Fear?* 37.

370   Abrams, *Faith or Fear?* 65.

371   Student Response, BB (F) Messiah College.

372   Student Response, SS (F), Messiah College.

373   Neill, *The Christian Faith and Other Faiths*, 21.

374   Neill, *The Christian Faith and Other Faiths*, 39.

375   Phan, "Jesus as the Universal Savior," 134.

376   Frymer-Kensky et al., *Christianity in Jewish Terms*, xvii.

377   Vermes, *The Religion of Jesus the Jew*, 214–15.

Timeline of Events in Jewish History

C.1290 (or 1225) B.C.E.—Suggested dates for exodus of Israelites from Egypt

C.1000 B.C.E.—Commonly held dates for the supposed kingdoms of David and Solomon

C. 950 B.C.E.—First Temple built

C. 822 B.C.E.—Israel splits into two kingdoms, Northern and Southern

722 B.C.E.—Sargon of Assyria conquers Kingdom of Israel

586 B.C.E.—Destruction of the First Temple

539 B.C.E.—Edict of Cyrus

517 B.C.E.—Completion of the Second Temple

167 B.C.E.—Revolt of the Maccabees (Hasmoneans) against Seleucid Rule

164 B.C.E.—Hasmoneans capture Jerusalem; Hasmoneans dynasty

40–4 B.C.E.—Reign of Herod the Great, King of Judea

66–74 C.E.—Great revolt; Sack of Jerusalem by Romans (70 C.E.)

77–78—Flavius Josephus writes *Jewish War*

115–17—Diaspora revolt

132–35—Bar Kochba revolt

C. 220—Mishnah completed

C. 415—Jerusalem Talmud compiled

589—Babylonian Talmud completed

1045–1105—Rashi

1096—Jews massacred by Crusaders in the Rhineland

1138–1204—Maimonides

C. 1275—*Zohar* compiled

1488—First printed Hebrew Bible

1492—Jews expelled from Spain

1534–72—Isaac Luria

1654—First Jews Arrive in New Amsterdam

1626–76—Shabbetai Zvi

1698–1760—Baal Shem Tov, founder of Hasidism

1729–86—Moses Mendelssohn

1730—First public synagogue in New York

1817—First Reform Congregation in Hamburg, Germany

1873—Union of American Hebrew Congregations

1882–1903—First *Aliyah* (Zionist immigration to Israel)

1885—Codification of Reform Judaism—The Pittsburgh Platform

1886—Founding of the Jewish Theological Seminary of America

1897—The First Zionist Congress

1917—The Balfour Declaration

1933–45—Nazi Persecution and the Holocaust

1936—World Jewish Congress

1948—State of Israel founded

1967—Six Day War

1973—Yom Kippur War

2013—Overland Park, Kansas Jewish Community Center Shooting

2018—Tree of Life Synagogue Shooting, Pittsburgh

Glossary of Selected Jewish Terms, Subjects, and Names

Aggadah (Aggadic): The term refers to homiletic and legend-like portions of rabbinic literature.

Amidah: An integral part of Jewish worship services, the Amidah consists of both communal and personal prayers and blessings; it is generally recited silently while standing.

Ashkenazim (Ashkenazic): Refers to Jews who settled in Eastern, Middle, and Northern Europe and are distinguished through their language, food, and many other social and religious customs from those Jews who were from Spain and the Mediterranean countries (Sephardic Jews).

B.C.E. (before the Common Era): An attempt to use a neutral designation for the period traditionally labeled "B.C." (Before Christ) by Christians. The related term **C.E.** (Common Era) is an attempt to use a neutral designation for the period traditionally labeled "A.D." (In Latin, *anno domini,* or "year of the Lord").

Ba'al Shem Tov: The term *Ba'al Shem Tov* is a title that means "Master of the Good Name." The historic teacher and mystical leader who founded a Jewish movement known as Hasidism. He was originally born as Israel ben Eliezer (in Poland) in 1698.

Bar/Bat Mitzvah: The term refers to the "son" or "daughter of the commandment." This term marks the point in time when a young boy or girl—aged twelve or thirteen—is seen to have become an adult in terms of being responsible for their own behavior (and sins). In this ceremony the child is brought into the life of the religious community with a ceremony followed by a celebration. Each community has distinct ways that these ritual celebrations are conducted.

Bimah: Raised area at the front or center of a synagogue from which the Torah is most usually read.

Cantor: A person in a Jewish worship service who leads the congregation in those portions of the service that are to be sung or chanted. A cantor is usually trained in liturgical music and often assists the rabbi in other parts of the service as well.

Haggadah (Hebrew; "telling"): Liturgical manual used in the Jewish Passover Seder.

Halacha (Halachic) (Hebrew; "walking the path"): Law or custom ratified by rabbinic jurists and teachers. Colloquially, if something is deemed halachic, it is considered proper and expected behavior.

Hanukkah: A winter holiday within the Jewish tradition that commemorates the victory of the Maccabees over unjust Seleucid rulers. Their uprising led to the rededication of the Temple in Jerusalem in 164 B.C.E.

Hashem: A Hebrew term which means "the Name." It is one of the terms used to refer to God.

Hasidism (or Chasidism) (Hasidic): A historical and ultra-orthodox movement in Judaism that was begun through the teachings of the Ba'al Shem Tov. The movement began in Eastern Europe at the beginning of the eighteenth century and sought to return pious spirituality and mystical experience into daily life.

Holocaust Remembrance Day: A day set aside each year (based on the date that Auschwitz was liberated) to remember the victims of the Nazi Holocaust against the Jewish people. The Hebrew name for this day of commemoration is *Yom HaShoah.*

Israeli Independence Day: This holiday commemorates the founding of the State of Israel in 1948. The Hebrew name for this day of commemoration is *Yom HaAtzma'ut*. The date is set in the Hebrew calendar as the 5th of *Iyar*, usually mid-May.

Kabbalah: A term that refers to Jewish mysticism. One of the central books of mysticism is the *Zohar*.

Kaddish: This is the prayer conducted by those who are mourning within the Jewish tradition. The words of the Kaddish prayer do not directly relate to death but call those who mourn to an attitude of submission to the will of God and gratitude for the blessings that those who live can still enjoy.

Kashrut(h): The Jewish term to refer to those dietary rules and restrictions that were established in the Bible and have been elaborated throughout history by many rabbis.

Kibbutz: An Israeli agricultural cooperative or collective; many of which focus on tourism or manufacturing.

Kippah: A cap or skullcap customarily worn by men in a synagogue service to show a person's devotion to God. It is sometimes worn only for prayer but can be worn at any time. Some women in North America have also begun to wear a kippah. The Yiddish term for this cap is *yarmulke*.

Kol Nidre: This is a special prayer service that begins the Yom Kippur observance. It is a chant that is recited just before sunset that releases one from vows made that cannot be fulfilled.

Maimonides, Moses (1134–1205): medieval Jewish philosopher and legal expert also known as Rambam (acronym for Rabbi Moses ben Maimonides).

Megillah: The word means "scroll" and often refers to the scroll on which the Books of Esther, Ruth, Song of Songs, Lamentations, and Qoheleth is written and from which the festival of Purim is recounted.

Menorah: The word itself means "lamp" and refers to the seven-branch candelabra that the priests of Temple times were responsible for maintaining. A nine branch *Hanukkiah*, or *Hanukah menorah*, is used during the celebration of the feast of Hanukkah.

Messiah: From the Hebrew meaning "anointed one" (in Greek, *Christos).* Ancient priests and kings (and sometimes prophets) of Israel were anointed with oil. In early Judaism, the term came to mean a royal descendant of the dynasty of David who would restore the unity of the kingdom of Israel and Judah and usher in an age of peace, justice, and plenty. The concept developed in many directions over the centuries. The messianic age was believed by some Jews to be a time of perfection of human institutions; others believed it to be a time of radical new beginnings, a new heaven and earth, after divine judgment and destruction. The title *Christos* came to be applied to Jesus of Nazareth by his followers, who were soon called "Christians" in Greek and Latin usage.

Mezuzah: A small container attached to a doorpost within which is a selection of readings from the Book of Deuteronomy along with three Hebrew letters that are used to spell one of God's Names.

Midrash (Hebrew, "interpretation"): A general term for rabbinic interpretation of Scripture, as well as for specific collections of rabbinic literature.

Mikvah: The ritual bath used by some observant Jews for ritual cleansings in preparation for Shabbat or for some women as part of their regular monthly cycle; also used in conversion ritual.

Minyan: A quorum of ten adults, which is the minimum required to form a congregation to meet for the purposes of prayer. In the Orthodox tradition, ten men are required to meet this obligation.

Mishnah (Hebrew, "second teaching"): An authorized compilation of oral rabbinic laws, codified c. 210 C.E. by Rabbi Judah Ha-Nazi. See "Talmud."

Mitzvah (Hebrew, "commandment"), plural, mitzvoth: A ritual or ethical duty or act of obedience to God's will. According to Moses Maimonides, there are 613 religious commandments referred to in the Torah (and elaborated upon by the rabbinic sages). In general, a mitzvah refers to any act of religious duty or obligation; more colloquially, a mitzvah refers to a "good deed."

Rabbi: A Hebrew term that literally means "my teacher"; spiritual leader of a Jewish congregation.

Rashi: Acronym of Rabbi Shlomo ben Yitzhak (1040–1105), who wrote classical commentaries on both the Tanakh and the Talmud (see below).

Shavuot: The term means "weeks" in Hebrew and refers to the holiday that celebrates the ingathering of the harvest; it falls in late spring, seven weeks after Passover and remembers the deliverance of the Ten Commandments to Moses on Mount Sinai.

Sephardim (Sephardic): Refers to those Jews who came from Spain, North Africa, and other Mediterranean regions. These Jews speak a different language and have entirely different rituals than Ashkenazim.

Shema: Title of the fundamental, monotheistic statement of Judaism, found in Deut 6:4 ("Hear, O Israel, the LORD Our God—The LORD is One"; *Shema Yisrael adonai elohenu adonai echad*). This statement avers the unity of God and is recited daily in the liturgy (along with Deut 6:5–9, 11:13–21; Num 15:37–41, and other passages) and customarily before sleep at night. This proclamation also climaxes special liturgies (like Yom Kippur) and is central to the confession before death and to the ritual of martyrdom. The Shema is inscribed on the mezuzah and the tefillin (phylacteries); in public services, it is recited in unison.

Shoah (Hebrew, "destruction"): The term used for the destruction of European Jewry by the Nazis during World War II. The English term "holocaust" comes from the Greek meaning "wholly burnt," which is itself a translation of a Hebrew term, *olah*, found in the Tanakh, referring to a sacrifice that was completely burnt. When applying the word "holocaust" to the Nazi destruction of European Jewry, the images of sacrifice and of being wholly burnt are troubling to Jews, who are increasingly using the term "Shoah," as are Christians who are sensitive to these same concerns.

Simchat Torah: This holiday commemorates the completion of reading the book of Deuteronomy, which is the last of the five books of Moses.

At this time, the Torah is immediately begun again with a reading from Genesis. The occasion is marked by joyful singing and dancing with the Torah in celebration.

Sukkot: The autumn festival which celebrates the harvest, and which commemorates the forty years that the people wandered in the desert, living in portable dwellings, before entering the Promised Land.

Tallit: A prayer shawl that contains special fringes (*tzitzit*) at the four corners. It is worn because God told Moses: "Speak to the Children of Israel and bid them to affix fringes to the corners of their garments" (Num 15:38). This was done to remind the people of the commands that God had given.

Talmud (Hebrew, "study" or "learning"): Rabbinic Judaism produced two Talmuds: the one known as "Babylonian" is the most famous in Europe (completed around the fifth century C.E.); the other, known as the "Palestinian" or "Jerusalem" Talmud, was edited perhaps in the early fourth century C.E. Both have as their common core the Mishnah (see above), a collection of early rabbinic law, to which the *amoraim* (teachers) of the respective locales added commentary/discussion *(Gemara)*. Gemara has also become a colloquial, generic term for the Talmud and its study, popularly applied to the Talmud as a whole, to discussions by rabbinic teachers on Mishnah, and to decisions reached in these discussions.

Tanakh: An acronym for the Jewish Bible, made up of the names of its three parts: Torah (Pentateuch or Law), Nevi'im (Prophets), and Ketuvim (Writings).

Tefillin: Also known as phylacteries, Tefillin are small boxes containing parchment, which includes selected verses from the books of Exodus and Deuteronomy. These are attached with leather straps and fastened to the left arm (right arm if left-handed) and on the forehead during weekday morning prayers.

Tikkun Olam: A Hebrew term meaning "repairing the world." The world is improved through *mitzvot*—good deeds—and through following the 613 Commandments as well as working for social justice.

Tisha B'Av: This festival is also called the "Day of Lamentation" because it commemorates the destruction of the First and the Second Temples in Jerusalem as well as other events of destruction. The day is marked by reading Lamentations and by fasting and other traditional Jewish signs of mourning.

Torah: The scroll that contains the Five Books of Moses (Pentateuch); Genesis, Exodus, Leviticus, Numbers, and Deuteronomy, which were given by God to Moses, according to tradition, throughout his life. Other scholars think that the Torah was pieced together over many centuries. The term "to study Torah" also refers to any form of Jewish learning and study in general.

Yahrzeit: A Yiddish term for the commemoration of the anniversary of a loved-one's death. It is marked by prayer and the lighting of a candle that burns for that entire day. The Yahrzeit candles are sometimes lit on other festivals as well such as Passover and the eve of Yom Kippur.

Yiddish: The language spoken by the Jews of Germany and Eastern Europe (the Ashkenazim). Yiddish is a combination of Hebrew and Low German with various phrases from other languages also included.

Yom Kippur: The Jewish "Day of Atonement," which is the holiest and most solemn day of the Jewish liturgical calendar. On this day, some Jews believe, one's fate in the coming year is pre-determined.

Zohar: A "discovered" book of Jewish mysticism and commentary on the Torah that appeared in the thirteenth century. It claims that it reveals secrets hidden since the time of creation.

Selected Bibliography

Abrams, Eliot. *Faith or Fear? How Jews Can Survive in Christian America*. New York: Free, 1997.

Aitken, James K., and Edward Kessler, eds. *Challenges in Jewish-Christian Relations*. Mahwah, NJ: Paulist, 2006.

Arendt, Hannah. *Anti-Semitism: Part One of The Origins of Totalitarianism*. New York: Harcourt, Brace, & Company, 1968.

Ariel, David S. *What Do Jews Believe? The Spiritual Foundations of Judaism*. New York: Schocken, 1995.

Ariel, Yaakov. *Evangelizing the Chosen People: Missions to the Jews in America, 1880–2000*. Chapel Hill, NC: University of North Carolina, 2000.

Ateek, Naim Stifan. *Justice and Only Justice: A Palestinian Theology of Liberation*. Maryknoll, NY: Orbis, 1989.

Avery-Peck, Alan J., and Jacob Neusner. *Judaism and Christianity: New Directions for Dialogue and Understanding*. The Brill Reference Library of Judaism 28. Leiden: Brill, 2009.

Baeck, Leo. *Judaism and Christianity: Essays*. Translated by Walter Kaufmann. Philadelphia: Jewish Publication Society of America, 1958.

Barnett, Victoria J. *Bystanders: Conscience and Complicity during the Holocaust*. Contributions to the Study of Religion 59. Westport, CT: Praeger, 1999.

Barth, Karl. *Church Dogmatics*. Vol. 2. Edinburgh: T. & T. Clark, 1957.

Barton, Carlin A., and Daniel Boyarin. *Imagine No Religion: How Modern Abstractions Hide Ancient Realities*. New York: Fordham University Press, 2016.

Baum, Gregory. *Is the New Testament Anti-Semitic? A Reexamination of the New Testament*. Mahwah, NJ: Paulist, 1965.

Beck, Norman A. *Mature Christianity: The Recognition and Repudiation of the Anti-Jewish Polemic of the New Testament*. Cranbury, NJ: Associated University Press, 1985.

Beker, Avi. *The Chosen: The History of an Idea, the Anatomy of an Obsession*. New York: Palgrave Macmillan, 2008.

Bemporad, James, and M. Shevack. *Our Age: The Historic New Era of Christian-Jewish Understandings*. Hyde Park, NY: New City, 1996.

Ben-Shea, Noah. *Jacob the Baker: Gentle Wisdom in a Complicated World*. New York: Ballantine, 1989.

Bergen, Doris L. *Twisted Cross: The German Christian Movement in the Third Reich*. Chapel Hill, NC: University of North Carolina, 1996.

Berkowitz, Allan L., and Patti Moskovitz. *Embracing the Covenant: Converts to Judaism Talk about Why and How*. Woodstock, VT: Jewish Lights, 1996.

Bernis, Jonathan. *A Rabbi Looks at Jesus of Nazareth*. Bloomington, MI: Chosen, 2011.

Block, Gay, and Malka Drucker. *Rescuers: Portraits of Moral Courage in the Holocaust*. New York: Holmes & Meier, 1992.

Boadt, Lawrence, Helga Croner, and Leon Klenicki, eds. *Biblical Studies: Meeting Ground of Jews and Christians*. Mahwah, NJ: Paulist, 1980.

Bonhoeffer, Dietrich. *The Cost of Discipleship*. Translated by Reginald H. Fuller. New York: Touchstone, 1996.

———. *No Rusty Swords*. New York: Harper and Row, 1965.

Boyarin, Daniel. *A Radical Jew: Paul and the Politics of Identity*. Berkeley: University of California Press,1994.

Boys, Mary C. "The Enduring Covenant." In *Seeing Judaism Anew: Christianity's Sacred Obligation*, edited by Mary C. Boys, 17–25. New York: Rowman and Littlefield, 2005.

———. *Has God Only One Blessing? Judaism as a Source of Christian Self-Understanding*. Mahwah, NJ: Paulist, 2000.

———, ed. *Seeing Judaism Anew: Christianity's Sacred Obligation*. New York: Rowman & Littlefield, 2005.

Bratton, Fred Gladstone. *The Crime of Christendom: The Theological Sources of Christian Anti-Semitism*. Santa Barbara, CA: Fithian, 1994.

Bray, John. *Israel in Bible Prophecy*. Lakeland, FL: John Bray Ministries, 1983.

Braybrooke, Marcus. *Children of One God: A History of the Council of Christians and Jews*. Elstree, UK: Valentine Mitchell, 1991.

———. *Time to Meet: Toward a Deeper Relationship between Jews and Christians*. Philadelphia: Trinity, 1990.

Brueggemann, Walter. *The Land: Place as Gift, Promise, and Challenge in Biblical Faith*. Overtures to Biblical Theology. Philadelphia: Fortress, 1977.

Bruteau, Beatrice, ed. *Jesus through Jewish Eyes: Rabbis and Scholars Engage an Ancient Brother in a New Conversation*. Maryknoll, NY: Orbis, 2001.

Buber, Martin. *Eclipse of God: Studies in the Relation between Religion and Philosophy*. Atlantic Highlands, NJ: Humanities International, 1996.

———. *I and Thou: A New Translation with a Prologue "I and You" and Notes by Walter Kaufman*. New York: Scribner's Sons, 1970.

———. *Moses: The Revelation and the Covenant*. New York: Harper and Brothers, 1958.

———. *On Zion: The History of an Idea*. Translated by Stanley Goodman. New York: Schocken, 1973.

———. *Two Types of Faith: The Interpretation of Judaism and Christianity*. New York: Harper and Brothers, 1961.

Burrell, David, and Yehezkel Landau, eds. *Voices from Jerusalem: Jews and Christians Reflect on the Holy Land*. Mahwah, NJ: Paulist, 1992.

Carroll, James. *Constantine's Sword—The Church and the Jews: A History*. New York: Houghton Mifflin, 2001.

Carter, Warren, and Amy-Jill Levine. *The New Testament: Methods and Meanings*. Nashville, TN: Abingdon, 2013.

Catalano, Rosanne M., and David Fox Sandmel. "Introduction: Speaking Theologically Together: Loving God with All Your Mind." In *Irreconcilable Differences? A*

Learning Resource for Jews and Christians, edited by David F. Sandmel, Rosanne M. Catalano, and Christopher M. Leighton, 1–10. Boulder, CO: Westview, 2001.

Charlesworth, James H., ed. *Jews and Christians Exploring the Past, Present, and Future.* Shared Ground among Jews and Christians: A Series of Explorations, 1. New York: Crossroads, 1990.

————, ed. *The Messiah: Developments in Earliest Judaism and Christianity.* Minneapolis: Fortress, 1992.

Chazan, Robert. *European Jewry and the First Crusade.* Berkeley: University of California Press,1987.

Cook, Michael. "The New Testament: Confronting Its Impact on Jewish-Christian Relations." In *Introduction to Jewish-Christian Relations*, edited by Michael Shermis and Arthur E. Zannoni, 34–62. Mahwah, NJ: Paulist, 1991.

Cohen, Asher and Bernard Susser. "Reform Judaism in Israel: The Anatomy of Weakness." *Modern Judaism* 30 (2010) 23–45.

Cohen, Jeremy, ed. *Essential Papers on Judaism and Christianity in Conflict: From Late Antiquity to the Reformation.* New York: New York University Press, 1991.

Cohen, Shaye J. D. "Judaism and Jewishness." In *The Jewish Annotated New Testament*, edited by Amy-Jill Levin and Marc Zvi Brettler, 513–15. New York: Oxford University Press, 2011.

Cohn-Sherbrook, Dan. *The Crucified Jew: Twenty Centuries of Christian Anti-Semitism.* London: Harper Collins, 1992.

————. *Messianic Judaism: A Critical Anthology.* New York: Continuum, 2001.

Cornwell, John. *Hitler's Pope: The Secret History of Pius XII.* New York: Viking, 1999.

Cox, Harvey. *Common Prayers: Faith, Family, and a Christian's Journey through the Jewish Year.* New York: Houghton Mifflin, 2001.

Cragg, Kenneth. *To Meet and to Greet: Faith with Faith.* London: Epworth, 1992.

Croner, Helga, ed. *Stepping Stones to Further Jewish-Christian Relations: An Unabridged Collection of Christian Documents.* London: Stimulus, 1977.

Crossan, John Dominic. *The Historical Jesus: The Life of a Mediterranean Jewish Peasant.* New York: HarperCollins, 1991.

————. *Who Killed Jesus? Exposing the Roots of Anti-Semitism in the Gospel Story of the Death of Jesus.* San Francisco: HarperCollins, 1995.

Cunningham, Philip A. *Proclaiming Shalom: Lectionary Introductions to Foster the Catholic and Jewish Relationship.* Collegeville, MN: Liturgical, 1995.

————. "Covenant and Conversion." In *Seeing Judaism Anew: Christianity's Sacred Obligation*, edited by Mary C. Boys, 151–62. New York: Rowman and Littlefield, 2005.

Cunningham, Philip, and Arthur F. Starr, eds. *Sharing Shalom: A Process for Local Interfaith Dialogue between Christians and Jews.* New York: Paulist, 1998.

Davies, Alan T., ed. *Anti-Semitism and the Foundations of Christianity.* Mahwah, NJ: Paulist, 1979.

————, ed. *Anti-Semitism and the Christian Mind: The Crisis of Conscience after Auschwitz.* New York: Herder and Herder, 1969.

Davies, W. D. *Christian Engagements with Judaism.* Harrisburg, PA: Trinity, 1999.

Dawidowicz, Lucy S. *The War against the Jews, 1933–1945.* New York: Holt, Rinehart, and Winston, 1975.

Dawe, Donald G., and Aurelia T. Fule, eds. *Christians and Jews Together: Voices from the Conversation.* Louisville, KY: Theology and Worship Ministry Unit, Presbyterian Church, USA, 1991.

DeLange, Nicholas. *An Introduction to Judaism.* New York: Cambridge University Press, 2000.

Dorff, Elliot N., and Louis E. Newman, eds. *Contemporary Jewish Theology: A Reader.* New York: Oxford University Press, 1999.

Dupuis, Jacques. *Toward a Christian Theology of Religious Pluralism.* Maryknoll, NY: Orbis, 1998.

Eck, Diana. *Encountering God: A Spiritual Journey from Bozeman to Banaras.* Boston: Beacon, 1993.

Eckhardt, A. Roy. *Jews and Christians: The Contemporary Meeting.* Bloomington, IN: Indiana University Press, 1986.

Eckstein, Yechiel. *What Christians Should Know about Jews and Judaism?* Waco, TX: Word, 1984.

Ellenson, David. "A Jewish View of the Christian God: Some Cautionary and Hopeful Remarks." In *Christianity in Jewish Terms,* edited by Tivka Frymer-Kensky, David Novak, Peter Ochs, David Fox Sandmel, and Michael A. Signer, 69–76. Boulder, CO: Westview, 2000.

Ellis, Marc H. "Jews, Christians, and Liberation Theology: A Response." In *Judaism, Christianity, and Liberation: An Agenda for Dialogue,* by Otto Maduro, 141–50. Maryknoll, NY: Orbis, 1991.

Ernst, Anna Marie. *Discovering Our Jewish Roots: A Simple Guide to Judaism.* Mahwah, NJ: Paulist, 1996.

Evans, Craig A., and Donald A. Hagner, eds. *Anti-Semitism and Early Christianity: Issues of Polemic and Faith.* Minneapolis: Fortress, 1993.

Fackenheim, Emil. *To Mend the World: Foundations of Post-Holocaust Jewish Thought.* Bloomington, IN: Indiana University Press, 1994.

Falk, Harvey. *Jesus the Pharisee: A New Look at the Jewishness of Jesus.* Mahwah, NJ: Paulist, 1985.

Farmer, William R., ed. *Anti-Judaism and the Gospels.* Harrisburg, PA: Trinity, 1999.

Feher, Shoshanah. *Passing over Easter: Constructing the Boundaries of Messianic Judaism.* London: Alta Mira, 1998.

Feldman, Emanuel. "How to Reply When the Doorbell Rings." In *The Jerusalem Post* July 2, 2008, accessed October 26, 2011 at http://www.jpost.com/Opinion/Op-EdContributors/Article.aspx?id=106321.

Fischer, John. *The Olive Tree Connection: Sharing Messiah with Israel.* Rev. ed. Downers Grove, IL: InterVarsity, 1983.

Fisher, Eugene J., ed. *Interwoven Destinies: Jews and Christians through the Ages.* Studies in Judaism and Christianity, Mahwah, NJ: Paulist, 1993.

———, ed. *The Jewish Roots of Christian Liturgy.* New York: Paulist, 1990.

———, ed. *Visions of the Other: Jewish and Christian Theologians Assess the Dialogue.* New York: Paulist, 1994.

Fisher, Eugene J., A. James Rubin, and Marc H. Tannenbaum, eds. *Twenty Years of Jewish-Catholic Relations.* New York: Paulist, 1986.

Flannery, Edward H. *The Anguish of the Jews: Twenty-three Centuries of Anti-Semitism.* Studies in Judaism and Christianity, Mahwah, NJ: Paulist, 1985.

Fleischner, Eva. *Judaism in German Christian Theology since 1945: Christianity and Israel Considered in terms of Mission.* ATLA Monograph Series 8. Metuchen, NJ: Scarecrow, 1975.

———. "The Shoah and Jewish Christian Relations." In *Seeing Judaism Anew: Christianity's Sacred Obligation*, edited by Mary C. Boys, 3–14. New York: Rowman and Littlefield, 2005.

Flusser, David. *Judaism and the Origins of Christianity.* Jerusalem: Magnes, 1988.

Fornberg, Tor. *Jewish-Christian Dialogue and Biblical Exegesis.* Studia Missionalia Upsaliensia 47. Uppsala, Sweden: Svenska Institutuet for Missionsforskning, 1988.

Forward, Martin. "Jewish-Christian Relations in the Interfaith Encounter." In *Challenges in Jewish-Christian Relations*, edited by James K. Aitken and Edward Kessler, 218–242. Mahwah, NJ: Paulist, 2006.

Fredriksen, Paula. *Augustine and the Jews: A Christian Defense of Jews and Judaism.* New York: Doubleday, 2008.

———. *From Jesus to Christ: The Origins of the New Testament Images of Jesus.* New Haven, CT: Yale University Press, 1988.

Fredrickson, Paula, and Adele Reinhartz, eds. *Jesus, Judaism, and Christian Anti-Judaism: Reading the New Testament After the Holocaust.* Louisville, KY: Westminster John Knox, 2002.

Frymer-Kensky, Tikva, David Novak, Peter Ochs, David Fox Sandmel, and Michael A. Signer, eds. *Christianity in Jewish Terms.* Boulder, CO: Westview, 2000.

Goldberg, Michael. *Jews and Christians: Getting our Stories Straight: The Exodus and the Passion-Resurrection.* Valley Forge, PA: Trinity, 1991.

Greeley, Andrew M., and Jacob Neusner. *Common Ground: A Priest and a Rabbi Read Scripture Together.* Cleveland, OH: Pilgrim, 1996.

Greenburg, Irving. *For the Sake of Heaven and Earth: The New Encounter between Judaism and Christianity.* Philadelphia: Jewish Publication Society, 2004.

———. "Judaism and Christianity: Their Respective Roles in the Strategy of Redemption." In *Visions of the Other: Jewish and Christian Theologians Assess the Dialogue*, edited by Eugene Fischer, 7–27. Mahwah, NJ: Paulist, 1994.

Greenstein, Howard R. *Judaism—An Eternal Covenant.* Philadelphia: Fortress, 1983.

Gregg, Joan Young. *Devils, Women, and Jews: Reflections of the Other in Medieval Sermon Stories.* SUNY Series in Medieval Studies. Albany, NY: State University of New York Press, 1997.

Hagee, John. *Beginning of the End: Final Dawn over Jerusalem; Day of Deception.* Nashville, TN: Thomas Nelson, 2000.

———. *Day of Deception: Separating Truth from Falsehood in These Last Days.* Nashville, TN: Thomas Nelson, 2000.

Halivni, David Weiss. *Breaking the Tablets: Jewish Theology after the Shoah.* Edited by Peter Ochs. Lanham, MD: Rowman and Littlefield, 2007.

Hargrove, Katherine T., ed. *Seeds of Reconciliation: Essays on Jewish Christian Understanding.* North Richland Hills, TX: Bibal, 1996.

Harkins, Franklin T., ed. *Transforming Relations: Essays on Jews and Christians throughout History in Honor of Michael A. Signer.* Notre Dame, IN: University of Notre Dame, 2010.

Harrelson, Walter, "Contemporary Christians and Israel's Ancient Scriptures." In *Seeing Judaism Anew: Christianity's Sacred Obligation*, edited by Mary C. Boys, 115–23. New York: Rowman and Littlefield, 2005.

Harrelson, Walter, and Randall M. FaLuke. *Jews and Christians: A Troubled Family.* Nashville, TN: Abingdon, 1990.

Harris-Shapiro, Carol. *Messianic Judaism: A Rabbi's Journey through Religious Change in America.* Boston: Beacon, 1999.

Harvey, Richard. *Mapping Messianic Jewish Theology: A Constructive Approach.* Milton Keynes, UK: Paternoster, 2009.

Heinz, Hanspeter. "Contempt for the Jews and Disregard for the Old Testament: The Reestablishment of the Tridentine Rite in the German Perspective." In *Transforming Relationships: Essays on Jews and Christians Throughout History,* edited by Franklin T. Harkins, 421–41. Translated by Johanna Schmid. South Bend, IN: University of Notre Dame, 2010.

Herford, R. Travers. *Christianity in Talmud and Midrash.* London: Williams and Norgate, 1903.

Heschel, Abraham Joshua. *God in Search of Man: A Philosophy of Judaism.* New York: Farrar, Straus, and Cudahy, 1955.

———. *Israel: An Echo of Eternity.* New York: Farrer, Straus, and Giroux, 1967

Hilberg, Raul. *The Destruction of the European Jews.* New York: Homes and Meier, 1985.

Hilton, Michael. *The Christian Effect on Jewish Life.* London: SCM, 1994.

Hilton, Michael, and Gordian Marshall. *The Gospel and Rabbinic Judaism: A Study Guide.* London: SCM, 1988.

Hirschman, Marc. *A Rivalry of Genius: Jewish and Christian Biblical Interpretations in Late Antiquity.* Translated by Batya Stein. SUNY Series in Judaica: Hermeneutics, Mysticism, and Religion. Albany, NY: State University of New York Press, 1996.

Hocken, Peter. *The Challenges of the Pentecostal, Charismatic, and Messianic Jewish Movements: The Tensions of the Spirit.* Ashgate New Critical Thinking in Religion, Theology, and Biblical Studies. London: Ashgate, 2009.

Jocz, Jakob. *The Jewish People and Jesus Christ: A Study in the Controversy between the Church and the Synagogue.* London: SPCK, 1949.

Jodock, Darrell. "Christians and Jews in the Context of World Religions." In *Covenantal Conversations: Christians in Dialogue with Jews and Judaism,* edited by, Darrell Jodock, 129–46. Philadelphia: Fortress, 2008.

———, ed. *Covenantal Conversations: Christians in Dialogue with Jews and Judaism.* Minneapolis: Fortress, 2008.

Juster, Daniel C. *Jewish Roots: A Foundation of Biblical Theology.* Shippensburg, PA: Destiny Image, 1995.

Juster, Daniel, and Peter Hocken. *The Messianic Jewish Movement: An Introduction.* Dallas, TX: Towards Jerusalem Council 2, 2004.

Kasimow, Harold, and Byron L. Sherwin, eds. *No Religion Is an Island: Abraham Joshua Heschel and Interreligious Dialogue.* Maryknoll, NY: Orbis, 1991.

Kee, Howard Clark, and Irvin J. Borowsky, eds. *Removing Anti-Judaism from the Pulpit.* New York: Continuum, 1996.

Kenny, Anthony. *Catholics, Jews, and the State of Israel.* Studies in Judaism and Christianity. Mahwah, NJ: Paulist, 1993.

Kjaer-Hansen, Kai. *Joseph Rabinowitz and the Messianic Movement: The Herzl of Jewish Christianity.* Grand Rapids: Eerdmans, 1995.

Klenicki, Leon, ed. *Toward a Theological Encounter: Jewish Understandings of Christianity.* Studies in Judaism and Christianity. Mahwah, NJ: Paulist, 1991.

Knitter, Paul, ed. *The Myth of Religious Superiority: Multifaith Explorations of Religious Pluralism*. Faith Meets Faith Series. Maryknoll, NY: Orbis, 2005.

Koenig, John. *Jews and Christians in Dialogue: New Testament Foundations*. Philadelphia: Westminster, 1979.

Kogan, Michael S. *Opening the Covenant: A Jewish Theology of Christianity*. New York: Oxford University Press, 2008.

Korn, Eugene B., and T. John Pawlikowski, O. S. M., eds. *Two Faiths: One Covenant? Jewish and Christian Identity in the Presence of the Other*. The Bernardin Center Series. Lanham, MD: Rowman and Littlefield, 2005.

Kraemer, Ross Shepard. *Her Share of the Blessings: Women's Religions among Pagans, Jews, and Christians in the Greco-Roman World*. Oxford: Oxford University Press, 1992.

Kushner, Lawrence. *Jewish Spirituality: A Brief Introduction for Christians*. Woodstock, VT: Jewish Lights, 2001.

Lachs, Samuel Tobias. *A Rabbinic Commentary on the New Testament: The Gospels of Matthew, Mark, and Luke*. Hoboken, NJ: KTAV Publishing and Anti-Defamation League of B'nai B'rith, 1987.

Langmuir, Gavin. *Toward a Definition of Anti-Semitism*. Berkeley: University of California Press, 1990.

Lazowski, Philip, ed. *Understanding Your Neighbor's Faith: What Christians and Jews Should Know about Each Other*. Jersey City, NJ: KTAV, 2004.

Leaman, James R. *Faith Roots: Learning from and Sharing Witness with Jewish People*. Nappanee, IN: Evangel, 1993.

Leffler, William J., II and Paul H. Jones. *The Structure of Religion: Judaism and Christianity*. Lanham, MD: University Press of America, 2005.

Levenson, Jon D. *The Death and Resurrection of the Beloved Son: The Transformation of Child Sacrifice in Judaism and Christianity*. New Haven, CT: Yale University Press, 1993.

———. "Judaism, Christianity, and Islam in their Contemporary Encounters: Judaism Addresses Christianity." In *Religious Foundations of Western Civilization*, edited by Jacob Neusner, 581–608. Nashville, TN: Abingdon, 2006.

Levin, Jeff. "Divine Love in the World's Religious Traditions." In *Divine Love: Perspectives from the World's Religious Traditions*, edited by Jeff Levin and Stephen G. Post, 3–22. Conshocken, PA: Templeton, 2010.

Levin, Jeff, and Stephen G. Post, eds., *Divine Love: Perspectives from the World's Religious Traditions*. Conshohocken, PA: Templeton, 2010.

Levine, Amy-Jill. *The Misunderstood Jew: The Church and the Scandal of the Jewish Jesus*. San Francisco: HarperOne, 2006.

———. *The Social and Ethical Dimensions of Matthean Salvation History*. Lampeter, UK: Mellen, 1988.

———. *Short Stories by Jesus: The Enigmatic Parables of a Controversial Rabbi*. San Francisco: Harper One, 2014.

Levine, Amy-Jill, Dale C. Allison, and John Dominic Crossan, eds. *The Historical Jesus in Context*. Princeton, NJ: Princeton University Press, 2006

Levin, Amy-Jill, and Marc Zvi Brettler, eds. *The Jewish Annotated New Testament*. New York: Oxford University Press, 2011.

Levy, Richard S., ed. *Anti-Semitism in the Modern World: An Anthology of Texts*. Sources in Modern History Series. Lexington, MA: Heath, 1991.

Lewis, Bernard. *Semites and Anti-Semites*. New York: Norton, 1986.

Linafelt, Tod, ed. *Strange Fire: Reading the Bible after the Holocaust*. New York: New York University Press, 2000.

Lipton, Sara. *Images of Intolerance: The Representation of Jews and Judaism in the Bible Moralise*. Berkley: University of California Press,1999.

Littell, Franklin H. *The Crucifixion of the Jews: The Failure of Christians to Understand the Jewish Experience*. Macon, GA: Mercer University Press, 1986.

Littell, Marcia Sachs, and Sharon Weismann Gutman. *Liturgies of the Holocaust: An Interfaith Anthology*. Valley Forge, PA: Trinity, 1996.

Lloyd-Jones, Gareth. *Hard Sayings: Difficult New Testament Texts for Jewish-Christian Dialogue*. London: Council of Christians and Jews, 1993.

Lochhead, David. *The Dialogical Imperative: A Christian Reflection on Interfaith Encounter*. London: SCM, 1988.

Locke, Hubert G. "On Christian Mission to the Jews." In *The Holocaust and the Christian World: Reflections on the Past, Challenges for the Future*, edited by Carol Rittner, Stephen D. Smith, and Irena Steinfeldt, 204–6. London: Kuperard, 2000.

Lodahl, Michael E. *Shekinah Spirit: Divine Presence in Jewish and Christian Religion*. Studies in Judaism and Christianity. Mahwah, NJ: Paulist, 1992.

Lohfink, Norbert. *The Covenant Never Revoked: Biblical Reflections on Christian-Jewish Dialogue*. Mahwah, NJ: Paulist, 1991.

Lotker, Michael. *A Christian's Guide to Judaism*. Mahwah, NJ: Paulist, 2004.

Lutz, Charles P., and Robert O. Smith. *Christians in a Land Called Holy: How We Can Foster Justice, Peace, and Hope*. Minneapolis: Augsburg Fortress, 2006.

Maccoby, Hyam, ed. and trans. *Judaism on Trial: Jewish-Christian Disputations in the Middle Ages*. The Litman Library of Jewish Civilization. Portland, OR: The Litman Library of Jewish Civilization, 1993.

Maduro, Otto, ed., *Judaism, Christianity, and Liberation: An Agenda for Dialogue*. Maryknoll, NY: Orbis, 1991.

Martin, Vincent. *A House Divided: The Parting of Ways between Synagogue and Church*. Studies in Judaism and Christianity. Mahwah, NJ: Paulist, 1995.

Maybaum, Ignaz. *Trialogue between Jews, Christians, and Muslims*. London: Routledge, Kegan, and Paul, 1973.

McGarry, Michael B. *Christology after Auschwitz*. Mahwah, NJ: Paulist, 1977.

———. "The Land of Israel in the Cauldron of the Middle East: A Challenge to Christian-Jewish Relations." In *Seeing Judaism Anew: Christianity's Sacred Obligation*, edited by Mary C. Boys, 213–24. New York: Rowman and Littlefield, 2005.

McInnes, Val A., ed. *Renewing the Judeo-Christian Wellsprings*. New York: Crossroads, 1987.

Merkley, Paul Charles. *Christian Attitudes towards the State of Israel*. Montreal & Kingston: McGill Queen's University Press, 2001.

Michaels, Annie. *Fugitive Pieces*. Waterville, ME: Thorndike, 1996.

Molloy, Michael. *Experiencing the World's Religions: Tradition, Challenge, and Change*. 7th ed. New York: McGraw Hill, 2018.

Mroczek, Eva. *The Literary Imagination in Jewish Antiquity*. New York: Oxford University Press, 2016.

Nanos, Mark D. "Paul and Judaism." In *The Jewish Annotated New Testament*, edited by Amy-Jill Levin and Marc Zvi Brettler, 551–54. New York: Oxford University Press, 2011.

Neill, Stephen. *The Christian Faith and Other Faiths: The Christian Dialogue with Other Religions*. Oxford: Oxford University Press, 1970.

Neusner, Jacob. "Divine Love in Classical Judaism." In *Divine Love: Perspectives from the World's Religious Traditions*, edited by Jeff Levin and Stephen G. Post, 80–108. Conshocken, PA: Templeton, 2010.

———. *Jews and Christians: The Myth of a Common Tradition*. Philadelphia: Trinity, 1991.

———. "Judaic Social Teaching in Christian and Pagan Context." In *Judaism and Christianity: New Directions for Dialogue and Understanding*, edited by Alan J. Avery-Peck and Jacob Neusner, 29–60. Leiden: Brill, 2009.

———. *A Rabbi Talks with Jesus: An Intermillenial, Interfaith Exchange*. New York: Doubleday, 1993.

———, ed. *Religious Foundations of Western Civilization: Judaism, Christianity, and Islam*. Nashville, TN: Abingdon, 2006.

———. *Telling Tales: Making Sense of Christian and Judaic Nonsense: The Urgency and Basis for Judeo-Christian Dialogue*. Louisville, KY: Westminster John Knox, 1993.

Neusner, Jacob, and Bruce Chilton. *The Intellectual Foundations of Christian and Jewish Discourse*. New York: Routledge, 1997.

———. *Jewish-Christian Debates: God, Kingdom, and Messiah*. Minneapolis: Fortress, 1998.

Nirenberg, David. *Communities of Violence: Persecution of Minorities in the Middle Ages*. Princeton, NJ: Princeton University Press, 1996.

Novak, David. *Jewish-Christian Dialogue: A Jewish Justification*. Oxford: Oxford University Press, 1989.

———. *Talking with Christians: Musings of a Jewish Theologian*. Grand Rapids: Eerdmans, 2005.

Oesterreicher, John M. *The New Encounter between Christians and Jews*. New York: Philosophical Library, 1986.

O'Hare, Padraic. *The Enduring Covenant: The Education of Christians and the End of Anti-Semitism*. Valley Forge, PA: Trinity, 1997.

Olitzky, Kerry M. *Introducing My Faith and My Community: The Jewish Outreach Institute Guide for the Christian in a Jewish Interfaith Relationship*. Woodstock, VT: Jewish Lights, 2004.

Olitzky, Kerry M., and Daniel Judson. *Jewish Holidays: A Brief Introduction for Christians*. Woodstock, VT: Jewish Lights, 2007.

Papademetriou, George C. *Essays on Orthodox Christian-Jewish Relations*. Bristol, IN: Wyndham Hall, 1990.

Parkes, James. *End of an Exile: Israel, the Jews, and the Gentile World*. New York: Schocken, 1982.

Pawlikowski, John T. "The Challenge of *Tikkun Olam* for Jews and Christians." In *Seeing Judaism Anew: Christianity's Sacred Obligation*, edited by Mary C. Boys, 227–38. New York: Rowman and Littlefield, 2005.

———. *What Are They Saying about Jewish-Christian Relations?* Mahwah, NJ: Paulist, 1984.

Perlemuter, Hayim Goren. *Siblings: Rabbinic Judaism and Early Christianity at Their Beginning*. Mahwah, NJ: Paulist, 1989.

Perlemuter, Hayim, and Wilhelm Wuellner, eds. *Paul the Jew: Jewish/Christian Dialogue.* Protocol of the Colloquy of the Center for Hermeneutical Studies in Hellenistic and Moderne Culture 60. Berkeley: Center for Hermeneutical Studies, 1990.

Pessah, Amy, Kenneth J. Meyer, and Christopher M. Leighton. "How Do Jews and Christians Read the Bible." In *Irreconcilable Differences? A Learning Resource for Jews and Christians*, edited by David F. Sandmel, Rosanne M. Catalano, and Christopher M. Leighton, 53–74. Boulder, CO: Westview, 2001.

Pettit, Peter A. "Covenants Old and New." In *Covenantal Conversations: Christians in Dialogue with Jews and Judaism*, edited by Darrell Jodock, 26–41. Philadelphia: Fortress, 2008.

Pettit, Peter A., and John Townsend. "In Every Generation: Judaism as a Living Faith." In *Seeing Judaism Anew: Christianity's Sacred Obligation*, edited by Mary C. Boys, 95–112. New York: Rowman and Littlefield, 2005.

Phan, Peter C. "Jesus as the Universal Savior in the Light of God's Eternal Covenant with the Jewish People: A Roman Catholic Perspective." In *Seeing Judaism Anew: Christianity's Sacred Obligation*, edited by Mary C. Boys, 127–37. New York: Rowman and Littlefield, 2005.

Poliakov, Leon. *The History of Anti-Semitism.* 4 vols. Philadelphia: University of Pennsylvania Press, 2003.

Pollak, Michael. *Mandarins, Jews, and Missionaries: The Jewish Experience in the Chinese Empire.* Philadelphia: Jewish Publication Society, 1980.

Power, Patricia A. "Blurring the Boundaries: American Messianic Jews and Gentiles." *Nova Religio: The Journal of Alternative and Emergent Religions* 15 (2011) 69–91.

Radoush, Daniel. *Rapture Ready: Adventures in the Parallel Universe of Christian Pop Culture.* New York; Scribners, 2008.

Raphael, Marc Lee. *Profiles in American Judaism: The Reform, Conservative, Orthodox, and Reconstructionist Traditions in Historical Perspective.* San Francisco: Harper and Row, 1988.

Ratzinger, Joseph Cardinal. *Many Religions, One Covenant: Israel, the Church, and the World.* Translated by Graham Harrison. San Francisco: Ignatius, 1999.

Rausch, David A. *A Legacy of Hatred: Why Christians Must Not Forget the Holocaust.* Chicago: Moody, 1984.

———. *Messianic Judaism: It's History, Theology, and Polity.* Texts and Studies in Religion. New York: Mellen, 1982.

Reinhartz, Adele. *Cast out of the Covenant: Jews and Anti-Judaism in the Gospel of John.* Lanham, MD: Lexington, 2018.

Reuchlin, Johannes. *Recommendation Whether to Confiscate, Destroy, and Burn All Jewish Books: A Classic Treatise against Anti-Semitism.* Studies in Judaism and Christianity. Translated and edited by Peter Wortsman. Mahwah, NJ: Paulist, 2000.

Reuther, Rosemary Radford. *Faith and Fratricide: The Theological Roots of Anti-Semitism.* New York: Seabury, 1974.

Rittner, Carol, Stephen D. Smith, and Irena Steinfeldt, eds, *The Holocaust and the Christian World: Reflections on the Past, Challenges for the Future.* London: Kuperard, 2000.

Rosen, Moishe, and Ceil Rosen. *Share the New Life with a Jew.* Chicago: Moody, 1976.

Rosen, Ruth, ed. *Testimonies of Jews Who Believe in Jesus.* 3rd. ed. San Francisco: Purple Pomegranate, 1992.

Rosenberg, Stuart E. *The Christian Problem: A Jewish View.* New York: Hippocrene, 1986.

Rothschild, Fritz A., ed. *Jewish Perspectives on Christianity: Leo Baeck, Martin Buber, Franz Rosenzweig, Will Herzberg, and Abraham J. Heschel.* New York: Continuum, 1996.

Rousmaniere, John. *A Bridge to Dialogue: The Story of Jewish Christian Relations.* Studies in Judaism and Christianity. Mahwah, NJ: Paulist, 1991.

Rubenstein, Richard L. *After Auschwitz: Radical Theology and Contemporary Judaism.* Indianapolis: Bobbs-Merrill, 1966.

Rubin, Miri. *Gentile Tales: The Narrative Assault on Late Medieval Jews.* New Haven, CT: Yale University Press, 1999.

Salmon, Marilyn. *Preaching without Contempt: Overcoming Unintended Anti-Judaism.* Fortress Resources for Preaching. Minneapolis: Augsburg Fortress, 2006.

Sanders, Jack T. *Schismatics, Sectarians, Dissidents, Deviants: The First One Hundred Years of Jewish-Christian Relations.* London: SCM, 1993.

Sandmel, David F., Rosanne M. Catalano, and Christopher M. Leighton, eds. *Irreconcilable Differences? A Learning Resource for Jews and Christians.* Boulder, CO: Westview, 2001.

Sandmel, Samuel. *Judaism and Christian Beginnings.* Oxford: Oxford University Press, 1978.

Saperstein, Marc. "Jews Facing Christians: The Burdens and Blinders of the Past." In *Challenges in Jewish-Christian Relations*, edited by James K. Aiken and Edward Kessler, 15–38. Mahwah, NJ: Paulist, 2006.

———. *Moments of Crisis in Jewish-Christian Relations.* Philadelphia: Trinity, 1989.

Sartre, Jean-Paul. *Anti-Semite and Jew.* Translated by George Becker. New York: Schocken, 1948.

Schiffman, Lisa. *Generation J: Call Us a Bunch of Searchers—Call us Post-Holocaust Jews—Call us Generation J.* New York: HarperCollins, 1999.

Schoen, Robert. *What I Wish My Christian Friends Knew about Judaism.* Chicago: Loyola, 2004.

Scholem, Gershom. *The Messianic Idea in Judaism: And Other Essays on Jewish Spirituality.* New York: Schocken, 1995.

Schrenckenberg, Heinz. *The Jews in Christian Art: An Illustrated History.* London: SCM, 1996.

Schwartz, Howard. *Reimagining the Bible: The Storytelling of the Rabbis.* New York: Oxford University Press, 1998.

Segovia, Fernando F. *Decolonizing Biblical Studies: A View from the Margins.* Maryknoll, NY: Orbis, 2000.

Sevener, Harold A. *A Rabbi's Vision: A Century of Proclaiming Messiah—A History of Chosen People Ministries, Inc.* Charlotte, NC: Chosen People Ministries, 1994.

Shanks, Hershel, ed. *Christianity and Rabbinic Judaism: A Parallel History of their Origins and Early Development.* Washington, DC: Biblical Archeological Society, 2002.

Shatzmiller, Joseph. *Shylock Reconsidered: Jews, Money Lending, and Medieval Society.* Berkley: University of California Press, 1990.

Sherman, Franklin. "The Road to Reconciliation: Protestant Church Statements on Christian-Jewish Relations." In *Seeing Judaism Anew: Christianity's Sacred*

Obligation, edited by Mary C. Boys, 241–51. New York: Rowman and Littlefield, 2005.

Shermis, Michael, and Arthur E. Zannoni. *An Introduction to Jewish-Christian Relations*. Mahwah, NJ: Paulist, 1991.

Simon, Merrill. *Jerry Falwell and the Jews*. Middle Village. New York: David, 1984.

Soulen, R. Kendall. *The God of Israel and Christian Theology*. Minneapolis: Augsburg Fortress, 1996.

Smith, Stephen. "The Effects of the Holocaust on Jewish-Christian Relations." In *Challenges in Jewish-Christian Relations*, edited by James K. Aitken and Edward Kessler, 137–52. Mahwah, NJ: Paulist, 2006.

Talmage, Frank E., ed. *Disputation and Dialogue: Readings in the Jewish-Christian Encounter*. New York: KTAV, 1975.

Tanenbaum, Marc H., Marvin R. Wilson, and A. James Rudin, eds. *Evangelicals and Jews in Conversation on Scripture, Theology, and History*. Grand Rapids: Baker, 1978.

Taylor, Howard. *World Hope in the Middle East*. Edinburgh: Handsel, 1986.

Taylor, Phyllis. "A Jewish Journey through Nicaragua." In *Judaism, Christianity, and Liberation: An Agenda for Dialogue*, edited by Otto Maduro, 65–72. Maryknoll, NY: Orbis, 1991.

Tec, Neachama. *When Light Pierced the Darkness: Christian Rescue of Jews in Nazi-Occupied Poland*. New York: Oxford University Press, 1986.

Teeple, Howard M. *The Literary Origin of the Gospel of John*. Evanston, IL: Religion and Ethics Institute, 1974.

Telushkin, Joseph. *Jewish Literacy: The Most Important Things to Know about the Jewish Religion, Its People, and Its History*. New York: Morrow, 1991.

Thiessen, Matthew. *Paul and the Gentile Problem*. New York: Oxford University Press, 2016.

Thoma, Clemens. *A Christian Theology of Judaism*. Studies in Judaism and Christianity. Translated by Helga B. Croner. Mahwah, NJ: Paulist, 1980.

Tonoyan, Lidia S. "Messianic Jewish Movements in Ukraine." Master's thesis, Baylor University Press, 2011.

Tucker, Ruth A. *Not Ashamed: The Story of Jews for Jesus*. Portland, OR: Multnomah, 1999.

Ucko, Hans, ed. *The Spiritual Significance of Jerusalem for Jews, Christians, and Muslims*. Geneva: World Council of Churches, 1994.

Van Buren, Paul M. *A Theology of the Jewish-Christian Reality*. Lanham, MD: University Press of America, 1987–88.

Vermes, Geza. *The Religion of Jesus the Jew*. London: SCM, 1993.

Vroom, Hendrik, ed. *Wrestling with God and with Evil: Philosophical Reflections*. Currents of Encounter 31. New York: Rodopi, 2007.

Walvoord, John F. *Armageddon, Oil, and the Middle East Crisis: What the Bible Says about the Future of the Middle East and the End of Western Civilization*. Grand Rapids: Zondervan, 1990.

Wasserman, Jeffrey S. *Messianic Jewish Congregations: Who Sold This Business to the Gentiles?* Lanham, MD: University Press of America, 2000.

White, Andrew P. B. "Israel within Jewish-Christian Relations." In *Challenges in Jewish-Christian Relations*, edited by James K. Aitken and Edward Kessler, 125–36. Mahwah, NJ: Paulist, 2006.

Wiesel, Elie. *A Jew Today.* Translated by Marion Wiesel. New York: Vintage, 1979.

Wigoder, Geoffrey. *Jewish-Christian Relations since the Second World War.* Sherman Studies of Judaism in Modern Times. Manchester: Manchester University Press, 1988.

Wilken, Robert L. *John Chrysostom and the Jews: Rhetoric and Reality in the Late 4th Century.* Berkley: University of California Press,1983.

Wilkinson, John. *God's Plan for the Jew.* London: Paternoster, 1947.

Willebrands, Johannes. *Church and Jewish People: New Considerations.* New York: Paulist, 1992.

Williamson, Clark M. *A Guest in the House of Israel: Post-Holocaust Church Theology.* Louisville, KY: Westminster John Knox, 1993.

———. "The Universal Significance of Christ." In *Seeing Judaism Anew: Christianity's Sacred Obligation,* edited by Mary C. Boys, 138–47. New York: Rowman & Littlefield, 2005.

Williamson, Clark M., and Ronald J. Allen. *Interpreting Difficult Texts: Anti-Judaism and Christian Preaching.* London: SCM, 1989.

Wilson, Marvin R. "An Evangelical Perspective on Judaism." In *Evangelicals and Jews in Conversation on Scripture, Theology, and History,* edited by Marc H. Tannenbaum, Marvin R. Wilson, and A. James Rudin, 2–33. Grand Rapids: Baker, 1978.

———. *Our Father Abraham: Jewish Roots of the Christian Faith.* Dayton, OH: Center for Judaic-Christian Studies, 1989.

Wylean, Stephen M. *The Jews in the Time of Jesus: An Introduction.* Mahwah, NJ: Paulist, 1996.

Wyman, David S. *The Abandonment of the Jews: America and the Holocaust, 1941–1945.* New York: Pantheon, 1984.

Wyschogrod, Michael. *Abraham's Promise: Judaism and Jewish-Christian Relations.* Edited by R. Kendall Soulen. Radical Traditions. Grand Rapids: Eerdmans, 2004.

Yoder, John Howard. *The Jewish-Christian Schism Revisited.* Edited by Michael G. Cartwright and Peter Ochs. Grand Rapids: Eerdmans, 2003.

Zannoni, Arthur E., ed. *Jews and Christians Speak of Jesus.* Minneapolis: Fortress, 1994.

Disfruta de más felicidad día a día...

Pide tus HERRAMIENTAS GRATIS FELIZ PORQUE SÍ en
www.HappyforNoReason.com/bookgifts

¡Enhorabuena! Has emprendido el viaje para ser Feliz porque sí, y serás cada día más feliz si pones en práctica lo que has aprendido en este libro. Para ayudarte a avanzar más rápido, he elaborado los siguientes regalos para ti:

Grabación sonora gratis
Highlights of the Happy 100 Interviews

Escucha varios de los extractos más inspiradores e instructivos de mis entrevistas con los 100 Felices. Escuchar a estas personas compartir sus extraordinarios relatos y reflexiones sobre cómo generar más felicidad en la vida alberga una fuerza especial.

Happy for no Reason Workbook gratis

Este libro de ejercicios descargable de 26 páginas incluye el cuestionario *Feliz porque sí*, los 21 ejercicios de Hábitos para la Felicidad y material extra especial.

Happy for no Reason eZine gratis

Cada pocas semanas te enviaré un magacín electrónico divertido e inspirador que incluye consejos prácticos y los últimos adelantos e ideas sobre felicidad incondicional.

EXTRA
Happiness Habits Miniposter gratis

Este bonito resumen en una página de los 21 Hábitos de Felicidad es ideal para colgarlo en tu tablero de propósitos o ponerlo en un lugar especial donde lo veas a diario y te sirva de recordatorio.

Para conseguir estos y otros regalos, visita la página web:
www.HappyforNoReason.com/bookgifts

Para acceder a los regalos, los usuarios deben registrarse,
con su nombre de pila y dirección electrónica.
Oferta sujeta a los artículos disponibles.